GRUB STREET STRIPPED BARE

The Coffee House Mob

'The Fleet Street presses now grow bold,
And num'rous lies in print were told . . .
The coffee tables now were spread
With all the lies that could be said.'
from Ned Ward's Vulgus Britannicus

GRUB St. stripped bare

The scandalous lives & pornographic works of the original Grub st. writers, together with the bottle songs which led to their drunkenness, the shameless pamphleteering which led them to Newgate Pris^on, *& the continual pandering to public taste which put them among the first almost to earn a fitful living from their writing alone.*

BY

Philip Pinkus

London: published by CONSTABLE and Company of Orange Street WC2 1968

Published by Constable and Company Limited
10–12 Orange Street, London W.C.2
© Philip Pinkus 1968
First published 1968
Printed in England by
Willmer Brothers Limited, Birkenhead
SBN 09 451470 4

Contents

Acknowledgements

I am indebted to the staff of the British Museum for their courtesy in helping me gather much of the material for this book; to my colleagues Professor Clarence Tracy who read the manuscript and offered useful criticism and Professor John Norris who saved me from several historical inaccuracies. But I owe a particular debt to my wife who helped me in my research.

A*

3

In this book, Grub Street refers to a particular time and place: London in the last years of the 17th and the first years of the 18th centuries. But Grub Street itself is a metaphor, evoking the eternal spirit of the hack writer. My problem was how to describe a metaphor without destroying the essence and leaving an arid abstraction. How does one do justice to the historical substance—the struggles and working conditions of the writers, the literary battles they fought, the tricks they used to keep ahead of the bum-bailiff, the commercial tactics of the publishers, all in the face of continual hostility from an erratic government—and still retain the spirit of the Grub Street world?

The method I chose was as far as possible to portray Grub Street in action, presenting the story of the Grub Street hacks through their own writings, and setting them in historical context by means of a running commentary. The result is substantially more Grub Street writing than commentary, but that, I think, is as it should be if one is to describe what Grub Street means. The reader may approach the book consecutively as a systematic history of the period or dip, as the fancy moves him, into a collection of Grub Street works.

How accurate a picture of Grub Street this method portrays it is difficult to say. Certainly the Grub Street hacks were not sitting back on their saintly objectivity when they wrote about their own condition. They were usually either glorifying their state or defiling it, stretching for effect, straining for sensation by being novel or obscene or lascivious, and always for the best of Grub Street reasons, because it might sell. What evolves from this will not be pure, laboratory-tested historical truth, but the usual amalgam of fact and fiction that contemporary writers create of their own world. Where it is not history it becomes legend, and legend has its own validity. Surely the legend that the hack writers created of themselves is as much a picture of Grub Street as any so-called objective study. The final effect, at least, is immediate, and what the reader cannot see he should be able to smell. Very little of this material has been published since the 18th century. Only in two major instances, Ned Ward's *The London Spy* and Tom Brown's *Amusements,* have I included texts published in the 20th century, and these for the sake of completeness. The texts chosen are, for the most part, the earliest printed. My concern was to present not a scholarly, collated text—which would serve no useful purpose—nor the revised text culled from many collected works, but the text roughly as it first appeared to the readers of the time, usually published separately in pamphlet or broadsheet form.

I have tried to follow one constant principle in my editing, to make the text as clear and accessible to the modern reader as possible, and to make no change that might distort the author's intent. Where it was necessary I have reproduced the fragmentary punctuation of the 17th century, which is largely rhetorical in its purpose—that is, where the printers' idiosyncrasies have not got in the way—rather than syntactical as ours is today. Where I felt the original to be somewhat obscure, I have modernized the punctuation. Since, for the most part, the works I have included here are not great literature, it seemed to me it would not be useful to include every comma of the original at the expense of the reader's comprehension. The spelling has been modernized. As for the deletions, I regret having to make so many, but the pressure of space made it necessary. Passages which were over-topical and required elaborate footnoting to be understood by the modern reader, and passages which were just plain dull, I have tended to remove. I can only hope that I have done this without destroying the continuity.

It may be objected that I have gone out of my way to reveal the salacious nature of Grub Street writing. But the salacious is one of the characteristics of Grub Street and I do not think that the emphasis I have given it is unrepresentative.

Finally, what justification is there for reviving the old Grub Street material when we have such rich specimens of our own? Some of the material is in itself worthwhile as literature. All of it provides an instructive back-stairs view of the authors and publishers, of the first raucous beginnings of professional writing in an exciting age. Mainly, their work needs no justification because it makes lively, entertaining reading in any age. It has a vinous exuberance, a soap-box vigour, that refuses to lie dead.

More a Way of Life than a Living

There was an actual Grub Street once. According to the *New English Dictionary* it is now called Milton Street, near Moorfields in London—which may or may not be relevant. But the Grub Street we know[1] is an eternal spirit that dwells in the heart of every author whose belly is at odds with his principles, inspiring a happiness greater far by the simple merchandising process of giving the customer what he wants. Today we have progressed enough to give Grub Street the dignity it deserves. It has become respectable. We call it Fleet Street or Madison Avenue, depending on whether it is selling soap or the latest Soho memoirs. Its members are solid citizens, leaders of the community, shaping the thought, the ideals, the desires of a whole society.

But in the years following the Restoration, especially the last part of the 17th and the first part of the 18th centuries, the hack writers of London—which we shall call the original Grub Street, time and space being interchangeable in the world of the spirit—were not well liked. To the blue-nosed tradesman, the hacks were a drinking, whoring lot, abandoned to every vice—worse, they were a blasphemy against the sacred principles of thrift, industry and cash payment. The gentleman class found

[1] *The first known reference to* Grub Street, *in the sense used here, was in 1630 by John Taylor, the 'Water-Poet', who was himself a kind of Grub Street hack. The term became more current during the Civil War when a large number of political pamphleteers sprang up who wrote for money. But it was not until after the Restoration that Grub Street became a term of common usage. Writers had attempted to earn a living from their writing as early as the Elizabethan period. But in the last part of the 17th century, when the professional writer became a familiar part of society, Grub Street came into its own.*

them rather useful in its political wars, at times entertaining, but always contemptible, because they wrote for bread. To be a professional was a violation of the gentleman's amateur standing. With some exceptions, the hack's view of life might be summed up in this pious prayer of Ned Ward's, one of the best of the Grub Street writers:

> O give me, kind Bacchus, thou God of the vine,
> Not a pipe or a tun, but an ocean of wine
> ....
> Thus, thus, would I live free from care or design,
> And when death should prevail I'd be pickled in wine,
> That is, tossed overboard, have the sea form my grave,
> And lie nobly entombed in a blood-coloured wave,
> That living or dead, both my body and spirit
> Should float round the globe in an ocean of claret.[1]

They were not always that drunk, of course. There were arid moments when they could not squeeze a shilling from their publisher or an ounce of credit from the tavern-keeper. But Ned Ward's lines seemed to reflect their dream, the Bacchanalian dream, which still has a certain nostalgic validity for Grub Street's respectable descendants. It is part of the myth that the Grub Street writers created for themselves, and, of course, it is only partly true. Many of the hacks lived austere, colourless lives; and writers like John Dunton were even rather Puritanical, in an equivocal way. Yet a sufficient number believed in the dream and aspired to it so that it became associated with the contemporary image of Grub Street. It is part of what Grub Street came to mean. And any general comment on Grub Street must take this into account.

Many of these Grub Street hacks were just as learned, intelligent and witty as the best of their present-day counterparts, but with fewer inhibitions. They were more daring, possibly because they took themselves less seriously, because they were poor, because, being less respectable, they had less to lose—and because the libel laws were lax. They lived wretchedly. The reading public was not large enough to support writers with dignity until the middle of the 18th century—and then only some of them. Even

[1] *From* The Wine Bibber's Wish.

Alexander Pope depended more on subscriptions from his wealthy and influential friends than on the direct sale of his writings in the open market. The more respectable writers, the gentlemen, had private incomes, or they were supported by their patrons, usually by some direct gift or a political sinecure, for which they often paid with fulsome dedications and political loyalty. By the beginning of the 18th century, however, even the author's relationship with his patron had changed: the author had become much more independent. But the hack writer had no patron; he depended entirely on his own efforts. In the 1690's, for the first time, it seemed possible for hack writers to live by their writing—or one should say almost possible, because the Grub Street hack who depended solely on his writing needed more agility than talent to escape a debtor's prison. It was a precarious independence, but it gave them the kind of moral assurance, in that heavy interval between their cups and their whores, to sneer at patron-seekers like Dryden.

Several factors brought about this improvement in the writer's status. A generation earlier the Civil War had shown that writers could be useful. Both sides felt the need to defend their position on paper, and since the important thing was to win, reasoned arguments alone were not to be trusted. To win they needed skilful writers, not scholars, who could ridicule and abuse and employ every blood-and-thunder tactic of paper warfare. Yet it was a hazardous business if you were on the wrong side. Disagreeing with the government could be interpreted as treason, with occasionally fatal consequences. The pamphlet war did not end with the Restoration, and the development of the news-sheet into something like the daily newspaper gave the war a new lift, with new opportunities for reaching Newgate on a libel action. When William III came to the throne the political party, not the court, became the centre of patronage, and the political value of the writer went up. He began to be wooed by the great political leaders. By the beginning of the 18th century all the great writers of the time—Addison, Steele, Swift, Prior, Defoe—were involved in politics, on one side or another of the party war. By 1710, Jonathan Swift, almost by the sheer force of his pen had become one of the most powerful men in England. But Swift was not Grub Street. The great rewards were for the prominent writers, for the gentlemen who were already comfortable, not for professional men like the Grub Street hack. Swift scorned payment for his work and when Harley offered him money Swift, like the amateur, non-union gentleman he was, angrily rejected it. In spite of this the Grub Street writer benefited from the increased status. He was found to be useful, at times he was even feared; and fear breeds a certain respect, and a great deal of interest which was beginning to be translated into cash payment, not by patrons this time, but by readers. Many of the Grub Street writers did not sell their pens to a political party. Writers like Tom Brown, William Pittis, Ned Ward, all Tories, risked their skins to support Tory policy, were ruinously fined, put in the pillory, imprisoned, not for political patronage, but simply because they were Tory —and possibly because they knew a good market when they saw one. Since they had no patrons they appealed to their readers, the first requirement of the professional writer.

The most important factor that changed the writer's status was the growing size of the reading public. An increasingly wealthy merchant class, mostly Dissenters centred in London, had acquired the leisure to read. Since the Dissenters were excluded from the regular schools they set up fine schools of their own which, together with the new Charity Schools, bred a new race of little readers. Most of this took place in London, and Grub Street by the end of the 17th century had acquired a compact, though not large, middle-class market of readers, with wider interests than the relatively narrow court circle of the previous generation. At the same time the growth of the coffee houses meant that there were many places in London where there was political and literary conversation, where a pamphlet or a poem immediately and almost literally became the talk of the town. The final factor was the lapse of the Licensing Act in 1695, which had somewhat erratically permitted printing only by government authority. The result was not a sudden bursting of the bonds and a full-blown emergence of the freedom of the press. The government still felt that every pamphlet attack was an abuse of privilege and a scandal to all decent people, and to the limit of its power did what it could to suppress the pamphlet and punish the author. But there was a sense of release, and writers had less fear about writing what they wished. In some respects writers had more freedom than today, particularly in their opportunities for personal libel, which makes this period so entertaining. In politics, however, they still had to be careful.

The combination of all these circumstances—more readers, less enforcement, a compact market, powerful political parties who needed writers—created a new situation which became increasingly apparent by the last part of the 17th century, where it was possible for the hack writer to achieve a kind of independence which had neither social status nor the slightest financial assurance. But his independence often landed him in another kind of bondage, to his bookseller-publisher. These were enterprising business-men like the 'unspeakable Curll', who kept stables of writers, slept them three to a bed, according to Amory,[1] advanced them money for work which, it must be confessed, they sometimes had no intention of completing but, finished or not, was never sufficient for expenses after they had paid their wine bill. The result was a familiar pattern. They got in debt, they went hungry, they skulked the streets to avoid the bum-bailiffs set on them by their landlord or their tailor, they even went without their wine. They could, of course, go into trade, like Ned Ward and Defoe, like the modern writers who join university faculties. But most of the Grub Street writers considered this demeaning, so their lives became a drunken decline, through brief periods of success and penury, marked by the odd physical beating by frustrated opponents, consumption, sponging houses—the temporary jails kept by bailiffs—and, finally, debtor's prison. It was a dubious kind of independence.

Very little of the enormous quantity of their writing deserves a permanent place in our literature, though much of it is good enough to deserve our interest. Because they wrote for a living they had to be particularly sensitive to public taste and to the requirements of their publisher. What they lacked as writers they frequently made up for in ingenuity and originality, in a stream of literary innovations to please the public palate. The result was a new kind of writing, lively, racy, at times salacious and deliberately shocking, but almost always interesting.

As for the publisher, he too took on new status about this time, becoming less and less the stationer and bookseller and more the publisher as we know him today. He learned quickly. There is hardly a trick of the publishing trade which he did not use, and a great many more that publishers might like to use today

[1] *See below, p. 52.*

but do not dare. All this—the hack writer and the hack publisher, their literature and their publishing tactics—form the subject matter which this book hopes to reveal through the medium of the Grub Street writings. Most of the selections will illustrate the various controversies of the time, the newspaper wars, the wars between author and publisher, between author and author, literary, religious, political and personal.

The Grub Street Mode

Grub Street was one long battle. One of the more flamboy-
ant battles was the fist-fight between Tom Brown, a major Grub
Street writer, and his publisher, Abel Roper, the editor of *The Post-
Boy,* one of the earliest London journals that might be called a newspaper. Fist-fights were not commonplace in Grub Street, even
between writer and publisher. Its inhabitants tended to fight with
words; though it should be added, their occupation was not without
physical adventure, such as being tossed in a blanket by unfriendly
readers, assaulted in dark alleys, paddled, or put in the pillory and
pelted with rotten eggs and rocks. But the Roper-Brown exchange
and the attendant skirmishes have a certain style which hardly can
be imagined in literary relationships in any other period in English
history. To recount the fist-fight, the events leading up to it and the
sequel, therefore, is to show enlarged the dominant mode of Grub
Street life.

Abel Roper met Brown professionally in 1691 when he
reprinted two of Brown's satires on John Dryden. Since that time
and through many publications they had fought, cheated and
maligned each other, appeared in court together, and in general
had a publisher-author relationship that was noteworthy even for
Grub Street. In 1698 Roper had undertaken to bring out a collection of Brown's poems and letters, which was to be accom-

panied by a preface. For two months he waited for Brown's preface. Finally Roper wrote it himself:

The Bookseller to the Reader

Methinks I see the reader under a great disappointment, to find a book of Mr. Brown's stealing into the world without the equipage of a flaunting dedication or a prefatory epistle, like a painted young whore in the frontispiece of a nanny-house, to inveigle customers. What, says the reader, has all his munificent patrons made their exits? has he dropped those necessary requisites of a mercenary pen, impudence and importunity? or has the fumes of a long debauch raised such fogs about his brains, that nothing could be pumped from his poet's fingers? No, Gentlemen, he is retired into the country with some yellow and white chips of the Tower, and now looks as much above a bookseller, as a privy councillor above a porter; and the devil a line can I draw from him, whilst he fancies himself Lord of India. This is an epidemical disease among some scribblers, who have no wit to sell, while they have money to spend, or can be trusted; but when they are reduced to a low ebb, they'll sneak, fawn, and cringe, like a dog that has worried sheep, and dreads the halter. Then 'tis, kind Sir, your most obedient humble servant, wherein, dear sir, does it lie in the sphere of my activity to serve you, and earn half a crown to procure me credit for a fortnight in a cellar in the Strand. Now since 'tis inconsistent with my interest, to wait any longer in expectation of a preface, I have adventured 'em to run the risk of censure, and shift for themselves without one. Nor indeed do I apprehend any necessity to detain the reader in the portal, where the inside abounds with such variety of excellent furniture, as will sufficiently delight the ingenious contemplator; here and there are interspersed some words bordering upon indecency, for which I hope Mr. Collier, Corrector General of the profane and debauched press,[1] will take my author into chastisement, amongst the rest of the smutty poets, and he'll oblige my grateful acknowledgement, in a bottle of wine and a neat tongue, for helping me to sell some thousands of these books more; but methinks I hear some say, how come a bookseller to write

[1] *One of the leaders of the movement for moral reform and author of* of A Short View the Immorality and Profaneness of the English Stage *(1698).*

prefaces; why not say I, for the conversation of the town, and keeping company with the wits will do much; for what would Mr. D——y have done, who was bred a scrivener, if it had not been for the conversation of the town; or what would become of the young Oxonians and Cantabridgeans, if they wanted conversation; if any designed for the Gospel, they must troop down to supply the country pulpits; or for the Law, they would be only fit to carry a green bag after a councillor. I beg my reader's pardon, for being so prolix, but I have now done, and remain his humble servant.

In February, 1699, Matthew Smith, a schoolfellow of Tom Brown's, published his *Memoirs of the Secret Service* in an effort to extract more money from his employers for some shady political spying. When this did not work he published a second pamphlet, *Remarks upon the Duke of Shrewsbury's Letter to the House of Lords.* This got results. In December, 1699, Smith was committed to Gatehouse Prison for libel. In the earlier pamphlet Smith made a passing reference to Richard Kingston, a Whig pamphleteer, to which Kingston replied at once with *A Modest Answer to Captain Smith's Immodest Memoirs,* charging, amongst other things, that the *Memoirs* were edited and partly written by Tom Brown. The episode at this point was getting shrill and out of hand. But it was only beginning. On January 4, 1700, Roper printed an announcement in his *Post-Boy* that on the following Saturday there would be an answer to Kingston's 'knavish and villainous pamphlet'. On the Saturday, in the January 6-9 issue of *Post-Boy,* Roper inserted the following:

Whereas in our last there was inserted a scandalous, lying, knavish, villainous paragraph, intimating that on Saturday next would be published a reply to Mr. Kingston's *Modest Answer to Captain Smith's Immodest Memoirs and Impertinent and Saucy Remarks upon the Duke of Shrewsbury's Letter;* this is to certify that the said paragraph was put in by that common reproacher of mankind, Tom Brown, a sharking, mercenary, infamous poet, that finding his criminal confederacy [with Matthew Smith] detected, according to his usual practice calls names in answer to matters of fact, which being done by a profligate wretch of this character, we presume nobody will regard it.

Brown was a seasoned fighter of Grub Street battles, but this was too much even for him. In a rage, stimulated by a friend and a bottle of brandy, he stalked down to Roper's shop to give him the beating he deserved.

In the January 9-11 issue of the *Post-Boy* the following was inserted: 'Last Tuesday happened a most terrible and bloody fight between Tom Brown and a bookseller, but the particulars not yet coming to our hands we refer you to the next [issue].' Roper was a newspaper man and a publisher to his fingertips. The account came out in the next issue of the *Post-Boy* and also in a broadsheet:

A Full and True
A C C O U N T
of a
TERRIBLE & BLOODY FIGHT
BETWEEN
TOM. BROWN, THE POET,
And a BOOKSELLER.

On Tuesday last Tom Brown's passive valour being raised above its ordinary pitch by a large dose of brandy, and meditating a dire and bloody revenge against a bookseller that had spoke a few words to his disadvantage. In all haste he runs to a cane-shop for a oaken plant, but for want of twopence to purchase that dead-doing weapon, or so much credit as to be trusted for it, he was forced to leave it behind him. *Non habit quo restim emat ad suspendium.* However this disappointment of a weapon was no abatement to his fury. He immediately marches to the bookseller's shop. Charges him with slandering and dishonouring a person of his quality, and swaggers about the shop like a bully in a brandy cellar. The bookseller justifies himself, says, 'twas no injury to call a spade a spade nor Tom Brown a rake-hell, that had tricked him of three guineas, in palming a false copy upon him for a true one. These bitter words put Brown, and the bookseller to loggerheads helter-skelter. To Brown's immortal praise be it spoken, he gave the first blow, and strutted back with so much celerity and conduct, that the bookseller, who was immured behind the counter, was not able to reach him a Rowland for his Oliver. Whilst daring Tom made use of this stratagem, and fought at a distance, the fate of war inclined to the poet's side; but as the best formed designs are liable to accidents and mutabilities, so the bookseller by surprise, catching hold on the poet's sleeve with one hand, so battered his chops with the other, that quite turned the scales, and 'twas whether for a groat which would have the victory. A gentleman in the shop taking away the poet's sword, gave the bookseller the advantage of leaping over the counter; which amazed the poet perceiving, he scours off into the backshop, in hopes of a reinforcement. The enemy with all speed pursues him, and renews the engagement. Brown, like a gib-cat, fighting upon his back, and the itch, or his fears, rendering him unable to clench his fists, he fought open-handed, and clawed and scratched the bookseller's face, till the blood run down his fingers.

This, with the loss of an old cravat, was all the damage the bookseller sustained in a bloody rencounter, that lasted thirteen minutes, and twenty seconds. Tom Brown, of the two, was the greater sufferer; for wanting eyes to ward off the blows, the bookseller so unmercifully belaboured the poet's lockram jaws, that put his phiz quite out of countenance, and his face was so swelled and begrimed with a mixture of blood, sweat, snot, and tears, that would have pierced a heart of stone, to see what a frightful figure he trooped off in.

This is inserted in vindication of Tom Brown's honour, and to prove, though he is not fond of fighting without great advantage, he can claw and scratch like a tiger upon occasion; though some have been so bold to affirm, he does neither.

With this kind of publishing efficiency even Brown was at a loss. But what truly must have confounded Brown was that in the January 23-25 issue of the *Post-Boy* Roper advertised Brown's *Collection of Miscellany Poems, Letters, etc.*, complete with Roper's Preface, as well as Brown's best-known book, *Amusements, Serious and Comical*, as if nothing had ever happened. What was a libel or two when there was business to be done? This was the end of the long relationship between Brown and Roper. But the Kingston affair continued. On February 15, 1700, Matthew Smith issued a reply from his home in Gatehouse Prison, *A Reply to an Unjust, and Scandalous Libel, Intituled, A Modest Answer to Captain Smith's Immodest Memoirs*, accusing Kingston of forg-

ing the evidence that showed Brown as part-author of the
Memoirs of the Secret Service. The final blow in the battle was
Kingston's, on February 20, 1700, an overwhelmingly abusive
libel, *Impudence, Lying and Forgery Detected and Chastiz'd, &c.*,
in which he attacked both Smith and Brown. How accurate were
Kingston's charges, it is difficult to say. But Kingston was an
angry man and much of his attack against Brown can be dis-
counted:

There is no greater sign in the world of a bad and baffled
cause, than its being supported by ill-words, instead of arguments;
railing, for want of reason, and false suggestions instead of answers,
to plain and positive proofs. In the *Modest Answer to Brown's
and Smith's Immodest Memoirs and Remarks*, I charge them
with matters of fact, and quote credible witnesses to prove every
allegation; and they being utterly unable to refute any one particular through the whole discourse, are pleased to drop the controversy, and fall upon me, in such a rude and barbarous dialect,
as none but things of their own characters could be guilty of.
And therefore if the provocations they have given me, shall sometimes make me so far forget myself, as to requite them in kind,
I hope the reader will forgive me, considering I am engaging
against a couple of infamous scoundrels, who in hopes that the
devil will always sit at their doors, defy law and justice, and are
sworn enemies to truth, as well as to good manners. But thanks
be to Heaven, our age is more wise, genteel and modest, than to
take the drivel of cankered mouths, and the nasty froth of ulcer-
ated lungs, for a reply to serious matter; but on the contrary,
will despise every author, that treats his antagonist, and manages
his cause after such a beastly manner as these poltroons have
done, who if they had been bound seven years to the Devil to
learn the arts of lying and slandering, they could not have been
more their craft's masters than they are; and for which abuses, if
I don't take my remedy at law against both the authors, printer,
and publishers, let all mankind conclude me guilty, and till then
they must not expect, I will so far credit their scurrilous reply,
as to take any notice of their egregious and supposititious calumnies,
which are assisted by no other proof, colour or pretence, than the
impudent assertions of a couple of exploded villains.

Now before I rejoin to this insignificant, incoherent, and scandalous reply, it will be necessary to acquaint the reader why they dropped the argument to take revenge upon me, and who the persons are, that industriously but ineffectually strive to blast my reputation; for which no other reason can be assigned, but that Brown and Smith are tools for a party, that are the common scandalizers of the government, and reproachers of every administration: against whose calumnies my pen having been thought too severe. That sort of malcontented humorists, have by all clandestine arts imaginable, endeavoured to weaken my credit in that kind, and having this opportunity, lived in hope to gain their point, and that their libels against the government might pass with greater currency, when they had nobody to oppose them. . . .

'Tis true in the *Modest Answer* I called Brown a scoundrel, and now I take the liberty to add that he is a common shark, an infamous scandalizer, a notorious cheat, and has long since forfeited his ears to the pillory, and this I will prove not by asking ridiculous questions, such as he concludes his libel with (and might be asked of any man in Christendom) but by matters of fact and irreproachable evidences, of which I have many more by me, though I now produce but one upon each head, for fear of swelling this rejoinder, and forestalling the History of his Life, where you will find them *usque ad nauseam*.

Now, to show you Smith's man of honour and great veracity, who is stigmatized by all that know him, for one of the greatest liars in the world, and a common cheat! Come out dear Tom. Show thyself in thy own proper shapes and colours. See how simply he looks now? How maladroit the poor passive villain makes his appearance, now he's entering upon his trial. First,

I charge him with borrowing a suit of very fine linen, some years since, of Mr. Henry Playford, bookseller near the Temple, and never returning it, nor making any satisfaction for it. Secondly,

I charge him with selling a copy of a book, called *The Welsh Levite Toss'd in a Blanket,* to Mr. Thomas Jones, bookseller, for four pounds, and receiving the money of him, and afterward took the copy from him, under pretence of adding something to it, and sold it to another bookseller for the same sum, without ever making Mr. Jones any kind of satisfaction to this day, as you will find by the following letter he sent to me:

Sir, According to your desire I have sent you a short account of Mr. Brown's dealing with me, viz. I bought of him the copy of his book called the *Welsh Levite* for four pounds, paid him the money, and after I had had the copy about three days in my custody, he came to my shop, and told me he would give the preface a flourishing stroke, which would cause the book to sell much better: whereupon I delivered him the copy, and he went immediately and sold it to another bookseller, by whom it was printed; but Mr. Brown never paid me a penny of my money back. This is the truth, and I will make oath of it when you please. Another time he was pawned at the Rose Tavern without Temple Bar for eleven shillings; he sent for me to discharge the reckoning, which I did; but he never repaid me. At the Ship Tavern I lent him half a crown, and he promised to treat me; but instead of that, he went away and pawned me for the whole reckoning. He bit Mrs. Rand that keeps a linen shop at the Black Lyon in Newgate Street, of as much linen as came to thirty shillings, for which she has not got her money yet. After the same manner he had like to have served Mr. Barrow the tailor, but he arrested him for his money, and Dr. D. became bail for him, and he suffered the doctor to be taken in execution for it. He came to my brother and borrowed Dr. Brown's and Oldham's Works, and went and sold them immediately at the next shop for ready money. He writ a lampoon of half a sheet upon the late Dr. H——k, for a dozen of beer, and some bread and cheese. If I had a day's time to refresh my memory, I could fill a whole sheet with his tricks; but this may suffice till I see you. In the meantime I am, Sir, your humble servant,

Febr. 19. 1699. T. Jones.

Mr. Roper, bookseller, at the Black Boy in Fleet Street, who had been Brown's special friend upon all occasions, employed him to write a banter upon the new sect called Philadelphians.[1] Brown went several times to Hungerford Market to hear them, and having as he said furnished himself with matter, undertakes it, gets money at several times of Mr. Roper, while Brown pretended the work was under hand, and hearing Mr. Roper was going out of town, Brown tells him the copy was almost finished,

---

[1] *A sect of religious mystics that appeared in London in 1670.*

and therefore desires him to leave order, that upon delivering the copy he might receive the rest of the money agreed for. Mr. Roper consented to his desires, and the very next day after Brown knew Mr. Roper was upon his journey, Brown sews up a parcel of useless papers under a marble paper cover, with the following title: *Speculum Haeresiarcharum; Or, the Impostures of the New Sect, that call themselves Philadelphians, laid open in Six Letters, by Mr. Brown;* and flourishes the title page with a verse out of Horace, which in truth is his own proper character, prayer, and practice.

> Da mihi fallere, da sanctum justumque videri,
> Noetem peccatis, & fraudibus objice nubem.

With this specious title, under which was not one word relating to the subject, Brown trots to Mr. Roper's shop, and showing a manuscript under the title above written, Mrs. Roper not suspecting so vile a cheat, pays Brown three pound, that her husband had ordered for him upon delivery of the copy agreed for; which fraud was undiscovered till her husband's return; but Brown never made any satisfaction for the cheat. And if these repeated frauds don't merit a pillory, I know not what does.

Having sufficiently proved him a shark, and cheat, my next affair is to prove him a common makebate[1] and slanderer, which though I might do sufficiently by reciting several of his pamphlets and lampoons, wherein he has blasphemed the gods, affronted kings, libelled princes, scandalized the court and city, and in his scurrilous petitions spared no sex, order, or quality of men or women whatsoever; yet I rather choose to do it under this pleasant relation.

A gentleman of a clear reputation, and a plentiful fortune near B——w in Essex, accidentally falling into Brown's company in London, he invites him to his house in the country, where he entertained him nobly for a month, took him with him to other gentlemen's houses, and at length sent him away with money in his pockets. Not long after the gentleman commending Brown as a pleasant fellow to some of his neighbouring gentlemen, at whose houses Brown had been, they all agreed that Brown was pleasant

---

[1] *A provoker of quarrels.*

in his humour, but said he was a very rascal in his nature, for he
had scandalously treated that gentleman behind his back, that
had been so kind to him. Upon which they premeditated a revenge, invite Brown again into the country, and down he comes
as bluff as a bully at an ordinary.

The neighbouring gentleman hearing of his arrival, came
to attend a ceremony that Brown little dreamed of; and having
repeated his foul crimes and misdemeanours to him, in reviling
a gentleman that had been so extraordinary civil to him, they
told him *nolens volens* he must with his own hand draw up, and
sign a confession of his fault, beg pardon upon his knees, and
submit to a punishment which was to be inflicted upon him.
Brown readily performed the first part of his penance, and then
was led into the gentleman's hall to perform the latter.

Now the servants rolled him upon the table, as they mould
cockle bread. Then they screwed him up in a blanket from head
to foot, leaving a place like the holes of a pillory to speak through,
and having soundly shaked his corpse to settle him in his gears,
they mount him upon a stool of repentance, set for that purpose
in the middle of the hall, and then let in the mob to be his
auditors, whilst with an audible voice Brown makes this confession.

I, Thomas Brown, do acknowledge and confess myself to
be a rogue, a scoundrel, and a rascal, that deserves not to live,
for speaking dishonourably of this worthy gentleman, (pointing to
the master of the house), that has been my great benefactor, for
which villainous offence I am heartily sorry, humbly beg his pardon, and promise never to commit the like offence against any
man for the future.

When Brown had duly performed this penance, in manner
and form as aforesaid, and the mob had exercised their wits upon
him, he was thrown into a turnip cart screwed up as above-
mentioned, and the cart environed by a strong mob, shouting and
hallowing: he was carried in triumph through the town, and at
the end of it was shot out of the cart's arse into a dirty puddle,
and half a crown being put in his hand was sent packing on
Bayard a-ten-toes to London.

Thus have I showed you in little, Smith's man of great
veracity, whose true character you see is a cheating, lying knave,
that never gave any man an ill word to his face, nor a bad one
behind his back. . . .

Brown and Smith have made very bold with the honour and reputation of several gentlemen, that have done the government very considerable service; but that I pass over with silence, since it proceeds from such polluted mouths that are the contempt of mankind, whom to tie up from their meat was to scandalize Tyburn, and spoil a couple of ropes that might serve for better purposes. The gentlemen are all known to be such, and Brown and Smith can't hope to escape a due chastisement from them, if their being such inconsiderable scoundrels is not a protection to their ears and their shoulders. . . .

It was therefore a foolish and malicious enterprise in Brown and Smith to think to advance their own ill designs by quarrelling with me, who am a volunteer in this service, and have averred nothing upon my single testimony, but what is confirmed by others; therefore if they designed to take off my evidence by these clandestine methods, their attempts were in vain, unless they could remove the other gentlemen also, who you see stand the test, though they have been often entreated and threatened to do the contrary.

But the poor shabs are in their trade, they must be traducing and slandering somebody, they care not who! And what in the name of ill luck have they gained by this trial of skill, but bruised bones, and broken heads, and seen themselves detected as notorious liars and slanderers in every paragraph of their libel. And since they threaten stilll, and have made the contest only mine, let them know, the more they stir the worse they'll stink; for since I find I can write more in three days, than they were both (with that shagrag Dod's assistance) able to produce a reply to in seven weeks, (though they promised in the *Post-Boy* to answer it in one) they have a full employment for their lives; for I will never give them over while these three poltroons are unhanged, or give over their trade of lying and slandering.

Whether or not Brown engaged in all these adventures, they are typical of Grub Street. In fact, together with Kingston's testiness and Roper's tactics, they represent that enthusiasm in literary matters that is the Grub Street style.

The Publishers

Abel Roper

There is a strange biography of Abel Roper entitled *Some Memoirs of the Life of Abel, Toby's Uncle. Composed, Collated, Comprized, Compiled, Digested, Methodized, Written and Illustrated,* by Dr. Andrew Tripe (1726). Dr. Tripe is the pseudonym of William Wagstaffe (1685-1775), a physician and an accomplished satirist. His biography of Roper is rather crude and digressive, but it is, perhaps, the only comprehensive account available of one of Grub Street's more colourful publishers:

... Abel was born in the year 1665, of honest parents, at a market town called Atherston in Warwickshire, about nine miles from the City of Coventry. His father having a great number of children, could not do much for him, but gave him grammar education; and when he was about twelve years old, his uncle, a wealthy bookseller in London, sent for him, and put him to school in that famous metropolis, where he got into Greek before he understood Latin; for you must know, he generally learnt his lessons by rote; and the usher neglecting him, Abel was utterly spoiled for a scholar.

Being arrived at the age of fourteen, or thereabout, he was bound apprentice to his aforesaid uncle Abel Roper, in Fleet Street. But his master happening to die within a year and half, he was turned over to Mr. Christopher Wilkinson,[1] (who was a strict churchman, and lived in the same street) to serve the rest of his apprenticeship, which he did very faithfully and honestly; and after having been journeyman a year with the same master, he had a mind to set up for himself, on the foundation of £100 which his uncle had left him by will, beside the sole right and title to all his copies of books, valued at about £100 more. Accordingly, he took one side of a Saddler's shop next to Bell-Yard, over against the Middle Temple Gate; and it being a little before the Happy Revolution,[2] he industriously, though privately, sold pamphlets tending to bring it about; particularly the Prince of Orange's Declarations. Moreover he was the first that printed the famous 'Ballad of Lillyburlero'; though fearing to sell them publicly, he did not get much by it. But soon after, when his Highness's success was out of the question, Mr. Richard Baldwin[3] was not so cautious; for he reprinted the same, with the tune pricked to it, which sold prodigiously.

Speaking of the Prince of Orange, puts me in mind of a story I had from Abel's landlord: Mr. Loggan, the noted engraver, comes to him one day, and shows him a picture of Oliver Cromwell mounted on a prancing horse, with armies and a fleet about him, and underneath, this inscription, viz. His Highness Oliver, Lord Protector. Says Abel to him, I will be concerned in working off the plate; but you must first raze out Oliver's head, and engrave that of the Prince of Orange in its room. Make him a handsome gentleman, with a Roman nose, a little pock-fretten, and it will look like him: and as to the words underneath, you may let His Highness stand, and instead of Oliver, Lord Protector, make it William, Prince of Orange. Loggan went away, and altered the plate according to Abel's directions; so got a number worked off, and they went partners in the sale, which proved very profitable, notwithstanding the difference in people's judgements about the resemblance; some asserting, that it was very like the Prince; others, that it was not like him at all....

By this time having picked up a little money, he removed

---

[1] *A publisher from 1669 to 1693 (H. R. Plomer,* A Dictionary of the Printers and Booksellers *(1922).*

[2] *1688.*

[3] *One of the best-known publishers of the period (1653?-1698) (Plomer). He was foremost amongst the publishers in fighting against press restrictions and was a strong supporter of the Revolutionary Settlement of 1688.*

to a better shop, next door to the Devil Tavern in the same street, where Mr. Starky[1] above-mentioned had formerly lived. And writing news-letters[2] into the country, as his master had done before him he happened to insert a paragraph in one of them, relating to some Turkey ships I remember, though the particulars I could never learn; for which he was carried before the Earl of N[ottingham], then one of the principal Secretaries of State to King William; and after having been asked several questions concerning that paragraph, his Lordship gently reprimanded him, telling him he must take more care for the future, and so dismissed him, to his great consolation, this being the first time he was taken up.

The second time of Abel's trouble of this sort, he was summoned before Mr. Secretary Trumball, for neglecting to license a play he had printed of Mr. Southwell's, upon the complaint of Mr. Cooke, a lawyer, then Licenser of the Press: And being examined by one of the Under-Secretaries in relation to the said non-licence, he answered that Mr. Cooke's complaint was nothing but malice, because he refused to comply with his demand, which was a book of 6s. price; too much (says Abel) to give for a licence, that costs other people but half a crown.[3] Whereupon he was discharged.

After this, he lay quiet a year or two, till putting Tom Durfey,[4] of snappish memory, (but at that time in great vogue for his songs) upon writing a copy of verses on Dr. Sherlock,[5] late Dean of St. Paul's taking the oaths to King William, being convinced (as he said) by reading Bishop Overall's Convocation-Book; Mr. Durfey gave his poem the title of *The Weasel*; and not content with being very satirical upon the doctor, he was

[1] *John Starkey published in London from 1658 to 1689 (Plomer).*
[2] *An early form of the newspaper. Originally it supplied domestic news to patrons. After 1640 it went on sale to the public. Since it offered little comment on the news it escaped the restrictions of Government Licensers. The news letters were expensive (£5 a year) and only the well-to-do and the coffee houses could afford them. With the advent of the official Oxford Gazette in 1665 (later* The London Gazette), *which sold for a penny each, the days of the 'Newes Paper' had arrived.*
[3] *By the Licensing Act of 1662 every printed book required a government licence. The Act lapsed in 1695.*
[4] *Durfey (1653-1723) was a song-writer and playwright with a considerable popular following.*
[5] *William Sherlock (1641-1707) had earlier refused to give the oath of allegiance to King William, then changed his mind and was made Dean of St. Paul's.*

charged with some heterodox notions of the Resurrection toward the beginning of this work, nay and that it squinted atheistically too. Whereupon Abel received a visit from Robin Stevens, alias Hog, then Messenger of the Press,[1] and was by him carried before Sir George Treby, Attorney-General, afterwards Lord Chief Justice of the Common Pleas, who you must understand had no great opinion of Dr. Sherlock; and being asked how he came to print the pamphlet, he answered, that he had no other thoughts in doing it, but to get a penny, the times being hard. Upon which Sir George turned his head aside, but was perceived by culprit to smile, whom he presently commanded to go about his business, as he joyfully did; and the first thing was to blow this accident well, which made the poem sell so extraordinarily, that the press was kept going upon it night and day for almost a week.

But the courtiers and great men of the law were not the only people Abel had to deal with. He had sometimes the honour to appear before the Lord Mayor and Court of Aldermen, and sometimes before single aldermen acting as justices of the peace; once, for instance, when he happened to offend Sir Humphrey Edwin, by reflecting (as he would have it) on the Reformation of Manners Men [a Low Church movement to reform the morality of the age]; a set of people, in plain truth, he had no better opinion of, than the Lord Chief Justice Holt had.

Having printed a book entitled *The Art of Cuckoldom*,

---

[1] *The Messenger of the Press was one of the assistants of the Surveyor of the Press, who was first appointed in 1663. His duties, briefly, were to act as 'informer', and he was authorized to enter and search any house or shop for unlicensed books. No one performed this job with more alacrity than Robert Stephens, known affectionately to the trade as Robin Hog. He was Messenger of the Press from 1676 to 1684. In 1689 he was given the lofty title of 'Inspector of Printing Presses', which he held until 1697, with the power 'to apprehend the authors of divers false, scandalous and seditious books, papers, news, pamphlets and intelligences [news sheets], daily printed and dispersed, containing idle and mistaken relations of what passes, with malicious reflections upon persons, to the disturbance of the public peace, which are published without any authority contrary to the law.' He was given a warrant by the crown 'to search in all printing houses and elsewhere and to apprehend such authors, printers, bookbinders, hawkers, news-writers and others as shall be found to distribute unlicensed seditious false and scandalous books, prints, manuscripts, papers, etc.'* (Calendar of State Papers, Domestic Series of the Reign of William and Mary [*London, 1895*], I, 3; II, 32; IV, 319; V, 498. *Quoted from* Literary, Political, Scientific, Religious and Legal Publishing, Printing and Bookselling in England, 1551-1700, *Vol. II, by* Leona Rostenberg (1965).

That is, despite the fact that the Licensing Act lapsed in 1695 Stephens was still going about his duties of entering and searching. Even though the press attained considerable freedom—so much so that the government became alarmed and issued proclamations to check it—the writers and publishers of this relatively unbridled period were still in danger of sudden arrest.

B

wherein Robin Hog the Messenger said there were obscene expressions, he got the grand jury to find a bill of indictment against Abel, which did not a little perplex him. However, he resolved to try what that universal friend money would do. He made an offer of some coin to Robin, which he refused! Thereupon he slipped a piece of gold and a crown piece into his pocket; not so privately, but that it was perceived, as he designed. Immediately Mr. Hog grunted, as swine generally do when you scratch them on the belly, and said he could not promise to do him any service; but he would use his endeavour. The money had so kindly an effect, that Abel heard no more of the prosecution; and so much for this indictment.

By that time the affair in relation to the *Book of Cuckoldom* was well over, Abel married his mistress, the widow of Mr. Christopher Wilkinson before mentioned, and so became the partner of her bed, as he was before in the shop. He was then in the 31st year of his age; and yet it was generally believed by his neighbours, that Abel had kept his virginity for her. I wish I could have the same opinion of him: but I mistrust him the more, because in my conversation with him, he would often talk amorously, though not obscenely.

The next ruffle Abel met with, after his marriage, was occasioned by some book[1] Dr. [James] Drake had written [that a plot had existed to exclude Queen Anne from the throne]; which not being to the taste of the court, he was severely prosecuted for the same; but upon a *necnon* in the indictment, the jury acquitted him. Our friend Abel inserted in his *Post-Boy*, that there was a flaw in the indictment, &c. Upon which he was, by his old acquaintance Robin, taken up and carried before the Under-Secretary; and being examined about it, he answered, that he knew nothing of it till he saw it in the *Post-Boy*, (though by the by he told an untruth) and he stood to this, notwithstanding all the threats and good words they could give him; insomuch that not knowing what to do with him they ordered Robin Hog to carry him to the Tilt-Yard Coffee House, Whitehall, for a few hours; and in the mean while the Under-Secretary sent for Mr. Borret, then Solicitor of the Treasury, whose business it was to manage prosecutions against such as libelled the government,

[1] The History of the Last Parliament *(1702)*.

or the like; who being come to the office, little Abel was recon-
ducted thither; and being carried before Mr. Borret, Come Mr.
Roper, said that solicitor, you had best own this paragraph, and
we will be very indulgent to you, or words to that effect; upon
which the intended answerer smiled, and shook his head at the
same time. But this was not to serve his turn, the Under-Secretary
still pressing him to own it, nay giving him the four Evangelists
to kiss, with these words, Do you know anything relating to this
paragraph about Dr. Drake? To which Abel, perhaps tired out,
or otherwise grown angry, answered, That is a nonsensical question. This put the gentleman into such a passion, that he loaded
poor Abel with hard names, and ordered him into the custody
of one Clarke, a messenger. This was on the Saturday evening;
but our paragraph-hunter threatening to bring a *habeas corpus,*
was admitted to bail the next day in the afternoon, about six of
the clock. Mr. Borret afterwards told the Under-Secretary, he
was in the wrong, and that he ought not to have put that question to Abel, for nobody was obliged to accuse himself.

I am not certain, that it was upon this occasion the following occurrence happened; but if not, it was in relation to something inserted in his paper much about the same time.

Abel being apprehensive that Mr. Beardwell, his printer,[1]
would be taken up and examined, went and said thus to him:
Mr. Beardwell, I believe you will be taken up: You know you
are often afflicted with the gout; be sure you lie abed longer than
ordinary tomorrow morning. This was, as I take it, the Sunday
evening, after he was bailed; and he added, My meaning is, if
you hear any stranger coming upstairs, be sure you cry out and
make a doleful noise, as if the gout was very strong upon you.
And just as Abel had guessed, two of the messengers coming upstairs the next morning, Mr. Beardwell acted his part as dextrously as any theatrical tragedian could have done; and a report
being made at the Secretary's office, of his bad state of health,
and that it might endanger his life to remove him, the stratagem
took so effectually, that the printer heard no more of that
affair. . . .

We shall now proceed to something more material. You
must know he still kept printing of books; one of which was

---

[1] *Printer of the* Post-Boy *from April 20, 1697 (Plomer).*

written by Capt. [Matthew] Smith, of about 2s. price, entitled
Memoirs of the Secret Service;[1] and as it was in relation to the
Duke of Shrewsbury, containing an account of what the author
called his Grace's ill usage of him, several copies of letters were
inserted, which concerned the Duke, who was then one of the
principal Secretaries of State. So as soon as this book appeared
abroad, Abel was taken up, and examined by his Grace's Under-
Secretary Mr. Vernon, who told him, that if he did not deliver
into his custody the whole impression, he should be severely prosecuted; and Abel fearing the ill consequences that might ensue
upon his refusal, actually sent him all the books, and thereby
put a stop to the prosecution. But I have heard him complain of
this as a great hardship; for soon after, it seems, Mr. John Darby
the printer[2] reprinted this very book by the author's directions,
perhaps with a few trivial alterations; and the same was published and sold with impunity, nobody being ever questioned
about it. . . .

The next thing remarkable in this man's life was, that
having printed a book of about 3s. 6d. price, entitled *The History
of The Conspiracy Against King William,* &c. written by Dr.
[Richard] Kingston,[3] wherein was inserted a list of several gentlemen, but instead of their names at length, only the two first letters
of them; there happened among these to be Sir W. C. Thereupon
Sir William Coryton, Baronet, came in a great hurry to Abel,
and demanded to know the reason why he inserted his name in
the list? Abel told him, he had not, that he knew of. Yes, said
Sir William, you have, pointing to the place in the book where
Sir W. C. was printed. Abel, to justify himself, pretended he did
not know Sir William was meant by it. Yes, said Sir William, I
am meant by it; and I will make my complaint to the House of
Commons, of which he was then a member. Sir, cried Abel, I
wish you would; for that will make the book sell the better. Upon
which Sir William went away in a great huff, and told Mr.
Timothy Goodwin, his bookseller,[4] who lived hard by, what had
passed, calling Abel an impudent and saucy fellow. No, Sir, says
Tim, the man is reckoned an honest and modest man; and is very

[1] *See above, p. 21.*
[2] *Printed in London, 1662-1704 (Plomer).*
[3] *See above, p. 21.*
[4] *An eminent publisher in Fleet Street from 1683 to 1720 (Plomer).*

right in his notion, for your complaint would certainly make the book sell; and therefore I believe you had better be silent. Accordingly Sir William took his advice, and dropped his intended complaint. This story I had from Mr. Goodwin's own mouth; and it puts me in mind of the following.

After the discovery of the Assassination Plot,[1] a General Council was held upon a Sunday, in which a proclamation was ordered for seizing several of the conspirators therein named, with £1000 reward for each of them. Abel gets a list of them that afternoon, and by six of the clock the next morning publishes what he called *A True Account of the Conspiracy*, with a list of the conspirators' names. This happened on the 23rd February, 1695. That afternoon (viz. Monday) the proclamation appeared and in it the names of the conspirators, as mentioned in Abel's paper published in the morning. There were particularly named in it, the Duke of Berwick, (then said to be come to London to forward the design), Sir George Barclay, Major Lowick, George Porter, Capt. Stow, Capt. Walbank, Capt. James Courtney, Dinant, Chambers, Boyse, George Higgons, Davis, Cardal, Goodman, Cranburn, Keys, Pendergrass, Byerly, Trevor, Sir George Maxwell, Durance, Chr. Knightly, King, Sir William Parkins, and Rookwood. Now several of these not knowing the plot was discovered, till they heard Abel's account cried about the streets, jumped out of bed, and made their escapes; which irritated the Government against him, so that he was taken up, and a prosecution ordered upon the same. Thus poor Abel, once more in the suds, has recourse to Mr. Gillibrand, I think then a messenger, but formerly a bookseller, and a man in good esteem among the great ones; and presenting him with four or five guineas, Gillibrand went and told them, he dared to say Abel had no design but to get money in publishing his account, without dreaming of the mischief he did by it; upon which the prosecution was dropped. . . .

Some time after [Roper's fight with Brown] when they were very good friends again, Tom Brown wrote a half-sheet poem entitled, *A Satyr upon the French King*. This, if I remember right, was immediately after the Peace of Ryswick;[2] and as no

---

[1] *A Jacobite plot to assassinate King William. The date was 1696, not 1695.*
[2] *Dr. Tripe is confused about his dates. The Treaty of Ryswick, the substance of the poem, was in September, 1697. Brown's fight with Kingston and Roper was 1699-1700.*

ambassador was yet arrived from France, Abel thought he might print it very safely; but was soon made sensible of his mistake, complaint being preferred against him by an agent of the court of France who was then in England; so he was taken up, with his author, for whom he was obliged to find bail, as well as for himself; but poor Tom was reported to be sent to Newgate, upon which Mr. Fleetwood Shepheard[1] wrote a very ingenious elegy upon him. . . .

Abel knew not what to do with this prosecution (for an indictment was drawn up against him), and dreading the consequences if proceeded on, goes to a friend of his, that was an intimate acquaintance of the Under-Secretary's, and puts him upon asking a letter in his favour to Capt. Baker (I think it was) then solicitor against men under his circumstance; which the Under-Secretary granted. This incendiary, as I may call him, was advised with the letter to carry a couple of guineas; and so he heard no more of the matter. This I had from Mr. Isted, then Chamber-Keeper of the Wine-Licence Office, who was a very good friend to Abel upon this occasion, induced thereto by his son's being bound apprentice to him, who is now a bookseller in the same street. . . .[1]

Brown's *Satyr upon the French King* was a clever bit of doggerel that exactly captured the issue of the moment. For most Englishmen the Treaty of Ryswick meant peace, the end of one of the several wars with France and the final defeat of James II. But to the Jacobites, who supported the deposed King James, it was a betrayal of the cause, since Louis XIV agreed to withdraw his support from James and recognize William. To the four hundred clergymen who were dispossessed of their living for refusing to swear allegiance to William, the Treaty meant ruin. In these verses Brown assumed the pose of a "non-swearing parson" who has just received the news of the treaty. The satire is more against Louis than the parson, but it delightfully burlesques the parson's distress, particularly his extreme partisanship, which is one of the stock satiric targets of this highly partisan age.

---

[1] *Sir Fleetwood Shepheard (1634-1698), a Restoration courtier, poet and satirist. He was considered one of the wits of the age.*
[2] *J. Isted published in Fleet Street from 1711 to 1725 (Plomer).*

A SATYR
upon the FRENCH KING.
Written by a Non-Swearing-Parson, and drop'd out of his
Pocket at Sam's Coffee-House.
Facit indignatio Versum.

And has thou left Old Jemmy[1] in the lurch?
A plague confound the doctors of thy Church.
Then to abandon poor Italian Molly,
That had the firking of thy bum with holly.
Next to discard the Prince of Wales,
How suits this with the Honour of Versailles?
Fourthly, and lastly, to renounce the Turks,
Why this is the Devil, the Devil, and all his works.
. . . .

Lord! with what monstrous lies, and senseless shams,
Have we been cullied all along at Sam's.
Who could e're believed, unless in spite,
Lewis le Grand would turn rank Williamite?
Thou, that hast looked so fierce, and talked so big.
In thy old age to dwindle to a Whig,[2]
By heaven, I see thou'rt in thy heart a prig.
I'd not be for a million in thy jerkin,
'Fore George thy soul's no bigger than a gherkin.
Hast thou for this spent so much ready Rhine?
Now, what the plague will become of *jure divine*?[3]
A change so monstrous I could ne'er ha' thought,
Though Partridge[4] all his stars to vouch it, brought
S'life, I'll not take thy honour for a groat.
. . . .

Thou makest me swear, that am a known Non-Juror.
But though I swear thus, as I said before,
Know, King, I'll place it all upon thy score.
. . . .

Since thou hast spoiled my prayers, now hear my curses.
May thy affairs, (for so I wish by heavens)

[1] *James II.*
[2] *For the most part the Whigs supported William.*
[3] *The Stuart doctrine of divine right of kings.*
[4] *John Partridge, a popular astrologer of the period.*

All the world o'er at sixes lie and sevens.
May Conti be imposed on by the Primate,
And forced, in haste, to leave the Northern climate:
May he rely upon their faith, and try it,
And have his bellyfull of the Polish diet.
May Maintenon,[1] though thou so long hast kept her,
With brand-venereal singe thy royal sceptre.
May all the poets, that thy fame have scattered,
Un-god thee now, and damn what once they flattered.
May Pope, and thou, be never cater cousins.
And fistulas thy arse-hole seize by dozens.
Thus far in jest; but now to pin the basket,
May'st thou to England come, of Jove I ask it,
Thy wretched fortune, Lewis, there to prop,
I hope thou'lt in the Friars take a Shop,
Turn puny-barber there, bleed lousy carmen,
Cut corns for chimney-sweepers and such vermin,
Be forced to trim (for such I'm sure thy fate is)
Thy own Huguenots, and us Non-Jurors gratis.
May Savoy with thee hither pack,
And carry a raree-show upon his back.
May all this happen, as I've put my pen to't,
And may all Christian people say amen to't.

Brown and Abel Roper, the printer, were arrested not for obscenity, as the poem might suggest, but for disturbing the peace that the treaty between William and Louis implied. In his usual way, Abel Roper escaped being sentenced, as the *Life of Abel* describes. After six months the case collapsed and Brown also was released. But the very fact that Brown was arrested brought joy to some of his enemies. One of them, presumably Fleetwood Shepheard, as the *Life of Abel* suggests, wrote a 'Petition of Tom Brown, who was taken up on account of the *Satyr upon the French King*', which ended in the following lines:

But if you had rather convert the poor sinner,
His foul writing mouth may be stopped with a dinner;
Give him clothes to his back, some meat and some drink,
Then clap him close prisoner without pen and ink,
And your petitioner shall neither pray, write, nor think.

[1] *Louis XIV's mistress.*

There was also a 'Recantation', pretended to be written by Brown, which is even worse doggerel than the original satire:

And has this Bitch, my Muse, trepanned me:
Then I'm as much undone as can be;
I knew the jilt would never leave me
'Til to a prison she'd deceive me;
Cursed be the wretch, and sure he's cursed
That taught the trade of rhyming first;
. . . .

Alas! alas! I'm now in jail;
My wits are rather on the rack
To save my own poetic back:
. . . .

Believe me, sirs, as I am a sinner,
I writ that satire for a dinner:
And stamped it with a parson's name,
Not as I meant them any shame,
But since I must the matter tell,
I thought 'twould make the paper sell:
By all that's good, and all that true is,
I ever loved and honoured Louis:
He's great and wise: more could I say
But fear again to disobey;
And for his priests, I here protest,
I value them like all the rest:
And though I cursed them all, what then?
The men are honest, harmless men.
Next for King James and Prince of Wales,
I always wished them happy gales;
And for my saucy naming Molly,
I own 'twas impudence and folly.
Lastly, for naming the Non-Juror,
Why that was but poetic furor,
I know I have ungrateful been;
'Twas raging hunger drew me in
T'abuse those very friends that have
Almost preserved me from the grave;

B*

They're honest men, mark what I say,
If I love any priests, 'tis they.
I now confess 'tis highly base,
T'insult the gown in such a case:
And could the thing be done again,
I'd starve before I'd wrong such men.
. . . .
For three long weeks my muse and I
Had been shut up in garret high:
The cause, I think, I need not tell
Poet with pox convertible;
While thus I lay in desperate state,
In comes a bawd, whose name was Kate;
A rampant jade, where once I tabled,
Who finding me of strength disabled,
Not vows nor promises could save me,
But off she tears the clothes she gave me.
And thus of coat, e'en shirt bereft,
Poor naked Tom in bed was left.
. . . .
All friends I tried, not one was willing
To credit me with one poor shilling:
In this distress, without advising,
I fell to cursed satirizing.
Oh! pity me, or I am lost,
Far worse than when in blanket tossed;[1]
And if this time I'm spared from whipping,
If e'er again you catch me tripping,
May all the plagues that e'er befell
A poet poor, on this side Hell,
Seize me at once, and may I be
A public mark of infamy:
May all my whores and duns o'ertake me,
And all my friends (even Bess) forsake me;
And may the pox, with which I struggle,
Joined with the gout, afflict me double:
May I at last by inches die,
First lose my nose, and then an eye;

---

[1] *Another punishment Brown incurred for his writing labours. See above, p. 28.*

And when I'm dead, then may I have
A just memento on my grave.

[Not very subtle, but the spirit is pure Grub Street.]

After this [continues the *Memoirs of the Life of Abel, Toby's Uncle*], joining with others of the trade, Abel printed a half-sheet, entitled *The Auction of Ladies,* and prefixed to it the picture of a black ram; wherein several young ladies, especially tradesmen's daughters, were scandalously reflected on; and the bachelors, you must think, did not fare much better. The paper was witty, and some of them written by Tom Brown, and sold extraordinary well, till Numb. VIII. or IX. came out, on which ensued a prosecution, and so put a stop to that pernicious way of abusing young people. For their design was (as I have been informed) to go through the whole town with it. Their scandal was couched after an insinuating manner, as thus: a young lady that lives within a mile of Fleet Street, &c. for there were no names printed. But some of the persons so reflected on, employed Robin Stevens to carry on the prosecution, notwithstanding the paper was laid down; and it went so far, that they were found guilty of printing and publishing the said paper: whereupon their counsel moved to be heard in relation to the merits of the cause, viz. whether it was scandalous as set forth in the indictment; and, whether, when no names were printed, it could be proved that such and such persons were meant? For instance now, it was said in one of those papers, that a sly bachelor, not two miles from Temple Bar, had lately burnt his fingers in the cold bath. Why it was true, that Capt. Sly the haberdasher without Temple Bar had been unsuccessful in his undertaking of setting up a cold bath near Islington; but would anybody have thought the captain would for that reason contribute toward the prosecution, and even make himself one of the evidence against them at their trial? After this, my little libeller applies to his old acquaintance Hog, and gives him four or five guineas not to concern himself any more about it; which had so good an effect, that they heard no more of the matter: and when the gentlemen who clubbed to the prosecution came to Robin, and asked the reason why he did not proceed in that affair, he answered, that he had met with a very great misfortune; for he lost all the papers relating to the cause.

'The Auction of Ladies' or 'Characters of Several ingenious designing Gentlewomen, Who have lately put into the *Ladies Invention*' was printed in 1699, before the Kingston affair—not after, as the *Life of Abel* indicates. At that time lotteries were so popular they had become a national madness, which was reason enough for Grub Street to provide a burlesque lottery, the *Invention*, with the added attraction of the ladies who put their money in it. It was the mixture as ordered, fashionable gambling, sex and a whiff of scandal, guaranteed to sell on any Grub Street in the world. The portraits were coarse and libellous, in some instances so like their originals, who were prominent people of the town, that they attracted considerable attention. This was good for business. Unfortunately, not everyone understood the business requirements of Grub Street and Abel Roper, as the *Life* describes, was prosecuted for libel. The author of the libels, Tom Brown, was not discovered.

Some sections of the 'Characters' are worth quoting as an example of the pure Grub Street product, unadulterated by either subtlety or good taste!

II. A bonny buxom widow in the Strand, living at the sign of the Black Bull with the Golden Cod, has ventured the price of four gallons of cold tea in the same bank, in hopes that she shall have the picking of a second husband's marrowbones. As she was unluckily mistaken in the ability of her first man, she intends to take the same course in the choice of her next, as the citizens do in choosing a lecturer, and will make him preach in her pulpit, before she will give him presentation.

III. A young termagant widow of twenty-two, at the sign of the Reynard in Fleet Street, who some years ago ran away with a captain, since dead, and whose mother is a well-wisher to the Mathematics, has put in four and sixpence, in hopes to be lifted under another officer. She and her virtuous sister endeavour all they can, as obedient daughters ought, to promote their father's trade, and know what's the proper use of that necessary piece of household stuff, called a bed. . . .

VI. A cutler's daughter in Cheapside, who is true metal to the back, and will endure grinding to the end of the chapter, has ventured full 13s. and 6d. to get her a portion. To encourage all young fellows, to put in for the plate, she has promised beforehand, that let the worst come to the worst, if her husband brings his knife with him, she'll take care to find him a sheath for't, and a fork to boot, who never fails in bathing-time to take a turn down to the waterside, to see what materials the prentices carry about 'em.

VII. A tailor's carrot-pated daughter in Exeter Street, purloined so much cabbage from that old thief her father, as came to the sum of fifteen shilling, and ventured it last week in the lottery. She knows exactly how many inches goes to the making of a yard, and let her spark bring never so much stuff with him, she has a certain place called Hell, which is deep enough to receive it. . . .

IX. A venerable piece of antiquity, near Guildhall, aged sixty-five, but as good a maid as ever blew in a candle, who if you'll take her word for't spoiled her teeth with cracking of peach-stones when she was young, weary of lying alone, and loath to divert the Devil with leading of apes in his dominions, had the faith to venture four King Harry angels in the lottery. This ancient person may serve for a warning to the rest of the sex, for she that might have had coral enough given her gratis in her younger days to rub her gums with, is forced now to go the charge of buying it, and may thank her maker if she gets it. . . .

Since the invention was successful, it naturally attracted imitators who played their own variations on the theme:

A Continuation of a Catalogue of Ladies, to be set
up by Auction, on Monday the 6th of this instant
July.
Catalogues are distributed by the booksellers of
London and Westminster.

CONDITIONS of Sale

First, He who bids most is the buyer; and if any difference arises, she is to be put again.

Secondly, That no person shall bid less than £200 the first proposal, and always advance £100.

Thirdly, That all of them shall be bound up in silks; and if any shall happen to be otherwise, the Party that buys them shall be at liberty to take them away, or leave them.

By E. Cl——r, Auctioneer, that sold the young Heiress in
Q—— Street

		£
1.	One brisk underbuilt young widow near Temple Bar, who wants to be probed	1000
2.	A buxom young maid of 19 years of age, who stinks of powder, by the same Bar, provided her father hath not given the £800 to the poor, will be worth	2000
3.	A vintner's widow, who formerly lived against St. Dunstan's Church, by reason of her non-reputation	500
4.	Three sisters in Shier Lane, very brisk, but 2nd hand, and go for maids each	800
5.	An old maiden-sempstress in Fleet Street	500
6.	A bookseller's only daughter in St. Paul's churchyard, if her father's debts be all paid value	1600
7.	A rich widow, humped-back, and crooked legs, who has buried 2 husb.	100
8.	A country farmer's daughter, lately come to town, and lodges in Essex Street, a good face, but an ugly gait	1100
9.	A famous conventicler's daughter, near Covent Garden, provided he has a good gathering this year, will give her	1500
10.	A councillor's daughter in the Temple, very well accomplished, only loves brandy	2300
11.	An Irish lady, very tall, aged 16	2700
12.	A solicitor's daughter, not straight, but a good face	4000
13.	Two sisters, tall handsome women lodging by Shoe Lane, each	1000
14.	A plumber's daughter in Fleet Street, brisk and airy, not to be bought under a coach and 6	1200
15.	A tailor's daughter in the same court, with a flaxen tower to cover her carrot head, worth	800
16.	A fat widow of St. Bride's Parish, she is but a foolish, a lumping penny-worth	200
17.	An ale-house-keeper's daughter in Bell Yard, worth	10000

		£
18.	A barber's wife near St. Dunstan's Church, lately divorced from her husband, a pretty woman, and fit for service	What you please
19.	The widow of the famous Dr. S——fold, late student in Physic, Astrology and Poetry, besides her talent in a napkin	200 per ann.
20.	A young orphan right honourable by the father's side and right by the mother's	3000

Of the imitations of the *Invention,* the main one was probably by William Pittis (1674-1724) who published 'Characters of Gentlemen that have put in to the *Ladies Invention*'. Roper and Brown quickly published their own 'Characters of Gentlemen', with the following advertisement: 'Whereas there was a paper which came out on Friday last, with a stagshead for the device: this is to acquaint the world, that none are genuine but what have this crested ram prefixed.' And so the Grub Street battle continued.

Even though Roper escaped sentencing for his part in the *Invention,* there was still a hue and cry after the author. It was rumoured that it was Pittis. There was not much point in arresting Pittis, however, because he was already in jail for debt. But two months later appeared the following *Elegy* on the 'death' of Pittis, 'Author of the Characters'. Very likely Tom Brown had a hand in this—the real author attacking the supposed author for his shamefully libellous tactics—because the *Elegy's* epitaph later appeared in Brown's *Amusements.*

AN ELEGY

On the Death of the Author of the Characters, &c. of the Ladies Invention, who dyed on the 13th of this instant May at the Rose Spunging-house[1] in Woodstreet, under an Arrest. Written by a Young Gentleman whom he had abused in his Characters.

> He's dead! Lament ye mercuries and hawkers,
> And Mourn his timeless fall ye tavern-chalkers.
> . . . .

---

[1] *Sponging houses were kept by bailiffs to confine debtors, usually before they went to debtors' prison.*

Even I unknown to verse, a young beginner
Will dare to sing our late departed sinner.
    First for his courage, hear of what I'm treating;
He dared deserve, and sometimes, stood a beating;
Nor was our rhyming hero e'er afraid,
Of wife, or widow, spinster, or of maid;
All were abused, as was his just intention,
And underwent the lash of his invention;
. . . .
    But, grief prevails, and gains upon my spirits,
And I must e'en pass by his other merits,
For who can sing, and not be broken-hearted
So learned a soul, from such a corpse departed:
Methinks I see him sitting at the Goat,
His wig untwisted, and unlined his coat,
His eyes just dropping out, his cheeks a-glowing,
His head a-swimming and his tongue a-going;
One hand the pot is grasping by the handle,
And t'other deals about his stock of scandal;
Whilst porters laugh, and many a trading fool
Wishes his friends had sent him too to school;
Whilst Lewis shakes his sides, and men of Wales
Leave toasted cheese to feed upon his tales.
. . . .
    But I too long my tears, and sighs have spent,
And fruitless vows for Pittis upward sent,
To verse in vain my sorrows I've digested,
He'll ne'er return again to be arrested!

The EPITAPH

Reader, beneath this turf I lie,
    And I am e'en content;
Piss if you please, pray what care I?
    Since now my life is spent.
A marble stone indeed might keep
    My body from the weather,
And gather people as I sleep,
    And call more fools together:
But had'st thou been from whence I came,
    Thou'dst never mince the matter,

But show thy sentiments the same,
  And hate stone-doublets after.
I'm dead, and that's enough t'acquaint
  A man of any sense,
That if he's looking for a saint,
  He must go farther hence.
Between two Roses down I fell,
  As 'twixt two stools a platter.
One held me up exceeding well,
  T'other did no such matter.
The Rose by Temple Bar gave wine
  Exchang'd for chalk, and filled me,
But being for the ready coin,
  The Rose in Wood Street killed me.

If Brown was responsible for the *Elegy*, it may have had something to do with a public apology Pittis made in the July 5-7 *Post-Boy*: 'Mr. William Pittis . . . having scandalized Mr. Brown and others signed the following note yesterday, July 6th, 1698. "I do acknowledge that I lately scandalized Mr. Thomas Brown, in a late half sheet of paper, and am very sorry for doing it, and beg his pardon. William Pittis." ' How they wrung this humiliating apology out of Pittis, we can only imagine. His lampoon must have drawn blood. But Brown's response—if it was his *Elegy*—hounding Pittis for his own libel, must have been a sweet revenge. We return again to the *Life of Abel* [Roper]:

This same Abel, though amorous sometimes, would yet never own himself guilty of printing any obscene books, except one, which tended that way, entitled, *A Collection of Poems, &c.* written by Mr. Tho. Brown. He put his bookbinder's name to it, viz. William Sparkes, who still lives in Fetter Lane. Away goes Robin the Messenger to this binder's, and knocking at the door, enquires for Mr. Sparkes. Sparkes, though at work in the garret, heard him; and knowing his voice, answered Robin, that he was not at home; for which Robin called him an impudent fellow, &c. This reaching Abel's ears, he made a paragraph of it; but was forced to go to the Messenger's, and atone for it, by giving him a handsome gratuity. At this time, Mr. John Nutt[1] near Stationers Hall was Abel's publisher of pamphlets, and Robin's near neighbour; who understanding that Mr. Hog made a sort of property of his friend Abel, went to him and said, You have this fellow (Robin Hog) always grunting after you for money; if you will take my advice, give him no more; or else he will be perpetually plaguing you. I know his humour; he will do nothing for nought, as the saying is. He took his advice; and it proved just as Mr. Nutt had persuaded. This I had from Mr. Nutt himself.

Abel was once summoned before the Board of Admiralty at Whitehall; and being asked how he came to give an account, in his *Post-Boy*, of the departure of his Majesty's ships in time of war, by which means the enemy would be apprised of it, he answered, that he only printed the port news, and was not aware of any harm that could accrue from thence, by inserting it in his paper. He was therefore reprimanded, and told, that he should not for the future put in anything of that nature, but what he might take from *The Gazette*.[2] His answer was to this effect: that it would then be stale, and consequently no news. Upon which Mr. B—— said, Come to me, and I will inform you as to port news; but he never did. The author of the *Post-Man*[3] being also summoned at the same time, he answered and said nothing, but cringed and complimented, and promised to take care for the future; which made the worse for Abel, who was stiff, and would promise no such thing. . . .

Mr. George Ridpath, author of the *Flying-Post*,[4] having been tried at Guildhall for inserting in his paper some scandalous reflections upon Queen Anne, had not the curiosity to stay in court till the jury brought in their verdict, but wisely made off, and never stopped (after he heard they had brought him in guilty) till he reached the banks of Holland; where being in company

---

[1] *London printer and publisher from c. 1690 to c. 1710 He was the publisher of Swift's* A Tale of a Tub *(1704)*.
[2] The London Gazette, *the official Government paper.*
[3] *Jean de Fonvive, a Huguenot exile. He was regarded, with Abel Boyer, Dunton and Defoe, as the best of the newsmen.*
[4] *From 1696? to 1713 (Crane and Kaye).*

with several English gentlemen some time after, their conversation turned upon affairs of their own nation, and George asked Sir John Walter, Baronet, who was of the number, (then Clerk of the Green Cloth, and Member of Parliament for the City of Oxford) whether he knew Abel Roper, for he was a great rogue, &c. Sir John answered, I know Abel, and believe him to be a very honest fellow; but there is one Ridpath, whom I do not know, is a very rascal, &c. Upon which George was extremely humble and silent; but the rest of the company sneered.

George Ridpath's crime was not great. His main mistake was to be a powerful Whig writer when the Tories were in power. The Whigs valued him so highly they were prepared to subscribe for his defence. But Ridpath, fearing a severe sentence, broke bail, fled to Scotland and then to Holland.

As for Abel Roper, according to Plomer, he was still in business in 1726. But Abel's biographer does not take us this far:

'. . . having mislaid some other memorandums of him, particularly as to his amours, that of Lord William, &c. (which, however, I am in hopes of recovering, for I am sure they are somewhere among my papers), I must defer the rest till another time.' And the biography abruptly stops.

EDMUND CURLL

The publisher-booksellers of Grub Street were the first to discover the basic principles of popular publishing. They learned the importance of hawking well-known names even if they had small relevance to the book they were selling, of promising titillation on the title-page whether or not they could deliver it in the text, and of selling controversy, scandal, and muck-raking, even if they had to invent them. While their dignified descendants today have to buy their material—secret lives of newly-dead statesmen, confessions of duchesses and prostitutes—the early Grub Street publishers could acquire theirs by subtle thefts and trickery.

Of all the Grub Street booksellers,[1] the most famous is Edmund Curll. He was the flower of Grub Street, the most colourful literary pirate of the day, and was duly enshrined by Swift and Pope as Grub Street's very spirit. Thomas Amory, in his *Life of John Buncle* (1756), describes him as 'in person very tall and thin, an ungainly, awkward, white-faced man. His eyes were a light-grey, large, projecting, goggle and purblind. He was splay-footed, and baker-kneed.' Amory gives a capsule character of Curll which will serve as an introduction to the man: 'He had a good natural understanding, and was well acquainted with more than the title pages of books. He talked well on some subjects. He was not an infidel. . . . He told me, it was quite evident to him that the Scriptures of the Old and New Testament contained a real revelation.' However, Amory continues, 'he was a debauchee to the last degree, and so injurious to society, that by filling his translations with wretched notes, forged letters, and bad pictures, he raised the price of a four shilling book to ten. . . . And when I told him he was very culpable in this, and other articles he sold, his answer was, What would I have him do? He was a bookseller. His *translators* in *pay*, lay three in a bed, at the *Pewter-Platter* Inn in *Holborn*. . . .'[2]

---

[1] *It will be noticed that the terms 'bookseller' and 'publisher' are used almost interchangeably. In the early days of publishing the man who printed the book also published it and sold it retail. 'Bookselling' referred to each of these activities. As the number of published books increased and the market developed, booksellers began to vary their stock by exchanging the books they had printed for books printed by other presses. 'Hence the familiar form of the 17th-century title-page: "printed by A, and may be had of B, C and D" ' (Marjorie Plant,* The English Book Trade *[1965], p. 67, from which this note on the bookseller is taken). In this way the two capacities of the 'bookseller' came to be separated. 'In the first instance he has had personal dealings with the author, has helped to plan the final form of the book, and has arranged for and taken the financial risks involved in its printing and circulation; in the other he is merely offering for sale various works produced quite independently of him. Here we have the essential difference between publishing and bookselling; but for a long period no such difference was recognized in common speech.'*

The term 'publisher' came into use by the 18th century. But it was some time before the different capacities of 'bookselling' was clearly and permanently distinguished.

To complicate matters further, publishers were also sometimes called stationers since, in fact, they were not only printers and booksellers, but often paper-makers and binders as well. The name Stationers Company—membership of which was open to all those involved in the production and sale of books—indicates this emphasis. By the end of the 18th century the separate functions were being differentiated.

[2] *Pp. 382-383.*

Today's publishing laws would have inhibited Curll's best efforts.[1] But in his time (1683-1747) even the Copyright Act of 1709[2] gave no protection to the author and only slight protection to the publisher. If the publisher had listed his publication at Stationer's Hall and was prepared to bring action against the offending publisher, he could hope for some redress. Such actions were in fact rarely brought, and Curll's genius blossomed unimpeded.

The conventional literary pirate, such as Henry Hills, merely issued cheap reprints of a successful book without permission. A popular poem or pamphlet selling for 6d. or a shilling would suddenly appear in a new penny or twopenny edition with the Hills imprint, published, as Hills explained, for the best of reasons, to propagate learning amongst the poor. The original publisher, usually no philanthropist, would print warnings in the news journals that the edition was 'unauthorized' or that it was 'printed from an imperfect copy', that it was a fraud. But Henry Hills was not easily dissuaded from his charitable work. Sometimes, Straus points out, the publisher who issued a book without the author's permission might not be at fault. The manuscript might have been passed from one person to another till finally it reached some public-spirited citizen who felt that the world must not be deprived and would offer to sell the manuscript, perhaps even persuading the publisher that it was his to sell. Curll frequently got his manuscripts this way, though he was less curious than most about the legality of the transaction. The publishing problem was complicated further by authors who actually wanted the

---

[1] *For much of my comment on Curll I am indebted to Ralph Straus's excellent biography,* The Unspeakable Curll *(1927).*

[2] *Writing of literary piracy in the last part of the 17th century, the London publisher, John Dunton, writes in his* Life and Errors *(p. 56):* '... *there are Plots and Counterplots, and a whole army of Hackney Authors that keep their Grinders moving by the Travel of their Pens. These Gormandizers will eat you the very Life out of a Copy so soon as ever it Appears; for as the Times go,* Original *and* Abridgement *were almost reckoned as necessary as Man and Wife, so that I am really afraid that a* Bookseller *and a Good* Conscience *will shortly grow some* Strange *Thing in the Earth.'*

Marjorie Plant (The English Book Trade, *pp. 120-121), quotes a passage written in the mid-18th century showing that literary piracy still flourished: 'A work no sooner receives the Approbation of the Town, but some trading miscreant prints it in a smaller Volume, and, as he is not at the Expence of Copy-Money is able to undersell the original Proprietor, who ventur'd on the work when there was not such a Certainty of the Sale'* (R. Campbell, The London Tradesman *(1757), p. 133). Nor was the Copyright Act of much use, 'for either the Piracy is done so private as not to be detected, or carried on in the Name of some Bankrupt, who has nothing to lose' (ibid., p. 136).*

details of publication kept mysterious. This had many advantages. They could later protest that the book was published without their permission or their knowledge, before they could make it the consummate work of art of which they obviously were capable. Since gentlemen, by definition, were not professional scribblers, they could also protest they had no intention of publishing the book at all. It was merely a trifle, an amusement to while away a tedious summer, and to have it published was an affront to a gentleman's dignity. These complications gave Curll all the room he needed in which to operate. He was no ordinary pirate.

Curll set up shop in January, 1706, and within a year he had found his stride. In 1707 he got hold somehow of a collection of Matthew Prior's poems—how he got his material was always Curll's secret. When Jacob Tonson, Prior's respectable publisher, heard that Curll was preparing an edition of Prior's poems, he published an advertisement in the *Daily Courant* of January 24, 1707: 'whereas it is reported that there is now printing a collection of poems which the publishers intend to call Mr. Prior's, this is therefore to inform the world, that all the genuine copies of what Mr. Prior has hitherto written, do of right belong, and are now in the hands of Jacob Tonson, who intends very speedily to publish a correct edition of them.'[1] Curll's edition was out within the week. Tonson's 'correct edition' that was to have been speedily published, did not come out for almost two years. Having published Prior once, Curll naturally felt he had the right to publish him again. He issued a second edition of Prior's poems, to which Prior objected as strenuously and as publicly as he could—in print. But Curll was not going to let a mere author interfere with his legitimate rights as publisher, and he made the following reply: 'Whereas a nameless person has taken the liberty to make use of Mr. Prior's name, and pretended that he had his order for so doing: This is therefore to assure the public, that a book entitled *A Second Collection of Poems* ... are genuine, and published from his own correct copies: The two last poems in this collection, being satires, Mr. Prior has never yet publicly owned them. ...'[2]

In 1708, Curll announced that a translation by Nicholas Rowe of the Latin poem *Callipaedia* would 'speedily be pub-

[1] *Quoted from* The Unspeakable Curll, *p. 21.*
[2] Ibid., *p. 25.*

lished'. It did not appear until 1712, and then only one-quarter of it was Rowe's. But the trick was to be first in the field, to make public claim to a manuscript or an idea before anyone else, so that he would have legitimate cause for complaint if some unscrupulous publisher tried to squeeze him out. If he could not obtain his manuscripts cheaply or by deception, Curll had yet another device. In the *Post-Boy* of March 14, 1708, Curll advertised the publication of a new edition of the works of Rochester and Roscommon 'with some Memoirs'. But the book was not available. Curll explained that there had been a slight delay 'by reason of several papers sent yesterday' which, of course, must be included in the works. Then followed, Straus says, the first of many public appeals for assistance: 'Those gentlemen that have any papers by them of the Earl of Rochester's, or Roscommon's, if they please to send them as soon as possible, they shall have as many of the books neatly bound as is proportionable to what they communicate.' Out of the responses Curll might carve a book and if he did not have to wait too long, even a worth-while book. Again the important thing was to be first in the field.

If a great man died, Curll announced immediately that his 'Life' was in the press and would be speedily published. This might be true, but usually, Straus explained, Curll would then invite the public to make the proposed publication complete by contributing any biographical bits they might have. The result was usually a strange concoction of scraps of biography with anything else the great man might have written, to give the book the proper thickness. But it was between covers and selling long before the grieving family or friends could publish anything at all. If a scrap or two came in after publication, it was excuse enough for a second or a third edition. Curll played variations on this technique. A few verses might appear by an anonymous writer. Some weeks later there would be a 'biography' of the supposed writer. Then the two pamphlets would be issued together as 'Poems on Several Occasions, with Some account, etc.' Then a preface would be added, creating another edition. And if some brief comment on the book was then discovered, it also would be added to the text, which became 'The Poetical Works of . . .' And when the poet died his Last Will and Testament was incorporated and the book became 'The Whole Works of . . .' or 'The Life and Times'. In this way the poet received Curll's undivided professional attention, and perhaps little else, almost from the cradle to the grave.

Straus describes other publishing tricks. One was to use names like Mr. J. Gay or Mr. J. Addison on the title-page as the 'author' of the work—no relation, of course, to the famous John Gay or Joseph Addison. Another was to include the name of a well-known author on the title page, though his only connection with the book was some trifling paragraph or verse printed without permission at the end of the book. Curll knew that the title-page was the thing to sell the book. Content was irrelevant. And if the book did not sell, it was not the content but the title-page that needed changing.

Curll often sold his books by public auction. Tom Brown gives us an interesting description of a book auctioneer in his 'Elegy on the Death of Mr. Edward Millington':

> Methinks I see him still with smiling look
> Amidst the crowd, and in his hand a book,
> Then in a fine facetious pleasing way,
> The author's genius and his wit display.
> O all ye scribbling tribe, come mourn his death,
> Whose wit hath given your dying fame new birth:
> When your neglected works did mouldring lie
> Upon the shelves, and none your books would buy,
> How oft has he, with strained eloquence,
> Affirmed the leaves contained a world of sense,
> When all's insipid dull impertinence.
> Come, gentlemen, come, bid me what you please;
> Upon my word, it is a curious piece,
> Done by a learned hand, and neatly bound;
> What say you, come, I'll put it up one pound:
> One pound, once, twice? Fifteen : Who bids a crown?
> Then shakes his head with an affected frown;
> Good lack-a-day, 'tis strange; then strikes a blow,
> And in a feigned passion bids it go;
> Then in his hand another piece he takes,
> And in its praise a long harangue he makes;
> And tells 'em that 'tis writ in lofty verse,
> One that is out of print, and very scarce;
> Then with high language, and a stately look,
> He sets a lofty price upon the book.

Curll's tactics assured an eventful life. He thrived on controversy; it was good for business. But not all the controversy
worked to his advantage. Like other enterprising booksellers, Curll
kept a stock of quack medical books and even the 'infallible remedies' themselves, to supplement his income. In 1704 a certain
John Martin, who began his medical career as a barber's apprentice, issued a pamphlet announcing a way of curing the pox without mercury, and suggesting that anyone ignorant enough to prescribe mercury was a quack. He had in mind another former barber, a Mr. John Spinks. In 1708 Curll came out with a book called
The Charitable Surgeon, by T. C. Surgeon, also promising to cure
the pox without mercury, obliquely attacking Mr. Spinks, and
announcing that the medicines might be procured at the shop of
Edmund Curll. These excerpts are from the second edition:

The Charitable Surgeon:

OR,

The best REMEDIES for the worst
MALADIES, reveal'd.

Being a New and True way of Curing (without Mercury)
the several degrees of the Venereal Distemper in both Sexes,
whereby all Persons, even the meanest Capacities, may, for an
inconsiderable Charge, without confinement or knowledge of the
nearest Relation, Cure themselves easily, speedily and safely, by
the Methods prescrib'd, without the help of any Physician, Surgeon or Apothecary, or being expos'd to the hazardous attempts
of Quacks and Pretenders.

To which is subjoin'd,

A new discovery of the true Seat of Claps in Men and Women,
different from the commonly receiv'd Opinions of Authors.

AS ALSO

A peculiar Method of curing their Gleets and Weaknesses,
whether Venereal, Seminal, or otherwise; with some pertinent
Observations relating thereto, never before taken notice of.

Likewise

The certain easy way to escape Infection, tho' never so often accompanying with the most polluted Companion.

BY T. C. SURGEON.

THE

PREFACE

Showing

The Scope and Intent of the Book, and giving some general Directions necessary to be known and observed by every Patient.

In my juvenile years the practical part of physic and surgery was my delight; but as age and weakness crept on, and nature called for a country retirement from practice, that I could no longer in that capacity be useful, I thought it was a duty still incumbent on me, as I had leisure and ability, to communicate to the world in print, what I had found so serviceable to mankind in practice, and not live altogether an useless member to the Commonwealth, under which I was bred, and in which I have attained to the competency I enjoy.

Upon these considerations I took pen in hand, and wrote upon the subject of these following sheets, and also on diverse other parts of the physical and chirurgical practice, which if strength permits, and death trips not up my heels, may also speedly see the light.

But it may be a wonder to some of my friends, into whose hands this will probably fall, why I should pitch upon, and write on this subject, and why I should do it primarily? Others may also wonder why I or any one should write on the venereal subject, when the same has been done already by diverse authors, both ancient and modern; but when they are informed that this is not a treatise of the nature, causes, kinds, &c. of the disease, but a practical scheme of its cure, and the way to prevent it when one's in danger of getting it, (which I have never observed to be done by any author before, so as to be within the power of the patient to perform both, that is, to prevent the disease and cure it) it will, I hope, be a satisfaction to them why I did it; and as

I am the first in this method, will not think but that I may justly claim a right of prerogative therein.

In answer to the 2nd query, and why I should primarily publish on this subject, 'twas because in no disease besides, there is the like opportunity of committing mischiefs as in this; for people getting a misfortune, run for privacy to quacks, where they are frequently ruined, when if such a book as this, by which they might (as they may by this) have so easy access to for a cure, had been by any heretofore published, thousands might have been preserved which have in their hands been spoiled, and therefore the urgency of the thing encouraged the expedition, and the more because the longer so necessary a book was neglected, the greater mischiefs would still have been committed; and besides my advanced years sufficiently tell me I must not expect long life, and that if this, which I looked upon the most pressing of all that I designed to publish, was not done by me in my lifetime, very probably another might not have the thought, or at leastwise not so willing to communicate so freely as I have done, for the good and benefit of the injured and unhappy people, and so they still left to be exposed to the mercenary power of quacks and ignorant professors, whose ill practices this in all likelihood will put a stop to and restrain; for by this means the hazard of ruin to body, estate and reputation, will be prevented, and not one of those three dismal calamities fall to the lot of any, when probably in their hands they might have irretrievably been entitled to them all, as some thousands in this nation to their sorrow sufficiently witness. This was one inducement for my writing on the disease. . . .

And the plainer to demonstrate that the benefit of the people is intended by this publication, and to make good that part of the title page, that gives expectation of being cured for a very moderate charge, I hereby assure the reader, that the prices to each medicine, as charged in the catalogue hereafter mentioned, is very little more than the prime cost of them; and whatever the charge of each prescription, amounts to more than any apothecary would compound them for, is the price only of the concealed ingredient, which were it mentioned in the recipe, and made up by the honestest apothecary in the town, would not come to less. . . .

And this being so in fact, and the remedies effectual, to be had easily, and for a very moderate consideration, and that at all times, and for all conditions; and being also portable, and what are easy to be taken, and few of them sufficient to accomplish the cure, what can be a greater benefit to those that stand in need? What mistakes will by this means be prevented? What advantages gained by everyone? And particularly by the poor, who beyond whatever can be had elsewhere, will be relieved thereby, purchasing a cure for a very little money, when otherwise they might suffer the fate of the many disgraceful and noseless people we daily meet in the streets, and become perhaps like them, very miserable, if not irrecoverable, had they not this favourable opportunity of preventing it now presented them. . . .

Advertisement

Note, all the medicines prescribed in this book, are prepared by the author's own hands, and are left by him at Mr. Edmund Curll's a bookseller, at the Peacock without Temple Bar, where this book is sold. At which place, and nowhere else, they are always ready to be had, and will be delivered to any messenger that shall but ask for them by their names or numbers, or both, and pay the prices, as mentioned for each, in the following catalogue, viz.

	s.	d.
Numb. 1. The Purging Electuary,	5.	0.
Numb. 2. The Diuretic Powder,	5.	0.
Numb. 3. The Strengthening Electuary,	5.	0.
Numb. 4. The Anodyne Injection,	3.	6.
Numb. 5. The Anodyne Fotus,	3.	6.
Numb. 6. The Anodyne Powder,	4.	0.
Numb. 7. The Emetic Potion,	3.	6.
Numb. 8. The Healing Lotion,	3.	0.
Numb. 9. The Suppurating Plaster and Digestive Balsam each	2.	6.
Numb. 10. The Emetic Bolus,	3.	6.
Numb. 11. The Specific Electuary,	7.	6.
Numb. 12. The Cooling Gargle,	3.	6.
Numb. 13. The Detersive Injection,	3.	6.
Numb. 14. The Grand Preservative,	7.	6.
Numb. 15. The Sudorific Potion,	5.	0.
The Yard Syringe,	1.	0.
The Womb Syringe,	2.	0.

	s. d.
The Nose Syringe,	1. 0.
The Throat Syringe,	1. 0.

Note, for the greater conveniency of the patient, all these syringes may be had ready fitted for use (because not so at the pewterers), and sealed up with the same seal as the medicines are, where this book is sold.

N.B. Ask for the Yard Syringe by the name of the least syringe, and the womb syringe the great syringe.

Some general Directions in taking and applying the Medicines.

If by often taking the electuary the taste should seem in any wise disgustful to the palate or stomach, or if you cannot well take it from the point of a knife as usual, then pour a little syrup of marshmallows, poppies, or what else you like best, into a spoon; then put your electuary in the syrup from off the point of a knife, pouring a little more of the same syrup over it, and sup it off. By this means you will not taste the electuary; and thus you may take the bolus.

When you use either of the syringes, you must put the end of the syringe in the liquor you would inject, and therein draw the squirt to and fro till you find it makes a good stream.

The certain easy way to escape Venereal Infection, though never so often accompanying with the most Infected Companion.

What I have before laid down and asserted concerning the seat of claps in both sexes, is a sufficient indication to me that the infection may be prevented; and every one that considers the same, and believes the seat of it to be where I have given my opinion it is (and that not only speculatively, but practically, as well as by occular demonstration, having, as before hinted, observed the same upon dissections, and experimented the truth, numbers of times) will be of my mind, and no longer think it a whim, or imposture, as some have boldly said, for any one to attempt it.

I know that as there are many that will not allow any such way to be preserved from the disease, upon having to do with a polluted companion; so there are others that do verily believe such a preservative is to be had, but mightily exclaim against those that shall dare to reveal it, because, as they say, they will thereby prostitute their consciences by instructing them how to be preserved, in favour of a debauched conversation; for that numbers of people, who by inclination are libertines, would, upon having such a preservative, make nothing of the practice of whoring, the disease being all that they fear; like many young women, who would not value their virginity, were they but secured from that and a great belly; the two only things that have deterred many from the practice, not virtue, but fear; this, I say, is the opinion of many, who at the same time never consider what numbers of men, women and children, get the disease undeservedly, from which, it is but a piece of justice to preserve them; and that many women that cannot help having to do with their husbands, even when they know they have the disease, who if they were provided with a preservative, might always engage without injury, and thereby not only preserve themselves, but secure to their posterity a good stamen, which otherwise would have been polluted, and the virus thereby transmitted to, it may be, many succeeding generations; the mature consideration of which chain of evils would make a man of any honour shrink, and choose rather to be hanged outright than be the occasion of such sad, deplorable, and too often irreparable mischiefs. So that upon the whole, I cannot but conceive, that the service such a medicine may do to the innocent people that get it undeservedly, will vastly tantamount what licentiousness may be committed by libertines, in their knowing where to be provided with it; for which reason, without any further apology, or thinking otherwise than that in revealing it, I do my country a more than ordinary service; I shall proceed in making it known, how the infection may be prevented.

There are some authors say, and that very confidently, that it is to be done by inward antidotes only; others that a certain application to the privities of both parties, must before engagement take place, than which nothing is more absurd and ridiculous, more especially when the nature and seat of the disease is considered to be as before laid down. Therefore, without heeding the various propositions of authors, or the many frivolous objections that can by any others be raised against it, the only certain easy way to escape the infection, and which everyone will find upon trial, is as follows, viz.

After a man has had to do with a woman, let both parties forthwith wash their privy parts with the following lotion, either warm or cold, but best warm, in the winter especially; the man also is to inject some of it into the passage of his yard, with a yard syringe, and the woman also to inject some of it into her womb, with a womb syringe; and thus to do three or four times a day daily, two syringes full each time, for two or three days together; by which time, whatever malignity was received, will be washed off, and destroyed, before the particles of the venereal poison are fixed and put into a ferment by the heat of the parts; and this it will certainly do, if used within six or eight hours after engagement, without the necessity of taking anything inwardly, or undergoing any other trouble; and that the patient may not be left wholly ignorant what this medicament is, I shall here give the prescription of it, only, as in every other medicine herein set down, I shall also in this conceal one, and the chiefest ingredient in it, which is no detriment to any person, since they may at any time, at the same place, as easily have it, as any of the rest of the medicines by paying the price of it, as mentioned in the foregoing catalogue. The medicament is this, and called, Numb. 14. The Grand Preservative. Take Zedoary, Virginian Snakeroot, Gentian and Birthwort roots, of each two drams, of my *sine pari* an ounce and half, Venice treacle three drams; boil all these in three pints of water, till a pint be boiled away, strain it, and add brandy a quarter of a pint, mix them together and when well settled, it is fit for the purpose, which use as above directed, and which will not be painful or cause smart or uneasiness, but will be pleasant, neat and easy, and so certainly effectual, as that a man or woman by having it with them, may without fear or danger ramble all the world over, and not scruple having to do with the most infected companion that is. . . .

Quacks and Emperics being all by wise men deemed the scorn, reproach and contempt of the world, in all ages and all countries. As the best method therefore, for the unfortunate and indigent, to avoid all their alluring baits, and to assure the people that no one medicine, which is generally recommended by those mercenary practisers, to cure all the degrees of the distemper, is possible to do it, and consequently to preserve their healths and lives, was this written; which if it proves as serviceable as it was honestly intended (which it will, if the rules herein be observed)

I shall have attained my aim, which was, the people's safety, from the most miserable and disgraceful disease, so very terrible to all, and but little pitied by any; and therein hope it will be allowed I have purely and generously done my country service.

There was no immediate reply from Mr. Spinks. He was in Fleet Street Prison at the time, for financial reasons. But in 1709 a pamphlet appeared, *Quackery Unmask'd*, which not only attacked Martin's latest treatise but asserted that Martin and T. C. Surgeon were the same man.

Quackery Unmasked

or,

*Reflections
On the Sixth Edition of
Mr. Martin's Treatise of the
Venereal Disease, and
its Appendix;*
And the Pamphlet call'd,
The CHARITABLE Surgeon, &c.

Containing

A Full and Plain Detection and Refutation of some gross Errors, &c. of those Authors: Interspers'd with many new and useful Observations concerning the Venereal Disease; and the Method and Medicines proper for its Speedy, Safe, and effectual Curation. Proper Remarks on Mr. Martin's Admirable Medicine, and his Infallible Preservative. A Full and True Account of Quacks; and their Method of Practice. An Account of some Excellent Medicines, &c.

Highly necessary to be read by all Venereal Patients, who would prevent their own Ruin; and by all Physicians, Surgeons, and Apothecaries, who are here Vindicated from Mr. Martin's Aspersions.

By F. Spinks, Licens'd Practitioner
in Physick and Surgery

Who the real author of the sixth edition of the *Treatise of the Venereal Disease*, and its appendix is, I know not; but the

The Compleat Auctioner

name Martin being in their title pages, I must, till better informed, presume some gentleman, whose name is Martin, is their
author, and shall address him by that name. Doubtless, Mr. Martin, so learned a man as you are (being an author) well know that
whoever becomes an author, submits his book to the censure of
every reader; and if he be guilty of mistakes, for *humanum est
errare,* (asking your pardon for expressing myself in a language,
I fear, you do not at all understand) he ought to acknowledge
himself obliged to any person that shall better inform him. No
man, though never so learned, can be sure that some errors shall
not escape his pen. For this cause we may observe the most learned
authors (witness the renowned Boyle) usually deliver their sentiments with the greatest modesty, and treat other men, though of
inferior capacity, with candour and civility. But the notions in
your books, not transcribed from other authors, are so notoriously
erroneous, and your treatment of all physicians and surgeons, so
egregiously insolent, and so unbecoming a member of Surgeons'
Hall, a man of art or learning, or indeed a man of an ingenious
education, that, unless you imagined yourself beneath any man's
notice, you were certainly infatuated if you did not expect that
your errors and ignorance in the matters you were about, would
at one time or another be detected, your ill manners chastised,
and you thereby rendered contemptible to the learned and ingenious part of mankind.

March 1 1708/9. From my house at the Golden Ball in the dark
passage, three doors beyond the Sun Tavern in Honey Lane (or
Milk Street) Market, in Cheapside.

CHAP. I

Of the Essence and Nature of the Venereal Disease

I shall not, say you, (page 1.) trouble myself or the reader,
in this treatise, with the many different and indeterminate notions
of the natural cause of this distemper, as to its original production,
&c. It is sufficient, continue you, (p. 2.) that we know it to be a
distemper daily gotten, and know how to cure it. What, do you,
Sir, pretend that you know how to cure a disease, which, you confess, you know no more of, than that 'tis a disease daily gotten?
Is this talking like an ingenious surgeon? Or rather, is it not talk-

c

ing like a tampering old woman? Or (in your rhetoric) a scandalously ignorant quack? ...

There were several exchanges, Mr. Spinks repeatedly getting the better of them, till finally he announced that he had analysed Mr. Edmund Curll's medicine and was happy to say that it did contain mercury and evidently Martin, alias T. C. Surgeon, did not know mercury when he saw it. After that, Curll seemed to lose interest in curing the pox, and for a while, Straus points out, he advertised a 'Pulvis Anti-Ictericus ... a never-failing remedy against the yellow jaundice or such distempers as proceed from a vitiated gall,' and then he returned to bookselling, full time.

Curll's most famous battle was with Alexander Pope. A great deal has been written about this quarrel and much of it goes beyond our period, so it will only be touched on here. It began in 1716 when Curll, in his usual ingenious way, acquired some verses which he believed were written by Lady Mary Montagu, or possibly—he was not sure—even by Pope himself. The poems, Curll announced on the title-page, were 'Publish'd faithfully, as they were found in a pocket-book taken up in Westminster-Hall, the last Day of the Lord Winton's Tryal', [for high treason]. This was not a bad beginning. In the Preface, Curll archly remarked that some people attributed the poems to 'a lady of quality' (Lady Mary), some to John Gay, and one person, 'a gentleman of distinguished merit' said, 'Depend upon it, these lines could come from no other hand than the laudable translator of Homer,' Alexander Pope. Treason, intrigue, mystery, and the cumulative selling power of three of the most saleable names of the town—this was Curll in action. But Pope was no admirer of Curll's genius, and the following pamphlet written by Pope himself soon after the event, described what he did about it:

A Full *and* True
ACCOUNT
of a
Horrid and Barbarous
REVENGE by POISON,
On the Body of
Mr. *Edmund Curll,* Bookseller;
With a faithful Copy of his
Last WILL and TESTAMENT.

History furnishes us with examples of many satirical authors who have fallen sacrifices to revenge, but not of any booksellers that I know of, except the unfortunate subject of the following papers, I mean Mr. Edmund Curll, at the Bible and Dial in Fleet Street, who was yesterday poisoned by Mr. Pope, after having lived many years an instance of the mild temper of the British nation.

Everybody knows that the said Mr. Edmund Curll, on Monday the 26th instant, published a satirical piece, entitled *Court Poems,* in the preface whereof they were attributed to a Lady of Quality, Mr. Pope, or Mr. Gay; by which indiscreet method, though he had escaped one revenge, there were still two behind in reserve.

Now on the Wednesday ensuing, between the hours of 10 and 11, Mr. Lintott, a neighbouring bookseller, desired a conference with Mr Curll about settling the title page of *Wiquefoil's Ambassador,* inviting him at the same time to take a whet together. Mr. Pope (who is not the only instance how persons of bright parts may be carried away by the instigation of the devil) found means to convey himself into the same room, under pretence of business with Mr. Lintott, who it seems is the printer of his *Homer.* This gentleman with a seeming coolness, reprimanded Mr. Curll for wrongfully ascribing to him the aforesaid poems. He excused himself by declaring that one of his authors (Mr. Oldmixon[1] by name) gave the copies to the press, and wrote the preface. Upon this Mr. Pope (being to all appearance reconciled) very civilly drank a glass of sack to Mr. Curll, which he as civilly pledged; and though the liquor in colour and taste differed not from common sack, yet was it plain by the pangs this unhappy stationer felt soon after, that some poisonous drug had been secretly infused therein.

About eleven o'clock he went home, where his wife observing his colour changed, said, Are you not sick, my dear? He replied, Bloody sick; and incontinently fell a vomiting and straining in an uncommon and unnatural manner, the contents of his vomiting being as green as grass. His wife had been just reading

---

[1] *John Oldmixon (1673-1742), a prolific writer. He began his career writing poetry and plays, and was editor of* The Medley *(1710), which tangled with Swift's* Examiner. *His later career was as an historian with an extreme Whig bias.*

a book of her husband's printing, concerning Jane Wenham, the famous Witch of Hartford, and her mind misgave her that he was bewitched; but he soon let her know that he suspected poison, and recounted to her, between the intervals of his yawnings and retchings, every circumstance of his interview with Mr. Pope.

Mr. Lintott in the meantime coming in, was extremely affrighted at the sudden alteration he observed in him. Brother Curll, says he, I fear you have got the vomiting distemper, which (I have heard) kills in half an hour. This comes from your not following my advice, to drink old hock as I do, and abstain from sack. Mr. Curll replied, in a moving tone, Your author's sack I fear has done my business. Zounds, says Mr. Lintott, my author! —Why did not you drink old hock? Notwithstanding which rough remonstrance, he did in the most friendly manner press him to take warm water; but Mr. Curll did with great obstinacy refuse it; which made Mr. Lintott infer, that he chose to die, as thinking to recover greater damages.

All this time the symptoms increased violently, with acute pains in the lower belly. Brother Lintott, says he, I perceive my last hour approaching, do me the friendly office to call my partner, Mr. Pemberton, that we may settle our worldly affairs. Mr. Lintott, like a kind neighbour, was hastening out of the room, while Mr. Curll raved aloud in this manner, If I survive this, I will be revenged on Tonson, it was he first detected me as the printer of these poems, and I will reprint these very poems in his name. His wife admonished him not to think of revenge, but to take care of his stock and his soul; And in the same instant, Mr. Lintott (whose goodness can never be enough applauded) returned with Mr. Pemberton. After some tears jointly shed by these humane booksellers, Mr. Curll, being (as he said) in his perfect senses though in great bodily pain, immediately proceeded to make a verbal will (Mrs. Curll having first put on his night cap). . . .

With all the details of this will we need not concern ourselves. The sick man prays for forgiveness 'for those indirect methods I have pursued in inventing new titles to old books, putting authors names to things they never saw,' and 'publishing private quarrels for public entertainment.' Anything of his that may seem malicious is due to charity, he having made it his 'business to print for poor disconcolate authors whom all other booksellers refuse.' And Mr. Pemberton is begged 'to beware of the indictment at Hicks's Hall for publishing Rochester's bawdy poems, that copy otherwise' being his best legacy to his 'dear wife and helpless child.' The squib ends with the arrival of Mr. [John] Oldmixon.

Ah! Mr. Oldmixon (said poor Mr. Curll) to what a condition have your works reduced me! I die a martyr to that unlucky preface. However, in these my last moments, I will be just to all men; you shall have your third share of the *Court Poems*, as was stipulated. When I am dead, where will you find another bookseller? Your *Protestant Packet*[1] might have supported you, had you writ a little less scurrilously. There is a mean in all things.

Then turning to Mr. Pemberton, he told him, he had several taking title pages that only wanted treatises to be wrote to them, and earnestly entreated, that when they were writ, his heirs might have some share of the profit of them.

After he had said this he fell into horrible gripings, upon which Mr. Lintott advised him to repeat the Lord's Prayer. He desired his wife to step into the shop for a Common Prayer Book, fetched a groan, and recommended to Mrs. Curll to give forty shillings to the poor of the Parish of St. Dunstan's, and a week's wages advance to each of his gentlemen authors, with some small gratuity in particular to Mrs. Centlivre.

When a publisher with the ingenuity of Curll and a poet with the satiric power and brilliance of Pope begin to quarrel one can expect extraordinary results. Curll began his counter-attack, says Straus, with a mock advertisement, a 'Second Part of Mr. Pope's Popish Translation of Homer', together with an announcement that an 'Excellent New Ballad, call'd The Catholick Poet . . .' would be issued the following week. This came out along with John Dennis's[2] *True Character of Mr. Pope and his Writings*, which dwelled on Pope's physical deformity. Pope, in turn, wrote two more squibs attacking Curll, and Curll replied in kind. Then in 1728 Pope apotheosized Curll in his *Dunciad*, a vicious portrait, for which Curll will be remembered long after his publishing feats

---

[1] *1716.*
[2] *John Dennis (1657-1734), one of the great critics of the 18th century, whose attacks on Pope began in 1711 with his criticism of Pope's Esssay upon Criticism.*

are forgotten. Curll promptly printed a *Compleat Key* to the *Dunciad*, which spelled out in full the initials and stars Pope had used for names in his attack on the Dunces of Grub Street. According to Straus, it is likely that Curll even pirated an edition of the *Dunciad*.[1] He led the Dunces attack against Pope by publishing a series of ferocious squibs on Pope's private character, written by himself and some of the swarm of enemies Pope had made by his writing. If Pope got the better of the satire, 'financially speaking,' Straus points out, ' ... the bookseller had the best of the bargain.'[2] In 1733 Pope tricked Curll into publishing a pirated edition of Pope's Letters, among which was a letter to a peer which got Curll into trouble with the House of Lords. But Curll escaped unharmed and Pope's intriguing became known and with this the battle between the two geniuses came to a close.

Pope's emetic was not the only physical response to Curll's publishing genius. He was imprisoned, stood in the pillory and on one memorable occasion tossed in a blanket by the Westminster schooboys for printing a funeral oration without permission. The event was celebrated in *A Consolatory Letter from Mr. Dunton*[3] *to Mr. Curll*, anonymously written. Here is a fragment:

> Could none of thy poetic band
> Of Mercenary wits at hand,
> Foretell, or ward the coming blow,
> From garret high, or cellar low?
> Or else at least in verse bemoan
> Their Lord, in double sense cast down? ...
> From Tonson down to Boddington[4]
> Fleet Street and Temple Bar around,
> The Strand and Holborn, this shall sound:
> For ever this shall grate thine ear,
> Which is the way to Westminster?

Curll made money and lost money. He was never rich. At his most successful he kept several hack writers more or less per-

---

[1] P. 125.
[2] P. 134.
[3] John Dunton, in his own way, was as enterprising a Grub Street publisher as Curll.
[4] Jacob Tonson published in London from 1677 to 1720 (Plomer). He published works of Dryden, Addison, Steele and Pope. Nicholas Boddington published from 1687 to 1717.

manently employed, and had translators, pamphleteers and minor poets assume all sorts of strange *personae* to sell his wares. Despite Pope's allegations, Straus points out, there is no evidence of his bullying his hacks or keeping them on short rations.[1] But to be one of Curll's hacks could not have been an undiluted joy. In *The Author's Farce,* 1730, Henry Fielding describes what it must have been like. The setting is a room in the house of Mr. Bookweight, the publisher:

Dash, Blotpage, Quibble, *writing at several tables.*

Dash. Pox on't, I'm as dull as an ox, though I have not a bit of one within me.—I have not dined these two days, and yet my head is as heavy as any alderman's or lord's. I carry about me symbols of all the elements; my head is as heavy as water, my pockets are light as air, my appetite is as hot as fire, and my coat is as dirty as earth.

Blot. Lend me your *Bysshe,*[2] Mr. Dash, I want a rhyme for wind——

Dash. Why there! blind, and kind, and behind, and find, and mind—It is one of the easiest terminations imaginable; I have had it four times in a page.

Blot. Devil take the first inventor of rhyming, I say. Your business is much easier, Mr. Dash. Well, of all the places in my master's gift—I should most like to be clerk of the ghosts and murders. You have nothing to do but to put a set of terrible words together in the title page.

Dash. The business is easy enough, but it is at a very low ebb now. No, Mr. Quibble there, as clerk of the libels, would have the best place, were it not that few men ever sat in his chair long without standing on an odd sort of a stool in the street,[3] to be gaped at an hour or two by the mob.

Quib. We act on different principles, Mr. Dash; 'tis your business to promise more than you perform, and mine to promise less.

---

[1] *It was not unusual for the publisher to provide room and board for the author whose works he was publishing. According to* The Life of John Buncle, *Curll's 'Translators in pay, lay three in a bed, at the Pewter-Platter Inn in Holborn . . .' (p. 383).*

[2] *Edward Bysshe's* Art of Poetry *(1702), which includes a rhyming dictionary.*

[3] *The pillory.*

Blot. Pshaw! thy business is to perform nothing at all.

Dash. It becomes an author to be diffusive in his title page. A title page is to a book, what a fine neck is to a woman.—Therefore ought to be the most regarded, as it is the part which is viewed before the purchase.

SCENE IV. *To them* Bookweight.

Book. Fie upon it, gentlemen! What, not at your pens? Do you consider, Mr. Quibble, that it is above a fortnight since your letter from a friend in the country was published.—Is it not high time for an answer to come out—at this rate, before your answer is printed your letter will be forgot—I love to keep a controversy up warm—I have had authors who have writ a pamphlet in the morning, answered it in the afternoon, and compromised the matter at night.

Quib. Sir, I will be as expeditious as possible.

Book. Well, Mr. Dash, have you done that murder yet?

Dash. Yes, sir, the murder is done—I am only about a few moral reflections to place before it.

Book. Very well—then let me have the ghost finished by this day sevennight.

Dash. What sort of a ghost would you have, sir? The last was a pale one.

Book. Then let this be a bloody one.—Mr. Blotpage, what have your lucubrations produced?—[reads] Poetical advice to a certain—from a certain—on a certain—from a certain— Very good! I will say, Mr. Blotpage writes as good a dash as any man in Europe.

SCENE V. *To them,* Index

Book. So, Mr. Index, what news with you?

Ind. I have brought my bill, sir.

Book. What's here?—for adapting the motto of *Risum teneatis amici* to a dozen pamphlets—at sixpence per each—Six shillings.

For *Omnia vincit amor* & *Nos cedamus amori*—sixpence. For *Difficile est satyram non scribere*—sixpence. Hum, hum, hum —ah—a sum total, for thirty-six Latin mottoes, eighteen shillings;

ditto English seven, one shilling and nine pence; ditto Greek four, one shilling. Why, friend, are your Latin Mottoes dearer than your Greek?

Ind. Yes marry are they, sir: for as nobody now understands Greek, so I may use any sentence in that language, to whatsoever purpose I please.

Book. You shall have your money immediately: and pray remember that I must have two Latin sedition mottoes, and one Greek moral motto, for pamphlets, by tomorrow morning.

Quib. I want two Latin sentences, sir, one for page the fourth, in the praise of virtue; and the other for page the tenth, in the praise of beauty.

Book. Let me have those too.

Ind. Sir, I shall take care to provide them.

SCENE VI. Bookweight, Dash, Blotpage, Quibble, Scarecrow.

Scare. Sir, I have brought you a libel against the ministry.

Book. Sir, I shall not take anything against them [*Aside.*] for I have two in the press already.

Scare. Then, sir, I have another in defence of them.

Book. Sir, I never take anything in defence of power.

Scare. I have a translation of Virgil's *Aeneid*, with notes on it.

Book. That, sir, is what I do not care to venture on—you may try by subscription, if you please: but I would not advise you: for that bubble is almost down: people begin to be afraid of authors, since they have writ and acted like stock-jobbers. So to oblige a young beginner, I don't care if I print it at my own expense.

Scare. But pray, sir, at whose expense shall I eat?

Book. That's an empty question.

Scare. It comes from an empty stomach, I'm sure.

Book. From an empty head, I'm afraid. Are there not a thousand ways for a man to get his bread by?

Scare. I wish you would put me into one.

Book. Why then, sir, I would advise you to come and take your seat at my tables. Here will be everything that is necessary provided for you. I am as great a friend to learning as the Dutch

C*

are to trade.—No one can want bread with me, who will earn it. Besides, a translator will be of use to me: for my last is in New-gate for shoplifting. The rogue had gotten a trick of translating out of the shops as well as out of the languages.

Scare. I prefer anything to starving.

Book. Then, sir, if you please to throw by your hat, which you will have no more use for, and take up your pen.

Scare. But, sir, I am afraid I am not qualified for a trans-lator.

Book. How, not qualified!

Scare. No, sir: I understand no language but my own.

Book. What, and translate Virgil?

Scare. Alas, sir, I translated him out of Dryden.

Book. Not qualified!—If I was an emperor thou shouldst be my prime minister. Thou art as well versed in thy trade, as if thou had'st laboured in my garret these ten years.—Let me tell you, friend, you will have more occasion for invention than learn-ing here: you will be sometimes obliged to translate books out of all languages (especially French) which were never printed in any language whatsoever.

Scare. Your trade abounds in mysteries.

Book. The study of bookselling is as difficult as the law,— and there are as many tricks in the one as the other. Sometimes we give a foreign name to our own labour—sometimes we put our own names to the labour of others. Then as the lawyers have John-a-Nokes and Tom-a-Stiles, so we have Messieurs Moore near St. Paul's, and Smith near the Royal Exchange.

Curll's publishing tactics made him almost a myth in his own day. He became the target of some of the best satire on Grub Street and achieved a kind of inverted immortality. His name became so closely identified with the Grub Street publisher that Richard Savage in his *An Author to be Lett* could use it almost as a metaphor in his satire of the hack author. Savage's satire was published in 1729, a bit late for our period. But Savage had been a Grub Street writer himself, and Iscariot Hackney, his 'author to be lett', is perhaps, according to Straus,[1] a satiric portrait of Charles Gildon, one of Edmund Curll's hacks. Like Iscariot Hack-

[1] *Op. cit., p. 44.*

ney, Gildon also was forced to drudge for Curll, living 'in a garret in Chancery Lane, and his nightly drudgery by candlelight began to affect his eyesight.'[1] Gildon was a prolific writer—poet, playwright, biographer, editor and a critic of some note—but for much of his career he was an undoubted hackney author. Savage's portrait of the hack author is, of course, a distortion, as all satire is: no one man could have accomplished so much, not even in Grub Street. Yet the picture it draws of the Grub Street author and publisher rings true. *An Author to be Lett* is Savage's contribution to the War on the Dunces, the climax of which was Pope's monumental attack on Grub Street, *The Dunciad*:

... At my first setting out I was hired by a reverend prebend to libel Dean Swift for infidelity. Soon after I was employed by Curll to write a merry tale, the wit of which was its obscenity. This we agreed to palm upon the world for a posthumous piece of Mr. Prior.[2] However, a certain lady, celebrated for certain liberties, had a curiosity to see the real author. Curll, on my promise that if I had a present, he should go snacks, sent me to her. I was admitted while her ladyship was shifting; and on my admittance, Mrs. Abigail was ordered to withdraw. What passed between us, a point of gallantry obliges me to conceal; but after some extraordinary civilities, I was dismissed with a purse of guineas, and a command to write a sequel to my tale. Upon this I turned out smart in dress, bit Curll of his share, and run out most of my money in printing my works at my own cost. But some years after (just at the time of his starving poor Pattison[3]) the varlet was revenged. He arrested me for several months board, brought me back to my garret, and made me drudge on in my old, dirty work. 'Twas in his service that I wrote obscenity and profaneness, under the names of Pope and Swift. Sometimes I was Mr. Joseph Gay, and at others Theory Burnet, or Addison.[4] I abridged histories and travels, translated from the French, what

---

[1] Ibid.

[2] *Matthew Prior (1664-1721), poet and satirist. Curll had pirated a collected edition of his poems in 1707.*

[3] *Pope accused Curll of starving William Pattison, one of his poets, to death. Straus (op. cit., p. 41) rejects this and says that Curll, in fact, actually nursed him in his last illness.*

[4] *These were some of Curll's publishing tactics. Theory Burnet refers to Thomas Burnet (1635?-1715), author of* The Sacred Theory of the Earth *(1684-1690). Its imaginative conceptions were the admiration of many poets, even as late as Coleridge.*

they never wrote, and was expert at finding out new titles for old books. When a notorious thief was hanged, I was the Plutarch to preserve his memory; and when a great man died, mine were his remains, and mine the account of his last will and testament. . . .

But before all this happened, a young nobleman gratified me for letting some verses of mine be handed about at court in manuscript under his name. This was the first time that I ever heard my writings generally commended. But alas! how short-lived the applause? They unfortunately stole into print, lost their reputation at once, and I am now ashamed to write any more, as a person of quality. I am a great joker, and deal in clenches, puns, quibbles, gibes, conundrums, and carry whichits. Many a good time have I lashed the whole body of clergy, and cracked many a smart joke upon the Trinity. One of my books had the honour of being presented for a libel, by the Grand Jury, and another was made a burnt offering by the hands of the common hangman.

When an author writes a piece that has success in his own character, I abuse him; but if in a fictitious one, I endeavour to personate him, and write a second part to his work. I am very deeply read in all pieces of scandal, obscenity, and profaneness. [The writings of some of the dunces in Pope's *Dunciad*.] . . . From these I propose to compile a very grand work . . . and as this is designed for the use of young templers,[1] it is hoped they will promote my subscription. Since private vices have been proved to be public benefits,[2] I would venture to call it, *An Useful Body of Immorality*, and print it in a broad, pompous folio; but such a one as may very well be bound up with Dean Smedley's[3] intended *Body of Divinity*.

By the help of indexes, and technical dictionaries, I work on every branch of learning. I pore often over the volumes of state tracts, whence I collect paragraphs which I mix with remarks of my own, and range under several heads. Those against a discarded minister I sent to the London and British Journals, and others more virulent against a prime one (for I naturally hate

---

[1] *Apprentices at the Inns of Court, notorious for their profligacy.*
[2] *The allusion is to Bernard de Mandeville's* The Fable of the Bees: or, Private Vices, Publick Benefits *(1714). Mandeville earned a mention in Pope's* Dunciad.
[3] *Author of* Gulliveriana, *a vicious attack on Pope and Swift.*

my superiors) are for my very good friend the *Craftsman*.[1] Rather than stand out of play, I have penned panegyrics in *Mist*[2] on Rich's[3] Pantomimes, and Theobald's *Shakespeare Restored*.[4] I am always listed by Mr. Lun the harlequin, to hiss the first night at any of the Drury Lane performances. Sometimes I draw up challenges for the champions of Mr. Figg's[5] amphitheatre, and sometimes for the disputants of Mr. Henley's Oratory.[6]

I have an excellent knack at birthday odes, elegies, acrostics, anagrams, epithalamiums, prologues, recommendatory poems, rhymes for almanack-makers, and witty distichs for the signs of country inns and ale-houses. When with an audible voice I spout forth my own verses, marvellous is their effect! The very bellman has been touched with envy!—an author, who like Mr. Ralph, has distinguished himself by night; the shrillness of my clamorous, dunning landlady has been charmed into a still attention! Nay, the very bailiff, in act to rush upon me, has stopped short to listen, and for a minute suspended the rapacious palm that was to fall upon my shoulder! . . .

When a man of quality is distinguished for wit, or an encourager of it, I endeavour to strike him for a dedication; but I have generally been so unhappy as to disgust my patrons by praising them in the wrong place. For want of being acquainted with polite life, I have unwittingly complimented a person for an illustrious birth, who really owed his rise entirely to his merit. Thus have I caused his enemies to sneer, and, perhaps, to libel him for my squab compliment; when, had I left him to his choice, he had rather chose my satire than my panegyric. . . .

The time has been when, after an evening's hard boozing, my brother bards (who have been what we call seedy or crop-sick) have bilked the public house, and barbarously left me in pawn for the reckoning. On this emergency I have written an account of a sharp and bloody fight, a *Vision in the Air, or a Wonderful*

---

[1] *Bolingbroke's journal (1726), the principal Tory organ opposing the Walpole administration.*
[2] Mist's Journal, *Tory organ of Nathaniel Mist, attacked in* The Dunciad.
[3] *John Rich, master of the Theatre Royal in Covent Garden, also attacked in* The Dunciad.
[4] *Lewis Theobald's book (1726) attacked Pope's work as an editor of Shakespeare and he was made the principal dunce in* The Dunciad *of 1728 and 1729.*
[5] *A well-known boxer who kept a popular gymnasium.*
[6] *J. Henley, a popular preacher of the day, also in* The Dunciad. *He was a prolific writer on various subjects from theology and sermons to history and grammar.*

Prophecy to be hawked about streets. And (would you believe it?) even these productions of mine have passed for designed wit, and I have silently sneered, to find the merit of them claimed and boasted of by Jemmy Moore, and the above-mentioned knight. . . .

My pamphlets sell many more impressions than those of celebrated writers; the secret of this is, I learned from Curll to clap a new title-page to the sale of every half hundred; so that when my bookseller has sold two hundred and fifty copies, my book generally enters into the sixth edition. . . .

Another famous hack writer in Curll's employ was John Oldmixon.[1] The following portrait of Oldmixon from *Mist's Journal*, July 26, 1716, though a bit unfriendly, describes the kind of Grub Street activity that centred on Curll:

Whereas a noted author, one John Oldmixon, is lately retired from his garret and trade of drawing up indexes, making ballads, and writing of strange relations; this is to give notice, that he now resides at Bridgwater, in the County of Somerset,[2] and is Intelligencer-General for that place of that writer to celebrated fame and veracity the *Flying-Post* [Ridpath]; and that his old friends may not imagine that his excellent talent of writing, &c. is buried by him, they are to understand that they may suddenly expect from him these following treatises, viz. 1. A Letter of Advice to J——H F——w——ll in Ludgate, with general directions concerning the cadence of the voice, and the management of the shoe in begging; and an account of some particular modes of address which he himself invented when he was an inhabitant of that place. 2. An account of a young lady who presuming to spit in the face of a royal picture, in the presence of a militia captain and an half pay officer, was taken under protection by a lady of one of the colonels of the Guards. 3. The theory and practice of lying, in two parts; in which he acknowledges he has received great assistance, especially as to the latter part, from Mr. R——r H—— re. 4. A compendious method of carrying causes in

[1] *See above, p. 67.*

[2] *In 1716 Oldmixon was made Collector of the port of Bridgwater, a political plum for his Whig pamphleteering. It was a poor reward, for the returns were not great and Oldmixon soon wished himself back in London.*

Oldmixon was as prolific a writer as Gildon, and his life was equally wretched. In July, 1741, a year before he died, he wrote to the Duke of Newcastle: 'I am now dragged to a place I cannot mention [likely a sponging-house], in the midst of all the infirmities of old age, sickness, lameness and almost blindness, and without the means even of subsisting.'

any of his Majesty's Courts at Westminster and elsewhere, by the help of affidavits. N.B. He took the hint of this from Mr. R——t M——th——n, by whom any one may be furnished with affidavits of all sorts and sizes, ready drawn and sworn to at reasonable rates. 5. A collection of curious observations, grave reflections and sage sayings in matters theological, moral, political and natural, from the author's conversation with J——n G——b——t, Esq. J——h G——w——y, Gent. and James B——ker, tallow-chandler. 6. An humble address to the P——ment, praying, that all white rose bushes may be utterly extirpated out of the southern parts of Great Britain. N.B. That the objection of white rose water being good for sore eyes, will in this treatise be fully answered, and a succedaneum proposed by J——n A——n, M.D., F.R.S. Note farther that 'tis to be wished that the said J——n A——n would oblige the world with an account of his methods and success in giving quicksilver in cholics, and insert a particular account of the case of that gentlewoman who was like to have been cured by the new invented use of a pair of bellows; and that he would exactly delineate that operation upon the next dial which he draws. 7. A critical dissertation concerning the etymology, signification, and present use of the word shitsacks; with some useful remarks upon the lamentable abuse of that word in the western parts of Great Britain. 8. Observations upon the difference between lying in a gaol or garret, and being in an office gathered from his own experience....

These and many other as great curiosities he has with prodigious labour and diligence collected, there being not many ale-sellers (who in this country are as excellent antiquaries, historians, and naturalists, as they are in most others) but what he has consulted, and made great use of.

Perhaps the final comment on Curll is his own response to Defoe's anonymous attack in the *Weekly Journal,* later called *Mist's Journal,* April 5, 1718:

... There is indeed but one bookseller eminent among us for this abomination [some of Curll's bawdy publications], and from him the crime takes the just denomination of *Curlicism.* The fellow is a contemptible wretch a thousand ways: he is odious in person, scandalous in his fame; he is marked by Nature, for he has a bawdy countenance, and a debauched mien; his tongue is an echo of all the beastly language his shop is filled with, and filthiness drivels in the very tone of his voice.

... In a word, Mist, record it for posterity to wonder at, that in four years past of the blessed days we live in, and wherein justice and liberty are flourishing and established, more beastly unsufferable books have been published by this one offender, than in thirty years before by all the nation. . . .

On the eternal principle that a knock is as good as a boost, Curll promptly published a pamphlet entitled *Curlicism Display'd.* It was, in effect, a moral defence of his publications:

... With relation to the publishing these books, I am farther to assure your old man [the author of the attack], that they cannot by the laws of nature and nations be termed *bawdy* books, since they treat only of matters of the greatest importance to society, conduce to the mutual happiness of the nuptial state, and are directly calculated for antidotes against debauchery and unnatural lewdness, and not for incentives to them. For which reason I shall not desist from printing such books, when any occasion offers, nor am I either concerned or ashamed to have them distinguished by the facetious name of 'CURLICISM.'

Defoe was silenced and Curlicism flourished.

The progress of Curlicism, however, was not without setbacks. In 1725 the government finally caught up with him and arrested him for obscenity for publishing *The Nun in her Smock* and *The Treatise of Flogging.* There was a protracted court case during which Curll spent some months in the King's Bench Prison. In the same period he was also involved in a 'scandalous and seditious libel,' for publishing Ker's *Memoirs.* On February 13, 1728, the following announcement appeared in the *London Evening Post*:

Yesterday Mr. Edmund Curll received judgement... for the first two [amorous] offences he was sentenced to pay a fine of 25 marks each, to be committed till the same be paid, and then to enter into a recognizance of £100 for his good behaviour for one year; and for the last [political] to pay a fine of 20 marks, to stand in the pillory for the space of one hour, and his own recognizance to be taken for his good behaviour for another year.

Straus points out[1] that the seventy marks, which was not a large sum,[2] was paid. As for the pillory, the following report from the *State Trials* describes what happened:

This Edmund Curll stood in the pillory at Charing Cross, but was not pelted nor used ill; for being an artful, cunning (though wicked) fellow, he had contrived to have printed papers dispersed all about Charing Cross, telling the people that he stood there for vindicating the memory of Queen Anne; which had such an effect on the mob, that it would have been dangerous even to have spoken against him; and when he was taken down out of the pillory, the mob carried him off, as it were in triumph, to a neighbouring tavern.[3]

Curll's life was, perhaps, more adventurous than the average publisher would desire, but that seemed to be his style. He raised Grub Street publishing to artistic heights. And if there is some celestial place for publishing hucksters, Curll would be there, pirating unto eternity.

JOHN DUNTON

Perhaps one reason why no biography of John Dunton, born 1659, has yet been published, is because no one would believe it.[4] By his own reckoning he published some 600 books and pamphlets. He wrote a good many himself, ranging like a virtuoso singer from bass to coloratura, from dull sermons to scurrilous satire, assuming different identities from a country vicar to a madman.

---

[1] *Straus, p. 120.*
[2] *A mark was worth 13s. 4d.*
[3] T. B. *Howell,* A Complete Collection of State Trials, Vol. XVII *(1816).*
[4] *There is, however, a Harvard dissertation by Theodore M. Hatfield,* The True Secret History of Mr. John Dunton *(1930), and a biography in progress.*

Where he was dullest he often invented provocative titles suggesting that lecherous thrills lay just over the page. One can always recognize the books he printed because he mixed up his page types, as twentieth-century newspapers sometimes do, in what is called 'circus' make-up. In a Dunton book stretches of ordinary type suddenly change to light italic, then to dark Gothic or bold upper-case capitals, often all on the one page, and without any discernible logic. The effect is electrifying and confusing. One feels, as the type suddenly, mysteriously, changes style, that there must be some important reason for it, which tends to make a Dunton publication look exciting, however dull it might prove to be.

Dunton described and passed judgement on almost every Grub Street writer and publisher of the period. He set himself up as a national morality squad in his *Whipping Post or a Satyr upon Everybody* (1706); and considering how salacious some of his publications were this showed a remarkable impudence. He published and helped write one of the first successful journals with intellectual pretensions, the *Athenian Gazette,* which began publication March 17, 1690, and continued weekly until February 8, 1696. His autobiography, *The Life and Errors of John Dunton, Late Citizen of London; Written by Himself in Solitude. With an Idea of a New Life; Wherein is Shewn How he'd Think, Speak, and Act, might he live over his Days again ... Together with the Lives and Characters of a Thousand Persons now Living in London &c ....* (1705), is one of the queerest books ever written. Much of it is embarrasingly naïve, gusting with almost manic passions and anxieties. Out of this, however, emerges a comprehensive picture of his birth, apprenticeship, love affairs, publishing ventures and publishing sins, religious beliefs, as well as a portrait gallery of most of the publishers, printers and writers of Grub Street. It is at once an aggressive justification of his personal and professional life, a self-conscious repentance and a publishing enterprise designed for quick sale. There are lucid intervals in the *Life and Errors* and much of it has the racy vitality of a good Grub Street product. But it is also a whining, rambling, incoherent flood of words, digression upon digression, that leaves the reader bewildered. Yet he is always interesting for the light he throws on Grub Street—even if it is at times a distorted light—and for the picture he gives us of one of the strangest publishers of that strange society.

The effect of Dunton's prose is cumulative and it is difficult to provide a sampling that reveals him to advantage, but these excerpts give some slight indication of the man and the period. We shall begin with the *Life and Errors*. Dunton inserts, with a touching modesty, a candid portrait of himself as Philaret, the bold lover of his mistress, Iris, his future wife:

Philaret is of a middle stature, his hair black and curled, his eyebrows black and indifferently even, eyes almost black, quick and full of spirit, his nose rises a little in the middle, his lips red and soft; the whole composure of his face, though it is not so beautiful as some are, is yet rendered amiable by a cheerful sprightly air, his body is slender and every way well-proportioned. As for those beauties his mind is enriched with, he is not only free from those vices that most young men are inclined to, but is very pious. Heaven has blessed him with very plentiful wit, his way of writing is excellent, he has great skill in poetry, and I think the famous Cowley may from him learn a passionate strain. He is of an excellent sweet humour, carries it respectively to his superiors, and obligingly to his equals; and his humility is visible to all, when he converses with his inferiors. He certainly is the most passionate, constant lover living: his friendship is courted by all, for he's a true friend, and will not disclose a secret that he is instructed with, though the concealment may endanger his life: he is hard to be displeased, and when offended, easily reconciled: his spirit is tender and compassionate, something inclining to love; his modesty is more than usually great; and to finish this imperfect description, I must sincerely say, he has all those qualities that are necessary to render him an accomplished gentleman.

I blush to insert this character of myself; for the world, that has known Philaret a long time, will discover little of the original in the picture; however I'll endeavour to come up to it in my new life, though I have fallen far short in the old.

My great errors whilst a bachelor, were my over-eager concern in trade, my too frequent neglect of closet-prayer, with abundance of folly and extravagance in the affair of courtship; and I have often lamented that the very first occasion of it was taken, though undesignedly given, on the Lord's Day. These general hints may be sufficient to caution others, and I am altogether unobliged to make the confession more particular....

He is more explicit, however, about his experiences with the writers of Grub Street after serving his seven years of apprenticeship:

Printing was now the uppermost in my thoughts, and hackney-authors began to ply me with specimens, as earnestly, and with as much passion and concern, as the watermen do passengers with oars and scullers.

I had some acquaintance with this generation in my apprenticeship, and had never any warm affection for 'em; in regard, I always thought their great concern lay more in how much a sheet, than in any generous respect they bore to the commonwealth of learning; and indeed the learning itself, of these gentlemen, lies very often in as little room as their honesty; though they'll pretend to have studied you six or seven years in the Bodleian Library, to have turned over the Fathers, and to have read and digested the whole compass, both of human and ecclesiastic history. When, alas! They've never been able to understand a single page of Saint Cyprian, and can't tell ye whether the Fathers lived before or after Christ. And as for their honesty, 'tis very remarkable, they'll either persuade you to go upon another man's copy, to steal his thought, or to abridge his book, which should have got him bread for his life-time.

When you've engaged 'em upon some project or other, they'll write you off three or four sheets perhaps, take up three or four pounds upon an urgent occasion, and you shall never hear of 'em more. . . .

Looking back over his years of publishing, in *Life and Errors,* Dunton is not entirely displeased:

I give this account of my own copies, that you may see their impudence, who tell ye I printed nothing but trash; but, Reader, two of a trade can never agree, and there be men in the world, who will call the first and best book in the world trash, (I mean the Bible) and therefore well may others be so called: nor indeed is there anything more usual amongst booksellers, than to undervalue what does not agree with their own sentiments, or what they have not an interest in themselves: but admitting that in the six hundred books I have printed, there might be some trash, I would fain know what bookseller there is, who has none in his shop, yea, or what gentleman or divine is without it in his closet. . . .

Though I am but turned of my 40th year, and have always devoted my time and travels, to the knowledge of countries, books, and men; yet were I to correct the erratas of my short life, I would quite alter the press—Would time unweave my age again to the first thread, what another man would I be? But as willing as I am to confess this, yet where I have erred with respect to printing, I must cast the fault into the great heap of human error—I never printed a book in my whole life, but what I had a just end in the publication. But if others won't think to, I cannot help it, I must own. That having printed a great many books (and not reading through the twentieth part of what I print) some errors have escaped my hand; but this is my misfortune, and not my crime; and ill success ruins the merit of a good meaning; however, the way to amendment is never out of date—Repentance is a plank, we (book-merchants) have still left, on which we may swim to shore; and having erred, the noblest thing we can do, is to own it. He that repents, is well near innocent—Diogenes, seeing a lad sneaking out of a bawdy-house, bid him hold up his head, for he need not be ashamed of coming out, but of going in. And therefore as I grow in years, I alter my opinion of things; when I now print a book, I put on my graver spectacles, and consult as well with my judgement as interest: when I first began to print, I had then seen but the outside of the world and men, and conceived them according to their appearing glitter.

You know, Reader, youth are rash and heedless, green-heads are very ill judges of the productions of the mind. The first glance is apt to deceive and surprise: novelties have charms that are very taking, but a little leisure and consideration discovers the imposture, those false lights are dispelled upon a serious review, and second thoughts are wiser than the first. And this was my case with respect to *The Second Spira—The Post-Boy Rob'd of his Mail—The Voyage Round the World—The New Quevedo —The Pastors Legacy—Heavenly Pastime—The Hue and Cry after Conscience*—But (excepting these seven books) I have nothing to repent of with respect to printing; but for these, I heartily wish I had never seen them, and advise all that have them, to burn them. . . .

Thus have I freely confessed my errors in printing, but

as to bookselling and traffic, I dare stand the test with the same
allowances, that every man under the same circumstance with
me, would wish to have, for the whole trading part of my life—
Nay, I challenge all the booksellers in London to prove I ever
over-reached them or deceived them in any one instance.... But
if notwithstanding this hearty repentance, for my errors in printing, and scrupulous justice in trade, I have still enemies, 'tis no
wonder; better men than I have had them as much undeserved....

Dunton lists some of his elaborate publishing adventures
which he calls projects—a remarkable range of publications even
for Grub Street:

I am now to entertain the reader with the projects I have
engaged upon, for I have been sufficiently convinced, that unless
a man can either think or perform something out of the old beaten
road, he will find nothing but what his forefathers have found
before him. A bookseller, if he is a man of any capacity and observation, can tell best what to go upon and what has the best
prospect of success....

My first project was the *Athenian Gazette*.... I was one
day walking over St. George's Fields, and Mr. Larkin, and Mr.
Harris[1] were along with me, and on a sudden I made a stop, and
said, Well Sirs, I have a thought I will not exchange for fifty
guineas; they smiled, and were very urgent with me to discover
it, but they could not get it from me. The first rude hint of it,
was no more than a confused idea of concealing the querist and
answering his question.[2] However, so soon as I came home, I managed it to some better purpose, brought it into form, and ham-
mered out a title for it, which happened to be extremely lucky,
and those who are well acquainted with the Grecian history, may
discover some peculiar beauties in it....

When I had thus formed the design, I found that some
assistance was absolutely necessary to carry it on, in regard, the
project took in the whole compass of learning, and the nature of

---

[1] *George Larkin and Benjamin Harris were eminent London publishers.*
[2] *The idea, in fact, was a series of questions, supposedly from readers, on an astonishing range of subjects, with answers sometimes intelligent and profound, sometimes naïve and comic by modern standards, reflecting the learning, the prejudices and superstitions of the times. It makes dull reading today.*

it required dispatch. I had then some acquaintance with the ingenious Mr. Richard Sault;[1] who turned Malebranch into English
for me, and was admirably well skilled in the mathematics; and
over a glass of wine I unbosomed myself to him, and he very
freely offered to become concerned. So soon as the design was well
advertised, Mr. Sault and myself, without any more assistance,
settled to it with great diligence. . . . The project being surprising
and unthought of, we were immediately over-loaded with letters,
and sometimes I have found several hundreds for me at Mr.
Smith's coffee-house in Stocks Market, where we usually met to
consult matters. . . .

In a little time after, to oblige authority, we altered the
title of *Athenian Gazette*, into *Athenian Mercury*.

The undertaking growing every week upon our hands, the
impatience of our querists, and the curiosity of their questions,
which required a great deal of accuracy and care, did oblige us
to adopt a third member of Athens, and the Reverend Mr. Wesley[2] being just come to town, all new from the university, and
my acquaintance with him being very intimate, I easily prevailed
with him to embark himself upon the same bottom, and in the
same cause.

With this new addition we found ourselves to be masters
of the whole design, and thereupon we neither lessened nor increased our number.

The success of Athens growing so very considerable,[3] Mr.
[Tom] Brown and Mr. [William] Pate began to ape our design
in a paper they entitled the *Lacedemonian Mercury*, which immediately interfered with us under a title, which it is true, was
pretty and pertinent enough. Upon this, I was resolved one way
or other to blow them up, in regard, it was both ungenerous and
unjust, to interlope upon a man, where he has the sole right and
property, for the children of the brain, are as much ours, as those
we beget in lawful wedlock.

---

[1] *Sault (d. 1702) was a mathematician and editor. Dunton supplied him with a good deal
of literary work.*
[2] *Samuel Wesley, father of the Methodists Charles and John Wesley.*
[3] *It was, indeed, highly successful and was even eulogized by Jonathan Swift, 'a country
gentleman,' in one of his early poems, 'Ode to the Athenian Society', 'which being an
ingenious poem was prefixt to the* Fifth Supplement *of the* Athenian Mercury.'

The *Lacedemonian Mercury* was started in February, 1692, by Brown, William Pate[1] and Charles Gildon,[2] who after a few weeks deserted to Dunton and was duly enshrined in the *Life and Errors*. It was more a burlesque of Dunton's paper than an imitation, and it succeeded admirably in both enraging Dunton and capitalizing on a profitable publishing venture. Here are the opening lines of the first number:

Vol. 1.   Numb. 1.

THE LONDON [LACEDEMONIAN] MERCURY

in which will be answered all witty and ingenious questions, for the diversion as well as satisfaction of the *beau monde*, and the *Athenian Mercury* supplied with queries from the fair sex, of what degree or quality soever; with some others which shall be judged to fall within the province of that Society.

Last night being very restless in my bed, I thought fit to divert the time with sporting an author ... till fortune, that took care of my health, had, by I know not what means, laid one of those papers, called the *Athenian Mercury*, by me, being destitute of either opium or poppy-water. I had scarce run over one paragraph, when I found a heaviness descend on my eyes, the welcome harbinger of approaching slumbers, which soon followed after. . . .

Most of Brown's issues had a few questions in honour of the Athenian Society and the chaste Mr. Dunton:

Queries relating to the Fair Sex.

Quest. 1. A certain querist of the fair sex, though for quality a little dirty (but that's nothing, they are all ladies at Athens) having a terrible angry corn between her toes of the left foot, and a wart or mole on the inside of her right buttock, she begs to know of your Athenian worships, which of these two small tenements, thus placed as abovesaid, you think to be best situated for air and prospect?

Que. 2. Another lady querist of the like degree and quality, (for

---

[1] *William Pate (1666-1746) was a considerable scholar who was also a tradesman, an unusual combination for this period. He became a friend of Steele and Swift. Swift referred to him as his 'learned woollen draper.'*

[2] *See above, p. 74.*

she's troubled with corns too, but more with scruples) had lately
the misfortune to oblige two neighbouring apprentices in a carnal
manner, about the same time; and this she did in hopes to draw
on a marriage from one of them. But the arch rogues having already consummated, refuse to perform any other matrimonial ceremony; and she finding herself in a teeming condition, humbly
begs your advice to which of the two she ought to lay her kid,
for she cannot father it on both, and therefore suspects from something, that you have already answered in a like case (Vol. 5, No.
13) that she ought to charge it on neither; but if your wisdoms
please, she'll lay it to a third person, from whom she may expect
better advantage, though he never gave her earnest. Your speedy
answer to this, I beseech you for time, tide, and a great belly will
stay for no man.

Qu. 3. An Alderman's domestic of the fair sex, having casually
hurt her hand in spitting a pig, desires your opinion, Gentlemen,
on these three heads. 1. What you think the best salve for a green
sore? 2. Whether she may venture to wash it once a day in her
own water, she being now about twenty-two? and 3. Whether
she may in conscience loiter and neglect her work till her hand be
well again? ...

Some of Brown's questions and answers were even sensible,
but for the most part, when he was not gibing at Dunton's *Mercury* he was a 17th-century Ann Landers, for adults only. Even
this had the added spice of being a parody on the *Athenian Mercury*:

Query 6. About fifteen months ago I married a tripe-woman's
daughter in Wapping, and within a fortnight after was pressed
to sea, where, as my captain can witness, I have continued a ship-
board till the first day of March last. When I came home, I was
told (to my great joy you may think) that my wife (the devil
take her) was just brought to bed of a child. With that, upstairs
I ran, and asked her, You strumpet you, who is the father of this
brat? Why, you sauce-box, says she, who but you? How can that
be, says I, I have been out of the kingdom above these fourteen
months. That's all one, says she, you are the father, and are like
to provide for it.—When I saw I could do nothing with bluster-
ing and storming, I sat me down peaceably by the bedside, Kate,

says I, dear Kate, prithee tell me honestly and fairly, who got thee with child? Lord! says she, what a do is here about a child! Why you, and nobody but you, had a hand in the getting on it. But, my dear, replied I, that's impossible, for I have been so many months at sea. And then she told me it was customary in Wapping for a woman to go fourteen months with child, and sometimes seventeen, and sometimes twenty, as it happened. Nay, she told me of a neighbour of hers that went four years and upwards with child; and the reason of it was, because living by the cold water-side, a child would not ripen in their bellies, so soon as it would in other places. I would fain believe poor Kate if I could; so she desired me to send to your Society (as you call it) and I should receive full satisfaction.—And now, what is your opinion of the matter?

Answ. Since you tell us, friend tar, that you would willingly believe what your wife Kate has told you to be true, we shall be so far from staggering you in that pious belief, which perhaps we might do, if we were ill-natured people, that we'll contribute all we can to fix and settle you still in a better opinion of your spouse's virtues. We can tell you then for a certain truth, that though the vulgarly-received opinion has fixed it at nine months, yet every day's observation shows that rule to be as uncertain as the Jewish trial of maidenheads, or the swimming of old women to be witches. Several women, and those of no mean quality, at the other end of the town, have been delivered at five or six months after matrimony; nay, we have heard of some, who to be sure were of a sanguine complexion, that had occasion for a midwife after two. The other extreme is indeed not altogether so common, we mean in the city, or Westminster. But since the bone of your side fairly assures you it is customary in Wapping, and the adjacent places, we'd even adivse you not to mind what Aristotle or Culpepper [author of a quack treatise entitled *Aristotle's Midwife*] say, but to believe her, for fear of drawing the indignation of the rest of your neighbourhood upon you, which may hinder you from partaking in many a comfortable bowl of punch, and that you know would be no inconsiderable loss....

Dunton, of course, was not pleased with Brown's attack. The day after Brown's first issue, he replied in his *Athenian Mercury*:

Yesterday morning was published a paper interfering with our Athenian project ... we therefore here give public notice, that those questions which he pretends to answer shall be all answered again by us, that so neither our Querists, the Booksellers, nor the London coffee-houses may be imposed upon by buying questions twice answered, for they shall always find in our papers the best of his thoughts ... with remarks upon his errors. We shall now change one of our days of publishing into that of his, and oftener if he gives any further occasion.

In four months the battle was over and Dunton had won. The circumstances are mysterious. On May 28, 1692, Dunton was enraged to the breaking point by an announcement in the *Lacedemonian Mercury* that its first volume would be published in book form, including a 'Large Account of several Athenian Blunders.' Then Dunton announced:

I shall take occasion in a very little time to give the world a just and well attested character of him [Brown], as to the scandal he has been to academicians, schoolmasters, and all the rest of the world he has conversed with, (and shall reserve his way of dealing with booksellers for a 2nd part of his *Life*). Nor will I do him the least injustice in what I shall charge upon him; and then I'll leave the world to judge of his reputation and mine. . . . What I shall publish will give the world occasion to judge what value is due to his scandalous pamphlets.

It is hard to imagine what scandal could possibly have disturbed Brown, who already had one of the most scandalous reputations on Grub Street. However, a few days after Dunton published his threat Brown's *Mercury* ceased publication. To Dunton it was just one more provoking episode in a life that was full of them:

A second project of mine, which was set on foot by the Old Athenians, and lately published by the New,[1] is entitled—

---

[1] *When the popular* Athenian Mercury *ceased publication Dunton, like a good publisher, used the name* Athenian *for other publishing ventures.* The Athenian Oracle *(1703) and* Athenianism . . . Six Hundred Letters in Prose and Verse, *written with his [Dunton's] own hand* (1710), *were others of the family.*

The Athenian Spy, or the Secret Letters of Platonick Courtship, between the Athenian Society, and the most ingenious ladies, in the three kingdoms, with the Form of Solemnizing Platonick Matrimony, invented by the Athenian Society; To which is added their amorous quarrels on the disputable points, relating to love and wedlock—The Copy of an Act, to provide Maids with Husbands—As also a method for unmarrying those that are unequally yoked. Published to direct the bachelor and virgin in their whole amour. This *Athenian Spy,* will be continued to several volumes and the reader may meet with their various subjects in the Preface to the first volume. . . .

[Dunton's third project] for the promotion of learning, was a monthly journal of books printed in London, and beyond sea, which was chiefly extracted out of *The Universal Bibliotheque,*[1] and *Journal des Sçavans,*[2] and it first appeared under the title of a *Supplement to the Athenian Mercury,* but was afterwards called, *The Compleat Library.* This design was carried on about ten months, when Monsieur Lecrose interfered with me in a monthly journal entitled, *The Works of the Learned,* upon which I dropped my own design, and joined with Lecrose's bookseller, in publishing *The Works of the Learned,* but Lecrose dying, 'twas discontinued. . . .

The sub-title of J. de la Crose's *The Works of the Learned* is 'An Historical Account and Impartial Judgement of Books newly printed, both Foreign and Domestick, to be published monthly.' It was published in 1691 and is one of the first journals of literary criticism in the English language. It offers a literary judgement and gives some evidence to support it. The following excerpt from the November issue is a comment on Dunton's Supplement to the Third Volume of the *Athenian Mercury*—that is, Dunton's third project which La Crose supplanted:

The *Athenian Mercury,* and the Supplement to it, have found such a favourable acceptance in the learned world (if we

---

[1] *A collection of reviews of contemporary books published in 25 volumes from 1686 to 1693 in Amsterdam. The major editor was Jean le Clerc, assisted at the beginning by La Crose himself.*

[2] Le Journal des Sçavans, *a scholarly journal published in Paris almost continuously from 1665 to 1828. Some of the greatest French scholars were associated with this journal.*

may believe the authors themselves), that none of the ingenious
writers, whose works make up our journal, must take it ill if we
give the first place to this wonderful attempt of the whole Athenian Society. Above two-thirds of this Supplement are bare translations out of the *Universal Bibliotheque,* and the rest consists in
five abstracts of several learned persons, as they entitle themselves.

As to the translations, you may judge of their faithfulness
and elegance by the following examples. [The article proceeds to
list about a dozen inaccuracies of style and meaning in the Supplement's translation from the French,[1] and makes some un-
charitable remarks on the level of scholarship in the five abstracts.]

And this is the issue of those so vast and nauseously-repeated
promises and advertisements, and as if they thought all men as
dull as themselves, and such as may eternally be imposed upon
by their windy babblings; they have yet the confidence, at the
end of this Supplement, to reiterate their notorious lies, by promising to print, in their next, all the books (an abstract of them
they should say) which they have promised in their *Mercuries,* together with all other valuable English books that shall be published
before the coming out of their Supplement; though it be visibly
impossible ... that they should insert them all in ten or twelve
papers of the like bulk.

It is easy to see why Dunton was beaten out of the field.

[Dunton's] sixth project, was *The Challenge,* sent by a young
lady to Sir Thomas—entitled the *Female War,* wherein the present dresses and humours of the fair sex, are vigorously attacked
by men of quality, and as bravely defended by several ladies. In
this *Challenge* (or *Female War*) there was an absolute freedom
of speech allowed by both sexes, which was given, and taken, without the least offence. The whole encounter consists of several
challenges, in which the ladies attack the men with such strength
of reason, and wit and gaiety, that they generally come off with
victory.

My next project was entitled, *The Post-Boy Rob'd of his
Mail: Or, The Pacquet broke open,* containing five hundred
letters that were taken from several posts, discovering the secrets

---

[1] *Since La Crose was part editor and author of* The Universal Bibliotheque, *he had a
right to be critical.*

of men and women of all ranks and qualities. The club of gentlemen supposed to have been concerned in this frolic, make remarks
upon the letters as they break them up. This project obtained
so well, that both volumes are now out of print.

'Tis true, there are many unwary and profane expressions
scattered through these volumes, so that I'm heartily sorry I had
any concern in them: but the author sent the copy to the press
as he writ it off, and in regard, I had no suspicion of him, I did
not peruse the letters till 'twas past time to alter them; I don't
think the same reason will justify either the author or myself,
upon which our modern playwriters build so much, that because
there's wickedness in the life, the representation should be so too.
However, the project in general, was very well approved and will
in few months, be reprinted, and severely corrected, with a large
number of additional letters, by New-Athens. . . .

My eighth project, was a design to expose vice, entitled,
*The Night Walker, Or, Evening Rambles in Search after lewd
Women, with the various Conferences held with them, dedicated
to the Whores and Whore-Masters of London and Westminster.*
This project was so well received, that I purposed to continue it
monthly, till a discovery was made of the chief prostitutes in England, from the pensionary-miss, down to the common strumpet.
This journal was kept up about eight months, and then my author
was quite out at the elbows, for want of matter; however, to fill
up the last, that the public might not have it imperfect, two young
clergymen, in other habits, and myself (with the consent of Iris
[his wife]) began the rambles, for neither they nor I before, had
ever seen the humours of the town. I am well enough satisfied
with the innocence of our design, but indeed the prudence of it,
I know not how to justify. 'Tis true, there was no wickedness committed, however, we ran ourselves upon temptation; but I leave
that matter to those reverend clergymen who were neither both
of them Dissenters, nor yet both Conformists. As for my own part,
I am sorry for the frolic, and would not act it over again; but if
any of the discoveries we made, do but give others an abhorrence
of that wicked generation of Night-Walkers, I shall willingly bear
the little censures I may meet with, and I think I practised all
the severity of that nature upon myself, which others can possibly
do.

The first night, we resolved to ramble, Mr. T—— and

myself, made an appointment with our reverend knight-errants, to meet them at the Bull-Head, exactly at eight, with some game along with us; we kept to the assignation very punctually, and had picked up a young piece of wickedness, which might easily be known by her telling us where she lodged at the very first. Our gentlemen were not exact to the appointment, and so soon as miss and we had drank two or three glasses, she began to gather up a little too close with us, whereupon I rose up, and with as ghostly a look as I could well affect, I said,

Madam, keep off, you think I am flesh and blood; and I doubt not but that I imitate it near enough to deceive your sight; assure yourself, I am not what I appear. Reclaim, your whore-doms, or you are unavoidably lost, your life is almost run out, and the time you have to repent is very short. If you are other-wise resolved, view these features, and expect me to be a witness against you at the Day of Judgement. Upon this she waxed pale, and swooned away, which gave us the opportunity to slip off as though we had vanished. The next day we went to enquire and listen in the neighbourhood where she lodged, and we understood the gentlewoman had given it out how she had met with a spirit.

In our next rambles we made sure to have the benefit of the clergy, along with us, though 'twas but in masquerade, and strolling in Drury-Lane, we met a mask[1] and she led us to the Horse-Shoe, where she revealed herself, and brightened upon us at a strange rate, whereupon the Reverend Mr. —— told her if the blackness of her mind could as easily be laid aside as that of her face, she had a good hand at it, but he was afraid that would prove the greatest difficulty she had met with. Miss replied, Shuh! Never fear boy, those things are bugbears, for children, I am as sound as an eunuch, and that's the main point. Well Madam!, returned he, I would ask you one question in the solemn presence of Almighty God, whether you think whoredom to be a sin, or no? Upon this she was all in confusion, and answered, she thought it might be a sin, but she hoped God would forgive her, for she went to church every Sunday, forgave everybody, and at the age of thirty, she resolved to leave it off.

Mr. —— told her, he was very sorry to hear it, that she was better keep from church, than go thither upon such terms as these;

[1] *By Dunton's time the Restoration fashion of wearing masks was associated with loose women.*

as for repenting at thirty, she could have no assurance of life till then, and if she could not master her inclinations now, there was no hopes of victory and reformation, when the habits of vice were strengthened by such a length of custom and ill practice. Miss grew uneasy under the lecture, and interrupted, Fuh, I hate all this stuff, then fluttered him in the face with her fan, and languished upon him. Stand off, Madam, said he, If my former discourse ben't awakening enough, what d'ye think of Eternity and the flames of Hell? Are those nothing but childish bugbears? As certainly as there's a God, and a life to come, you shall spend an eternity in flames of sulphur, and in everlasting banishment from the presence of God and happiness unless you—— Here she started up, and said, What Gentlemen, d'ye bring me here to affront me? She took her leave, and so the conference broke up.

Leaving the Horse-Shoe, we steered next to the play-house, which is the rendezvous of all extravagance, or rather the shambles,[1] where both young and old are exposed to sale; coming too soon for the play, we took a turn in the lobby, where a black devil in a mask, strolled by, with some assurance. The moving engine looked very big upon her own dimensions, which were something mountainous. Her shadow swept before her, like a link-boy;[2] we saw 'twas no talking with such a body of sin, so we made up to the pit,[3] where, in a corner, we found a knot of quality (like Quevedo's Collection,[4] in a corner of Hell). Ladies were talking to gentlemen, and we supposed gentlemen to ladies too—We here took particular notice of a country squire, who had got an antiquated piece into a privacy; she was certainly a procurer, and the man too modest to take up at first hand. This superannuated strumpet, seemed at first to be a little coy, but agreed at last (for we dogged 'em out of the pit) to meet him at the Goat in H——. The country esq. makes the best of his way to the place of meeting, and the old harlot goes as fast to the Dog-Tavern, where calling for a room and looking glass she begins careening herself for the interview; she washes her bubbies, patches her face,

---

[1] *A meat market.*

[2] *A boy employed to carry a torch through the unlighted streets of the time.*

[3] i.e. *the pit for cock-fights, one of the popular diversions of this period.*

[4] *Quevedo's* Visions of Hell. *Quevedo (1580-1645) is one of the greatest writers of comedy and satire in Spanish literature. There were several English translations by Dunton's time.*

THE DISTREST POET.

A MIDNIGHT MODERN CONVERSATION

Top: The Distrest Poet. *Bottom:* A Midnight Modern Conversation

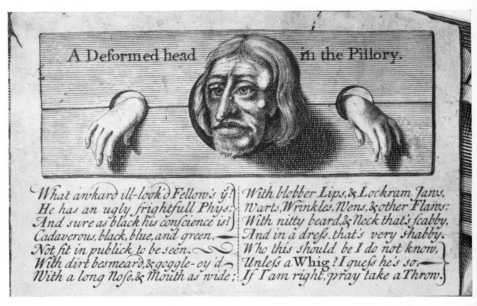

A Deformed head   in the Pillory.

What awkard ill-look'd Fellow's y?
He has an ugly frightfull Phys:
And sure as black his conscience is?
Cadaverous, black, blue, and green,
Not fit in publick to be seen.
With dirt besmear'd, & goggle-ey'd
With a long Nose, & Mouth as wide:

With blobber Lips, & Lockram Jaws,
Warts, Wrinkles, Wens, & other Flaws:
With nitty beard, & Neck that's scabby,
And in a dress, that's very shabby.
Who this should be I do not know,
Unless a Whig? I guess he's so,
If I am right, pray take a Throw.

Top: Daniel Defoe in the Pillory. *Bottom:* The Art and Mystery of Printing Emblematically Displayed. [In three sections, left to right: (1) Ass's head sets up type. (2) Hog's head inks type; horse's head pulls over the frame; greyhound's head puts his foot through a forme of *The Craftsman*, (a Tory journal edited by Bolingbrooke); Janus-headed printer looks on. (3) The Devil hangs printed sheets of paper to dry on lines stretched across the room.]

powders her hair, and sweetens her arm-pits. When she came to the place of assignation, she was told her spark had been waiting for her above an hour, and desired she'd come to his arms alone, and without so much as the company of a candle. She knew the night that concealed her guilt would do the same funeral office to the fingerwork of her dress; and therefore she could not away with it at first blush; however a strumpet's conscience being wide, and larger by two foot, than a Jacobite's, she submitted at last to the disadvantage; and felt her way to the bed; where the expecting lover was feeding on the metaphysical fare of fancy and anticipation; when the soft duel was over the gentleman sunk into a slumber; whereupon having a mind to gratify her eyes, with the sight of her conquest, she rises, springs a light, and coming to take a full view, saw the perfect phiz of her own dear husband in the sheets. For our own parts, we only followed her to the Dog-Tavern, and there left her, but going to the Goat-Tavern the next day, we had this whole account from the honest drawer.

We laid the scene of our third ramble towards Charing Cross, and stepping into a coffee-house, on the left hand of the passage into Pall-Mall, where designing a little friendly discourse, we asked for a convenient room, and being shown up one pair of stairs, and sat down, in comes a charming machine of wickedness, she sailed towards us in all the luring postures you can possibly imagine; she first asked our pardon for the rudeness, and indeed she was never more in the right of it; and then told us she thought we had been some gentlemen of her own acquaintance, but that was nothing, we should soon be acquainted. We asked her whether she was married? No, she never married, she replied, unless 'twas for a quarter of an hour, or so; Mr. —— then put the question to her, what misfortune it was that had thrown her upon that course of life? She answered, her father lived near Hampton-Court, where a club of rakes had made her drunk, and then debauched her, and so she had followed her pleasures. Ah, returned Mr. ——

When once debauched, your sex for ever burn
In lawless fires, virtue knows no return.

Really, Madam, continued he, I extremely pity you; you seem to be in the ready way to misery and unhappiness. 'Tis true, you

D

may sin on a while, and then die in an hospital. At this she began to weep, and said, she was very sensible of it, but she could not supply her necessities any other way; but if any gentleman would take a fancy to her, she could make the most faithful wife in Christendom. At these words, his reverence was something in confusion, and methought there was the appearance of an infant passion struggling in his breast, for really she was the fairest angel of flesh and blood, and rank inclination, I had ever seen. However, he got his soft sentiments conjured down, and then read her a severe lecture upon debauchery, both in this, and the next world; and so soon as miss saw we were nothing for her purpose, she rubbed off. But before she went we painted her in her own colours, and showed her there was no depending on a person of her principles, this gave her spleen some disturbance, and she was all overcast with frowns; I supposed we should shortly break up upon it, and calling for the reckoning, she melted all into smiles and affection on a sudden, and petitioned me for a pair of gloves. I asked her pardon that I could not encourage the practice, and so dismissed her under disappointment and melancholy. . . .

The night was well advanced, and the clock struck ten as we entered the street; however it was not too late to pursue another adventure; and as we were wholly engaged upon the scent, an old gentleman of the —— Inn in Leaden-Hall-Street, gave us the shoulder. We perceived he was pretty rampant, and had been with the oyster-wench; so we traced his doubles very diligently, till he pushed forward into a dark alley and meeting with —— &c. he addressed her, Madam! I wish I was twenty-seven for your sake. But if you have the charity to accept the service of an ——. Here she interrupted him, Sir, I am sorry you're no younger, if you want a wife; but if you're ranging for a whore, pray put on your spectacles, you've mistaken your woman; we're well acquainted, your name is T—— &c. My man of four-score was dumbfounded, and as he slid off, made the very figure of a cur disappointed of his bone. We were glad the lady's virtue could resist the attack, though the temptation 'tis true, had little of flesh in it. The night being far advanced, myself, Mr. T—— (and our two companions) retired to our lodgings, and let the world wag for that night.

These are all the discoveries we made, and I here give the reader a solemn caution, never to allow himself the same liberty;

for though the defence of these rambles may seem plausible enough, yet I am willing to number 'em among the errors of my life. . . .

Such are the hazards of publication.

With so varied a Grub Street background, Dunton is well qualified to pass judgement on the Grub Street world, which he does on almost everyone, with the same dubious candour that we have come to expect from him:

> I next reckon myself obliged in gratitude, to draw the characters of the authors for whom I printed, &c. and indeed my own life would appear but a broken thread, unless I should set both men and things in as fair a light as I can, so far as they have come within the compass of my own sphere. . . . Tom Brown (that incorrigible sinner) deserves the birch much better than the bays, for exposing Mr. Burgess.[1] But alas! The meeting and the play-house, the Temple of God, and the Synagogue of Satan, stand too near, to have any good harmony betwixt 'em. . . .
>
> Tom Brown is a good scholar and knows to translate either the Latin or the French incomparably well; he's enriched with a noble genius, and understands our own tongue as well, if not better than any man of the age. The poems he has writ are very beautiful and fine, but the urgency of his circumstances won't allow him time enough to lay out his talent that way. After all, I can't but lay that his morals are wretchedly out of order, and 'tis extreme pity that a man of so fine parts, and so well accomplished every other way, should spend his time upon a few romantic letters,[2] that seem purely designed to debauch the age, and overthrow the foundations of religion and virtue.
>
> Mr. Durfey[3] has but a low genius and yet some of his farces would make a body laugh. He has writ considerably in his time, and there are few authors have been more diverting. Yes, Durfey,

---

[1] *Referring to Brown's satire of Daniel Burgess (1645-1713) in his* Amusements Serious and Comical *(1700). Burgess was an extremely popular Presbyterian minister with a lively and eccentric manner of delivering sermons that made him the laughing-stock of the wits.*
[2] *The practice of writing letters on imaginary situations was a literary fashion of the time. Many of Brown's letters were indecent.*
[3] *Tom Durfey (1653-1723), popular playwright and song-writer, particularly bawdy songs.*

Thou canst play, thou canst sing
To a mayor, or a king,
    Though thy luck on the stage is so scurvy;
Such a beau, such a face,
Such a voice to disgrace,
    Such a mien, 'tis the de'il, Mr. D——

Mr. Ridpath is a considerable scholar, and well acquainted with the languages. He's a Scotsman, and designed first of all for the Ministry, but by some unfortunate accident or other, the fate of an author came upon him. He has writ much, and his style is excellent, and his humility and his honesty have established his reputation. He scorns to receive a farthing of copy money, till he knows what numbers are sold off. He was very fortunate in engaging in *The History of the Works of the Learned*, which was originally my own thought,[1] and the first I published under the title of *The Athenian Supplement*, and the next under that of *The Compleat Library*. He writes the *Flying Post*, which is highly valued, and sells well; but if the merits of an author must be determined according to the success of his works, the greatest genius of the age would suffer by it—'Twas this ingenious gentleman that invented the Polygraphy, or Writing Engine, by which one may with great facility, write two, four, six, or more copies of any one thing upon so many different sheets of paper at once; this writing engine is likewise attended with this advantage, that being moved by the foot, while the hand guides the pens, it keeps the whole body in warmth and exercise, which prevents many of the usual inconveniences of a sedentary life, besides the time which the engine saves in dispatch.

Mr. Daniel De Foe is a man of good parts, and very clear sense. His conversation is ingenious and brisk enough. The world is well satisfied that he's enterprising and bold; but alas! had his prudence only weighed a few grains more, he'd certainly have writ his *Shortest Way* [*with Dissenters*], a little more at length. . . .[2]

Had he writ no more than his *True Born Englishman*, and spared some particular characters that are too vicious for the very originals, he had certainly deserved applause; but 'tis hard to

[1] *See above, p. 92. Ridpath began the journal on La Crose's death.*
[2] *This satire was misunderstood by almost every reader in London and got Defoe into serious trouble. See below, p. 240.*

leave off when not only the itch and inclination, but the necessity of writing lies so heavy upon a man.

Should I defend his good nature, and his honesty, and the world would not believe me, 'twould be labour in vain. Mr. Foe writ for me the Character of Dr. Annesley,[1] and a Pindaric in honour of the Athenian Society, which was prefixed to the *History* of it, and he might have asked me the question before he had inferred either of 'em in the collection of his works, in regard he writes so bitterly against the same injustice in others.

Mr. Fuller[2] is not only a villain, but he's known to be so. He has something peculiar in his face that distinguishes him from the rest of mankind; but however, he has been such a mystery of iniquity, that the world had much ado to unriddle him. His looks are so honest and innocent, that you'd think 'twas impossible that any mischief should be lodged in his heart.

He has told the world in the *History of his Life*, that Mr. Baldwin and I, did improve his *Narrative of the Sham Prince of Wales*, on purpose to make it sell, which is the most formal lie I have met with; in regard the copy was printed off before we saw it.

In the same *History of his Life*, he pretends to make public every roguery he committed, but says nothing of his carrying Mr. Hayhurst and myself to Canterbury, and several other places, in quest of some state letters which were never in being; and of the great sum he's yet indebted to us, upon that account; so that if his penitence and his confession be in the same condition, they neither of them signify a farthing.

Mr. Gildon is well acquainted with the languages, and writes with a peculiar briskness which the common hacks can't boast of, in regard, they want the life and spirit, and the same liberty, and extent of genius. He was always very just in the engagements where I had any concern, and his performances were done, as well as the designs would admit. He writ *The History of the Athenian Society*, which contained the just merits of that cause.

---

[1] *Samuel Annesley, a well-known Dissenting minister of the time. Both Samuel Wesley and John Dunton married Annesley's daughters.*
[2] *William Fuller (c. 1670-1717), declared by the House of Commons in 1692 an 'imposter, cheat and false accuser' for concocting a story about Jacobite plots. His Life of* William Fuller *(1701) and his other writings earned him a stay in the pillory, a whipping and a heavy fine for his 'false' assertions.*

Mr. Philips,[1] a gentleman of good learning, and well born. He'll write you a design off in a very little time, if the gout (or claret) don't stop him. He translates *The Present State of Europe, Or, The Monthly Mercury*, incomparably well, which is one of the finest journals of the kind, the world has ever seen; I was once concerned in it, but had the misfortune to drop it. . . .

Mr. Bradshaw, the best accomplished hackney author I have met with; his genius was quite above the common size, and his style was incomparably fine. You could propose to him no design, within the compass of learning, but he knew to go through with it; he designed for the Ministry, till he had finished his studies and then fell off something like Tom Brown, though the comparison be a little too mean for him. He writ for me the *Parable of the Magpyes*, and many thousands of them sold. I had once fixed him upon a very great design, and furnished him both with money and books, which were most of 'em historical and geographical; but my gentleman thought fit to remove himself, and I'm not sure that I have seen him since. In a little time after, was published the first volume of the *Turkish Spy*, and so soon as I saw it, the very style, and the manner of writing, convinced me that Bradshaw was the author[2]. This gave me a little fresh uneasiness to find him out, and one day I met his wife in Grays-Inn; at first sight she was almost dumbfounded, but I was as civil to her as my nature would suffer me; I asked after her husband, and she gave me this account, that Dr. Midgely[3] had engaged him in a work which would take up some years to finish; she added, the Dr. gave him 40s. per sheet, 20s. per sheet he received, and the other twenty went to pay off some old arrears, betwixt him and the Doctor. Dr. Midgely owned to me he was well acquainted with Mr. Bradshaw, and said he was very ingenious, but unhappy, and something indebted to him. After this, I had no more intelligence of Mr. Bradshaw, but the *Turkish Spy* was for some years published. . . . If Mr. Bradshaw be yet alive, I here declare to the world, and to him, that I freely forgive him what he owes, both in money and books, if he'll only be so kind as to make me a visit.

Likely John Philips (1676-1709), author of The Splendid Shilling.
[2] *Isaac Disraeli* (Curiosities of Literature *[1888],I, p. 378) says that John Paul Marana, an Italian, was the author of* The Turkish Spy.
[3] *Likely R. Midgely, publisher of Peter Motteux's Gentleman's Journal (1692.)*

But I am afraid the worthy gentleman is dead, so he was wretchedly over-run with melancholy, and the very blackness of it reigned in his countenance. He had certainly performed wonders with his pen, had not his poverty pursued him, and almost laid the necessity upon him to be unjust.

Mr. Settle[1] has got himself the reputation of being a good poet, and perhaps he knows the art, at least, as well as his brethren of the quill. His Latin poem, dedicated to the Princess Sophia, has shown he's a man of learning. His *Character of a Popish Successor*, has deservedly given him the name of a wit, and most of his plays have been acted with great applause. Mr. Dryden found him smart enough, and could have wished himself safe out of his hands.

But, alas! after all, when I see an ingenious man set up for a mere poet, and steer his course through life towards that point of the compass, I give him up as one pricked down by fate for misery and misfortune. 'Tis something unaccountable, but one would incline to think there's some indispensable law, whereby poverty and disappointment are entailed upon poets. . . .

Mr. Shirley, (alias Dr. Shirley)[2] is a good natured writer as I know, he has been an indefatigable press-mauler, for above these twenty years. He has published at least a hundred bound books, and about two hundred sermons—but the cheapest pretty, pat things, all of 'em, pence a piece as long as they'll run—His great talent lies at collection, and he'll do it you for 6s. per sheet. He knows to disguise an author that you shan't know him, and yet keep the sense and the main scope entire. He's as true as steel to his word, and would stave off his feet, to oblige a bookseller. He's usually very fortunate in what he goes upon: he writ *Lord Jeffrey's Life* for me, of which six thousand were sold. After all, he subsists, as other authors must expect, by a sort of geometry. . . .

Robert Carr—— A small poetical insect, like Bays in everything but writing well—an odd mixture of lead and mercury—as heavy and dull as an old usurer, and yet as unfixed and maggoty as Parson Grubb—still changing, displeased, unquiet, uneasy,

---

[1] *Elkanah Settle (1648-1724), Restoration dramatist. He was satirized by Dryden as Doeg in* Absalom and Achitophel, II *and by Pope in* The Dunciad. *In his later years he was the 'City Poet' preparing pageants for the Lord Mayor's Shows.*
[2] *Likely Benjamin Shirley, a Fleet Street publisher (Plomer).*

a perfect contradiction to himself, and all the world. He writ *An Antidote against Lust*; and has nothing but his chastity to recommend him. . . .

Mr. Ames,[1] originally a coatseller, but had always some yammerings upon him after learning and the muses. He has almost writ as many pretty, little pleasant poems as Taylor the Water-Poet; you might engage him upon what project you pleased, if you'd but conceal him, for his principles did never resist in such cases. I printed a poem for him, under the title of 'The Double Descent'; at that time the French talked big of invading England, and we were making ready for a descent upon their coasts. Wine and women were the great bane of his life and happiness; he died in an hospital, but I hope he was truly penitent; for a little before his decease, he said to me, with a great deal of concern. Ah, Mr. Dunton! with what another face does the world appear, now I have death in view!

Much of Dunton's *Life and Errors* was written ostensibly with reformation in mind. The old Dunton, the negligent publishers who had erred and sinned, was no more. A new and reformed Dunton had arisen, even less censorious than the old, kind and generous, charitable and understanding, who would never malign a character merely to sell a book, whose awakened conscience was to guide him to the good life and better publishing. The following passage near the end of his book shows how much he has reformed. It is presented here, with some of Dunton's typographical flavour, as the final comment on the *Life and Errors*:

But as I was ever backward to censure others, my OLD LIFE, &c. may hope for a better Treatment; but the Criticks will scarce credit my NEW; for Men judge hardly of others, from a Sense of their own Guilt; There's *Squire Vinegar*, that is charg'd

---

[1] *Richard Ames, a student of Lincoln's Inn. Some of the 'pretty, little pleasant poems' he wrote are 'The Search after Claret' (1691); 'A Search after Claret . . . in answer to the late "Search after Claret"' (1691); 'A Farther Search after Claret' (1691); 'The Last Search after Claret in Southwark' (1691). 1691 must have been a poor year for claret. He also wrote 'A Dialogue between Claret and Darby Ale' (1691), and 'The Bacchanalian Sessions' (1693). But Ames did have other interests. He also wrote about women, specializing in satires on women, which he indignantly answered himself with poems like 'Sylvia's Revenge, or a Satyr against Man' (1699). A particularly lurid piece was his 'The Female Fire-ships, a Satyr against Whoring, etc.' (1691).*

with keeping a Whore at L——, of Debauching a Virgin at St. H——, of making a Nanny-House of T——'s Ware-House—— And of PRAISING the Widow S——, 'till he got to Bed to her (for what Business else cou'd he have with a *Platonick Mistress*, 'till Twelve at Night, when he had a Wife and Children Sobbing at home) yet even this RAKE has been the first in slandering his innocent Neighbour: I cou'd enlarge in this FELLOWS Character but 'twere endless to name all his fond Assignations in B——, L——, St. H——, and I——, S——, T——; and if Sir B—— may believe his eyes, even SUNDAY itself was spent in Caressing his *Spiritual Miss*—— And yet even this *Scoundrel* has had the Impudence to charge Sir B—— with *Forgery, Incest, and keeping of Six Whores*, when the poor Knight can scarce keep himself, and (as he told me lately) challenges all the World (and this TOWN-BULL, in a particular Manner) to prove him guilty of an ill Thing——*Good God*! when such a HE FRIEND (or Precise Stallion) shall have so little *Manners and Piety*, as to turn Informer, for Disguise, and to slander others, for no other End, but to Whore on without Suspition; certainly that's the DEVIL indeed! And such a DEVIL is *Squire Vinegar*; nay, he is the greatest Monster in Nature; he is a Trimmer in Religion,[1] and holds the Ballance even between God, and the DEVIL: And whereas the Atheistical Libertine, is happy here, and the Saint will Eternally be so, this scandalous Goat (without Repentance) both is, and will be, eternally miserable.

 Sir Know-Post is just such another Saint, and for that Reason, Sir B—— perswades me to publish *The Secret History of his Stoln Amours, &c.* as 'twas drawn up by his *She Confident* ... and found amongst her Papers, since her Death; and to these I might add, PEEVISH (*Tomazo's* Concubine)—Mrs. *To-and-agen* (the UNNATURAL Provoker of her own Sex [*Rom.* I. 26.] and Tempter of ours); neither shall *Minx Taundry* ... be forgotten in this SCANDALOUS HISTORY; but Sir B—— has a great Respect for the Fame of the young Ladies; and if they repent, he intends to forgive 'em; but if they go on in their Wickedness (or move, either Tongue or Pen, to abuse Sir B——) he resolves to cure 'em of *Private Slandering*, by publishing THE MIDNIGHT REVELS OF SQUIRE VINEGAR; and if Sir B—— shou'd request a Second

---

[1] *That is, in the spirit of compromise, uncommitted to any religion.*

D*

(as he's my Friend, and a Person of worth) I'll defend his Innocence, *as long as I can handle a Sword or Pen*; for tho' my *Dear
(and only) Brother,* had the Misfortune to be kill'd in a DUEL, I
shall never stick (in a Just Cause) to defend my Self (or Friend)
with a brighter Weapon than a Pen; and let the Ladies remember, if they force me to speak, I will speak out; neither can the
Publishing this BLACK HISTORY be thought ungenerous, for
Vinegar was the first Aggressor; and has had the Impudence to
charge Sir B—— with such vile Things, as *The Devil wou'd blush
to Name.* But I judge, by this, they see their *Sin in their Punishment*; and if they are true Penitents, we have nothing further to
say to 'em, but to advise 'em to Practice this NEW IDEA (*and
to Sin no more, &c.*) and then I hope we shall all meet in that
PURE and Holy Place, where none transgress so much as in
Thought.

Now wou'd I fain see the Faces of those Persons who find
their own here, but I can't guess at 'em without Book—— R——
Swells—— D—— Stutters—— P—— Raves—— F——Bites——
W—— Swears—— G—— Struts—— M—— Whines——
N—— Leers—— E—— Flatters—— B—— Conjurers——
and H *—nah tosses up her Nose, and so on, &c.* —— I hope
they'll fall upon the Author, Lampoon him to some purpose (as
they did once in *Vinegar's Nanny-House*) and then my Book's
made, it runs like Lightning; and I don't fear *Two Impressions.* . . .

And so much for that OLD Life I repent of, and that NEW
Idea I wou'd (seriously) practice, might I *live o'er my Days again.*

Directly after this incredible passage a line is drawn across
the page and Dunton continues:

Having here some VACANT PAGES, *I shall add a BRIEF
Character of some Eminent Persons,* whose Vertues, or Errors, I
shall have Occasion to mention in *The Second Part of my Life.* . . .

Such is Dunton's *Life and Errors.*

Dunton disapproved of fornication, professionally. In a
pamphlet called *The Whoring Pacquet* (1706), he published a
number of fornicating adventures to show the folly of loose living.
This is his concluding paragraph:

Would my room allow it, *The Whoring Pacquet* had been much larger, for I have just now received,

1. A Discovery how one maid got another with child, being a strange amusement to expose the marriage-haters.
2. A pleasant relation of a man who would believe he had made himself a cuckold.
3. News from Dublin of a young woman who is got with child by Al——n G—— with some serious advice to the aged whore-masters—with many discoveries of kept misses and great bellies &c.

All which we reserve as a proper Appendix to the *Concubine Pacquet.*

I shall only add, my next will be *The Wedding Pacquet.* If therefore any young gentlemen and ladies can send me[1] any pleasant discoveries (in verse or prose) as may properly be inserted in *The Wedding Pacquet,* if they send them to Claypool's Coffee-House in Swan Alley in Birchin-Lane, they shan't fail of a place in our next journal, with remarks thereon, if there be occasion.

It is not always easy to separate the Puritan from the publisher in Dunton. He was a strange mixture of contradictions. But in the midst of an autobiography full of repentance and recantations of old publishing sins and resolutions to publish in future only what is moral and worthy, the gleam of a new Grub Street venture beckons him again. Titles like *The Whoring Pacquet* were hardly intended to guide his readers to heavenly grace.

Dunton even tried to make a publishing profit out of his creditors: 'The Living Elegy: or Dunton's Letter (being a Word of Comfort) to his *FEW CREDITORS*: with the Character of a Summer-Friend. To which is added, The Lives, Religion, and Honesty of ... and the other Attackers of my Person and Goods. *Have patience with me, and I will pay thee all. Mat.* 18.26'. (1706). No comment can do this justice :

... As to the moneys I owe you, 'tis more than I can pay at present, but I don't owe more than I am willing and able to

---

[1] *A familiar publishing device of the time for creating books out of the thin air of a title. Its principal merit is that the publisher does not have to pay for the copy, though Dunton was usually fair in his dealings.*

pay; and therefore (as no man will lose a farthing by me) I presume, I have still a title to your good opinion. . . .

Gentlemen, how far I have deserved your good opinion, will appear by that full payment I hope to make you in a few months. I confess, I have just finished a merry paradox, proving —no man is honest, but he that is rich—But this is only a paradox to divert that melancholy I groan under, for being so long your debtor; for I'll make it appear that you are not deceived in Dunton, but that he is and will (always) be as honest as you can desire.

Gentlemen, whatever my losses in trade were, I still took effectual care they should be none of yours, (saving the waiting for your just debts a little longer than usual). And to convince you of this, I shall now (as a word of comfort after long waiting) tell you the very day when I shall pay you all to a farthing. 'Tis true, (as I said before) I had great losses in trade, (many of which have been owing to M——[1] telling me there was 400 sold of a book when there was not 60) and have had a much greater disappointment in the sale of my woods; for, on the account that the mortgage on my estate was expired, I was forced to sell that for £300 that (could I have helped it) should not have gone for six. But as good as the bargain was, (my three farms being jointured) had I not surmounted a hundred difficulties, been at a great expense to secure the title, and besides that, met with a generous chapman, (the only Good Samaritan, that would part with money to heal my wounds) I could not possibly have cleared so far as I did. But now (the mortgage being paid off) £200 is all I owe in the world; and could my sister B—— now pay me that £200 I can prove she owes me, I would clear with the whole world before I slept. However, this £200 is a further argument to convince my creditors that I shall pay 'em all at the time I promise; for my sister B—— is a very grateful and just person, and as I never asked her till now, for the money she owes me (in mere compassion to her great losses),[2] so now I expect to be paid in a few

---

[1] *Sarah Malthus, London publisher, who, as Dunton points out, attached his goods for debt. On the title page of Dunton's* Life and Errors *is the line: 'Printed for S. Malthus, 1705.' That is, Dunton did not publish his own autobiography.*

[2] *In his* Life and Errors *(1705), Dunton jogged her memory by publishing some of her original letters, 'which I have yet upon the file,' asking for money.*

months, out of her Jamaica windfall, which will amount to some hundred pounds. . . .

Then, how base was M—— and her two scoundrels[1] to call me dunderhead — simpleton — fractured bookseller — whipping spark (that can't hold it) bankrupt, jail-bird; and to tell the world I was starving, &c.—when none of my creditors ever questioned their money; and are here told to a day, when they shall be paid every farthing I owe them. . . .

Had M—— called me sot, or madman, for trusting such a hedge-publisher, perhaps those that did not know me, might have believed her; but to call me bankrupt, jail-bird, one that writes to prevent starving, is a malicious falsehood. Nay, says another of M——'s hackneys, (for she hired these fellows to blast my credit if possible) Would I hang myself, no chandler in town would trust me with a penny cord. So that if I'll die in a string, (if you'll believe a rake that has more w[hore]s than pence) I must be hanged upon mere charity. And the *Wandering Spy* (alias W[ard])[2] is so very hasty to send me to Tyburn, that he would have it death for me to print a word more, till my last dying speech and confession came out signed by the ordinary of Newgate. . . .[3]

Why scoundrels! Why M—— with what face can you publish such known and ridiculous lies as these. For, you can't deny my printers and stationers knew the misfortunes I laboured under, and as they had the product of their own trust to a farthing, (so far as I have yet received) 'tis both base and sordid to reflect thus for present deficiencies, seeing they'll be made good to a tittle. And 'tis yet the baser in these detractors as one of 'em is still in my debt; and the rest never saw my face. 'But,' as Philip said of the Grecians, 'if men slander me with no reason, what would they do if I should do them hurt?' But, (added he), they make me a better man, for I strive daily, both in my words and deeds, to prove them liars. That I may imitate Philip in this excellent practice, all I shall say to M—— and her two hackneys (the *Moderator* and *Wandering Spy*) is, what one said of scandals,

---

[1] *The authors of* The Moderator *and the* Wandering Spy.
[2] *Dunton had mistakenly assumed that Ned Ward, author of the* London Spy, *had written the* Wandering Spy. *Cf. H. W.* Troyer, Ned Ward of Grub Street *(1946), p. 226.*
[3] *It was frequently the practice for criminals to have the story of their life and their confession ghost-written and hawked at the foot of the gallows to the crowds waiting for the execution.*

'If I do not deserve, (saith he), what is thrown upon me, my life
will give them the lie; if I do, it's my duty to be patient and
amend'—And sure enough, I had need have patience to deal with
M——. For, D——y[1] when he attached my *Life*, and *Athenian
Oracle*, finding he had only attached the credit that printers gave
me, &c. was ashamed (or I'm sure he might) of what he had done,
and withdrew the attachment of his own accord; which M——
finding, she contrives that to her attachment mentioned before,
and did me all the private mischief she could.... 'Tis stabbing
a man behind, and is the worst sort of murder as it leaves no room
for defence. This way of attacking (or rather stabbing) is so un-
manly, that Anthony put those slanderers to death which could
not prove their accusations. But M—— never considered this,
and therefore (to revenge my going to another publisher) hired
the *Moderator* and *Wandering Spy*, to call me 'all the simple and
poor fellows in nature.' But though M—— and her little scoundrels, thought me so very low, that they might venture to trample
upon me; yet, ungenerous fools! I must here tell 'em, (for tread
on a worm and he'll turn again) that my printers and stationers
are willing to trust me as ever. I would give many instances to
prove this, were not the *Whipping-Post* (or *Satire upon Every
Body*)[2] and a diverting project I've now in the press, sufficient to
prove, that no disappointment in trade can lessen my credit with
such as know me; and as for others (I mean such that speak ill
of a man that they can't prove), 'their good word is a scandal.'
And for all such, I as little want their trust, as they need my
friendship. For as fractured and starving as M—— would now
make me; till I had great losses, I even dunned the printers to
take their money, and shall do it again in a little time—Then,
ain't it rare gratitude in M——, (who tells me in several letters,
'that I was the only friend in the world that had stood by her')
to hire a crew of hackneys (the *Moderator* and *Wandering Spy*)
to slander me at this rate. But if I hear any more of her, (except
it be to pay me for the 600 books she conveyed away), the world
shall know, I shall be able to show my head as long as M——
and her lousy authors will be able to show their ears—Ears! Have
they any left?[3]—For the *Wandering Spy* was sentenced in the

[1] *Likely Dowley, a London bookbinder (Plomer).*
[2] *Published 1706.*
[3] *By Dunton's time, it was no longer the practice to slice off the ears for libellous statements.*

Old Bailey, for a fabulous, obscene, scandalous writer: (or rather
beast in the shape of a man) whatsoever you say, he will draw to
bawdry. He makes christenings, and sometimes funerals, speak it.
He never sees a woman but he lusts after her, strips her naked,
and enjoys her straight in imagination. Everything with him is
incentive unto lust; and every woman, devil enough to tempt him
to it. Silk gowns and red petticoats are all alike to him, he playing
at women, just as he does at cards, while every suit, in their turns,
is turned up trump. Whence he has (as 'tis thought) more diseases
than an hospital, of which he lies in every spring and fall. His
very publisher was a midwife, his *Spy* is a pimp, and his wit is
never so quick as here. The pox only converts him, and that only
when it kills him. Joan's as good as My Lady. And since W[ard]
(the supposed author of the *Wandering Spy*) can't feast on other
men's goods, he is resolved to enjoy their wives. His whore in
Little Britain[1] besieged his door with a child from Sunday noon
to Sunday night; but came too late for admittance, his other
strumpet having been there with a bastard before her. His word
is, a merry life and a short. I know not how merry 'tis, but I'm
sure 'tis short enough, he consuming just like a candle at both
ends, betwixt wine and women; without which (in spite of his
fabulous morals) he holds there is no pleasure in this world. And
for the other, he would fain be an atheist, and believe there is
none at all, whilst his manners and ignorance supply his want of
faith; for he lives like one, and knows no soul he has. For, he can't
but own, he repents more the omitting an evil action (but more
especially whoredom and drunkenness) than any saint would the
committing it.—This is the lewd and scandalous life of the *Wandering* (or rather Earless) *Spy*; and I judge his death won't be
much better, for atheism is ever the refuge of such sinners as Ward,
whose repentance will be only to hang himself; for a deliberate
hanging at Tyburn (the death he'd prefer me to) is too great an
honour for such a libertine. For he makes a jest of repentance
and modesty, and is an artificial fool (or jack-pudding) that gets
his living by making others and himself ridiculous. In a word,
he is the rich man's antic, and the Devil's father, that by a strange
fable of invisibility, sends men laughing to Hell. And all this (with
lewder things that I hear of him) is the true character of the

---

[1] *One of the main areas of the publishing trade at the time.*

Wandering Spy. Ears! (can such a lecher as this have ears?) 'Tis to affront all the women he ever met, to say he has either ears, nose, or so much as genitals.[1]

As to the *Moderator,* he is rather worse than the former; for, being a designing hypocrite, (and mere hackney author) there is no hopes of his repentance, or amendment; whereas, the *Wandering Spy* owning himself a rake, may with the prodigal return at last. But there is no hopes of the *Moderator,* for all his papers are so abusive, dull, and foolish, they can be writ for no other end, but to get a penny and distract the kingdom. This fellow is a cunning archer, that looking to the public service, as the mark he aims at, yet squints aside at his own ends, (viz. bread to keep him from starving) which is the true butt all his *Moderator*s are shot at.... In a word, the *Moderator* is a very blank, wherein you may write anything that will make for his prefix: (with the hedgehog) he turns his den which way soever the wind of prosperity blows —To sum up his character (in three words) he's—a mercenary scoundrel. And for that reason proposes to have all papers, but his own, suppressed; but as a judgement upon him, (for telling so many lies of their kind reception) his own papers have led the way. So that all the honour the *Moderator* has, (after publishing thirty numbers) is now to wipe ——

Ears! Can such an ambidexter—parasite—scoundrel—nothing at all, &c. have ears?—No!—'Tis to call in question the understanding of men of learning and temper, to say he has had either ears or credit, ever since he disgraced that excellent virtue of moderation, in pretending to write for it.

Thus have I given a brief (but true) character of those careless fellows, (if they had their due) the *Moderator* and *Wandering Spy,* that (to oblige M——) said all they could to blast my credit with printers and stationers.

I come next to the *Whipster,* (drunken Alecto)[2] who stole my title of *Whipping-Post,* and then spits, and froths, and drivels

---

[1] *Part of Dunton's attack is probably true of Ward's early years, but most of this we can attribute to Dunton's usual enthusiasm for his subject. The irony, of course, is that Ward was not the author of the* Wandering Spy. *(See above, p. 109.)*

[2] *William Pittis (1674-1724) wrote the journal* The Whipping-Post *(1705) before Dunton's Whipping-Post came out, although Dunton announced his intention of using the title in an earlier publication. Pittis had an appetite for wine that was astonishing even in that liquid age.*

as much nonsense, malice and vanity at me, as Tom S——[1] would
pay him for. This sot of an author is a compound of all that's vile,
dull, and abusive in the *Moderator* and *Wandering Spy*, with
this addition, that P[itti]s is the greater sot—In order to his preferment, P[itti]s' friends sent him to Oxford, where he ate, and
drank, and slept, played a match or two at football, (perhaps)
stole a pig, ran away from the proctor, and studied three or four
years to as much purpose as was his stealing my Whipping title;
or if they did not steal my title, let 'em clear themselves by an
affidavit, and then I'll fairly own there's no thieving, but only
good wits jump in the case. But without this, let the world judge
how basely they have waylaid me; as it 'twas entailed upon
S——'s family, to steal both titles and projects from John Dunton,
for this bulk whipster is son to that very S——[2] who undermined
my question-project, till he lost about twenty pound, and then
flung up his *Lacedemonian Mercury*, (as his son has done the
Whipping-Post) as the just reward of an interloper. So that (if I
ain't mistaken) here is trim tram; or whatever the master is, sure
I am the rake, or tool he employs, is both sot and coxcomb. His
head [Pittis's] is like an Irish bog, a spongy quagmire, his brains
are in a perpetual souse-tub, the pickle (since he stole my title) is
only changed from ale to wine. This profound soaker (alias *Whipster*) is one of the common scorns of all civil people, as carrying
about him all the signs and tokens of a shameless sot—His eyes
are ready to tumble out of his head—his bacon-complexion is
greasy, and like the jelly of veal, and his breath and belchings are
strong enough to cause an infection—And as the beast hath on
him the drunkard's mark, so he hath their rewards, shame and
poverty—This parboiled rat (had his interloping succeeded) had
been accounted a rabbin[3] with Tom S——; but to everybody else,
his besotted countenance betrays and discovers his ignorant, dull,
stupid soul—This drunken whipster (if you dare take his word
for't) studies only at the tavern, in company with rakes and
scoundrels. For in his *Miscellanies over Claret*[4] he tells his readers,

---

[1] *Thomas Sawbridge published in Little Britain, 1669-1692 (Plomer).*
[2] *Likely George Sawbridge, who, according to Plomer (p. 263), was the son of Tom Sawbridge,
and succeeded him in his business.*
[3] *A learned scholar.*
[4] *A short-lived journal published in 1697.*

'but as Motteux[1] desired his letters (after postage paid) to be sent
to the coffee-house, so we have two or three among us such exceeding drunkards as to submit to no place but the tavern. At
present our office is kept at the Rose-Tavern without Temple Bar;
which may be as well called an office of credit as the Land-Bank,
for we pay our reckonings after the same manner Dr. Ch——n
does his salaries, that is, not at all. But no matter, our landlord
is an honest man (that he is) though I believe he'll soon be weary
of his pots, for we have just now chalked up a crown with him'—
These are his own words, in the Preface to his *Miscellanies over
Claret* by which he insinuates, he that drinks well, sleeps well;
and he that sleeps well, thinks no harm. The falsehood of which
may be soon confuted, because he staggers in the argument; and
which is yet worse, he glories in his drunkenness, for to convince
the world he's a shameless sot. In his dedication to the aforesaid
book, he tells his patron 'My Lord, we are four or five, some say
honest, others foolish, but all say drunken fellows, now drinking
your Lordship's health at the tavern; and our poetical inclinations are all attended with poetical pockets. Some of us have sixpence and eight farthings, some neither eight farthings, nor a
sixpence; so that the chiefest of our dependance is upon the
strength of this dedication. And since the majority of us are too
dirty for your levee, we have picked out the nicest spark of us
all, to make this present by. He is our plenipotentiary, and we
give full power to receive, &c. anything your Lordship shall order
towards the continuance of your Lordship's health. Your Lordship may guess by him, what a figure the rest make, for he's the
very quintessence of gentility among us all—But the rogue of a
drawer will bring up the reckoning, unless we call for more wine;
therefore, to avert that judgement, we beg leave (though abruptly) to subscribe—My Lord—your Lordship's most dutiful and
obedient servants, &c.—Thus (Gentlemen) you see that P[itti]s
(my Whipping enemy) is a drunken sot by his own contention;
and for that reason, (if he have any ears) the pillory or stocks is
the most likely place to find 'em. And that he might want no
accomplishment necessary for a town rake, he is as great a sharper
as he is a drunkard. For he'll offer a dinner, or bottle of claret,
out of his joy to see you; and in requital of this courtesy, you

---

[1] *Peter Motteux, a Huguenot exile, editor of* The Gentleman's Journal *(1692), a literary
journal of high quality.*

can do no less than pay for it. So that no man puts his brains
to more use than P[itti]s, for his life is a daily invention (for
punch and claret) and each meal a new stratagem. And I suppose
no man will question this, that reads his drunken letter to Dr.
Read,[1] which was signed with his own hand, and was to this
effect.—That he got drunk the night before, at the Rummer
Tavern at Charing Cross, that he was benighted, and forced to
lie at the Star Inn, where he was dipped over head and ears for
3s. 6d. and had no friend, &c.—

By means of such drunken adventures (as are here confessed) P[itti]s often wants a surgeon to plaster his countenance;
and is as often in danger of drowning, except when he rides at
anchor in Newgate, (where we find him often) the Round House,
or Bridewell—But it appears by his letter to Dr. Read, that his
most usual rest and repose is upon benches, and chairs, in petty
inns and tap houses, unless he chance to creep under some cart,
and get a pile of faggots to shelter him—Now (Gentlemen) I leave
you to judge who is—the greatest maggot,—or lunatic—(the epi-
thets this Whipster gives me) Dunton, or P[itti]s.—For, as to the
first, he can't do me a greater honour than to call me maggot;
for if a man must be called a maggot, for starting thoughts that
are wholly new, then farewell invention. (Even philosophy itself
had never been improved had it not been for new opinions.) And
as to his charge of lunacy, if new projects to pay my debts, and
to act justly, be a sign I have lost my senses, I desire to be so accounted. Though it must be owned, the loss of one's reason and
one's liberty at once, would break a body; and a statute of bankrupt might be awarded against me by the great Governor of the
intellectual world who has given me credit for my faculties, when
he's like to lose both principal and interest. But whatever Dunton is, (who has had enough to distract a stronger brain than his)
sure I am that man is absolutely mad (or worse) that like
P[itti]s, instead of quenching his thirst, drowns his soul—How
many brute beasts will rise up in judgement against P[itti]s, who
make the sufficiency of nature their standard, in eating and drinking—Then ain't this a special fellow to whip the age into so-
briety? But let him remember the story of Dives; there is no tippling in Hell—But he's a hardened sot, and there is no hopes of

---

[1] *Sir William Read, the Queen's oculist.*

his reformation: for he was famous even in Oxford by the name of drunken Pittis; but the sot (his brains a little settled) had the luck to reel out of Oxford to London, and from thence, in pursuit of adventures, to S—— in Little Britain, there to steal other men's projects, and to guzzle (had their whipping succeeded) as deeply in the juice of the grape as he had (whilst he lived at Oxford) swilled himself in that of good ale. But though Oxford has spewed him out, yet he has taken all his degrees in the school of Bacchus; and is now accounted a finished toper, a living conduit, a drunken rake, a sot all over—Gentlemen, this is the interloper that would whip the age into good manners! But I have given but a taste of his drunken practices, should I mention all, I should never have done—I might proceed to his other crimes (which are yet blacker) —As his swearing—profaning the Sabbath—jesting with sacred things, &c. . . .

    Ears! Can such a mercenary shameless toper as this, have ears? 'Tis to whip all the beadles of Bridewell, to say he had either ears, or a sound back, ever since he tricked Dr. Read of 3s. 6d. reeled to the Star Inn, &c. abused Dr. Willis for his healing sermon before the Queen, and stole my title of *Whipping-Post.*

    My last undeserved and public enemy (and consequently, the last I shall lash in public) is Lesley[1] (the tacking author of that scandalous paper called *The Rehearsal*)—this hackney writer has more wit and learning than either the *Moderator, Wandering Spy,* or *Drunken Whipster,* and therefore I would lash him more (severely) than I do those empty blockheads, did not his reverend gown protect him. . . .

    Dunton continues at some length in his *Living Elegy,* lashing his various enemies among the publishers and writers of Grub Street. It provides an interesting picture of the hurly-burly of sub-literary London. For despite the success of the *Athenian Mercury* and the abundance of his publications (600), Dunton's life, as we may gather, was the usual Grub Street round of getting into debt, dodging the creditors and the bum-bailiff, and finally debtor's prison. In the first years of his publishing Dunton was forced to flee to New England to escape his creditors. And as an old man, after some forty years of publishing, with the Grub Street wars behind him, he was still in debt, as he tells us in *Dying Groans*

[1] *Charles Lesley (1650-1722), a High Church divine and editor of* The Rehearsal.

from Fleet-Prison,[1] written about 1726, when he was sixty-seven years of age. *Dying Groans* was a public petition to George I for money, explaining that he was insufficiently rewarded for his pamphlet, *Neck or Nothing,* which he said exposed the plot of Oxford and Bolingbroke (the leaders of the Tory Party, 1710-1714) to restore the Pretender to the throne. *Dying Groans* contains perhaps the longest sentence ever printed in an English pamphlet.[2] This in itself is no great distinction, but as a literary filibuster it has no equal. It is one long winding protest against injustice, with the hint that the sentence will go on and on until the injustice is re-redressed, and the suggestion of blackmail—very daring in a petition to a king—and that they had better beware because there were still one or two kicks in the old boy yet.

If there was any question about how much life there was still in the old man, Dunton appended a list of publications that he was 'preparing for the press,' a list of seven 'Dying Farewells' with 'five hundred ninety three more that are to complete this *Farewell* project.'

The last years of Dunton's life are obscure. It is fairly certain, however, he fell even further into poverty and the 593 'dying farewells' he threatened to inflict on the world were not published. He died in 1733.

---

[1] *Dunton was neither dying nor in prison. The title was the usual Dunton melodrama, suggesting what might happen to him if he was not rewarded, because he was so much in debt.*
[2] Dying Groans, *pp. 2-10.*

The Authors

The most renowned of the Grub Street hacks was Tom
Brown. Today he is remembered slightly for his major work,
Amusements, Serious and Comical, and for the trifling epigram,

> I do not love thee, Doctor Fell,
> The reason why I cannot tell;
> But this alone I know full well,
> I do not love thee, Dr. Fell.[1]

He deserves better, though one could make a stronger case arguing
from the brilliant potential than the debauched reality. He was
born in 1663, educated at Christ Church, Oxford, and was
intended for holy orders, according to Dunton. He had the advantages of a classical education, the knowledge of several modern
languages, an excellent mind, and talent, and he ended up Tom
Brown, prince of the Grub Street hacks.

   This is not to diminish Tom Brown. It is no mean thing
to be a prince, and Brown's achievement was considerable. Swift
wrote of him, 'I read Mr. Thomas Brown entire and had the
honour to be his intimate friend, who was universally admitted to

---

[1] *Dr. John Fell was Dean of Christ Church, Oxford, when Brown was a student there.
Legend has it that he had given an order for Brown's expulsion for some misdemeanour
and promised to withdraw it if Brown could translate extempore one of Martial's epigrams.
The above lines were Brown's unhesitating response and the decree of expulsion was withdrawn.*

be the greatest genius of his age.' No doubt this is ironic. But it
does suggest in a left-handed way that Brown was a force to be
reckoned with. He was not an unprincipled hack, though there
are many pieces of his written to his publisher's specifications, or
according to his own instinct about what would sell. Many of his
works show a joy in being alive—frequently an obscene joy. And
his satire was serious. He did not compromise his political beliefs
—High Church Tory; he did not receive pay for his political writing; he held to fairly traditional principles of integrity and attacked those who violated them. Yet, in spite of these virtues, he
managed to devote his brief life to gay, irresponsible debauchery.
In 'Tom Brown's last Letter to his Witty Friends and Companions', looking back over the dissolute years, he defines the Grub
Street ethic:

> Whenever you have any money in your pockets, that you
> dedicate to the use of Bacchus's viceregents, be sure you take care
> to spend it in good company: men of wit, are both diverting and
> informing; and wine better worth half a crown a quart in an
> edifying conversation, than twelvepence a gallon in a dull cabal
> of stupified mechanics. Never keep a fool company at your own
> expense, or suffer yourselves to be plagued with his troublesome
> impertinence, except he treats you; for he has no way of discern-
> ing your merits but through his own folly, and the greater bubble
> he finds you make him, the more he will extol you for men of
> ingenuity. If a spunging friend is apt to be too burdensome to
> your pocket, every time you see him, complain first of your own
> deficiency, and you will find it a ready way to get rid of him.
> You that are men of wit and fortune, should always stand fast
> one by another, and never rail behind one another's backs, except
> it be at one that has got the start of you; and then if he shuts
> his fist against your humble requests, cry him down for a block-
> head, ridicule everything he writes, as we did *Prince Arthur* [by
> Richard Blackmore],[1] that the world may see neither knights nor
> niggards will be allowed by critics to be the true sons of Apollo,
> for though they once were, yet they forfeit their adoption by the
> change of their condition, as alms-men do their pensions when
> they lay aside their badges. For poets ought to be poor, and those

[1] *c. 1650-1729. He attacked the wits of the age for their alleged immorality and consequently
became a stock satiric target, particularly for Brown. See below, pp. 145 ff.*

that disdain the station, can have no true title to the honour.
Upon the initiation of a new brother just come from the university, make him but a journeyman to your society, till he has spent
his patrimony, that is, do you make his pains your profit, and
suffer nothing to be entirely his own, without your perusal and
correction, that if the whim takes, the reputation may be yours;
but if the darling dies an abortive, let the blame fall upon the
parent; and when he has spent all in the service of the muses,
give him a character for his wit, and let him go a begging for
himself in Apollo's name among the bountiful Maecenases. Whenever you dedicate a book, pick out a generous fool for patron,
and the less merit he has, be sure the more you flatter him; for
the more virtues you ascribe to him that has none, and the more
you magnify his wit, that has but little, the more he will think
himself obliged to you for your kindness, and will certainly reward
your labours with the more liberal gratuity. Talk soberly and
sparingly among wise men, vainly and viciously among beaux and
blockheads, wittily and warily among the cheerful and facetious,
respectfully and pleasantly among the female sex, and merrily
and loosely among your own fraternity, and you need not doubt
but all parties will be pleased with your company.

One of Brown's first satiric targets was John Dryden. Dryden
in 1687 startled the world by his poem, *The Hind and the Panther,*
an apology for Roman Catholicism, published shortly after his
poem, *Religio Laici,* an apology for the Church of England. The
shift happened to coincide with the succession of James II, the
Roman Catholic, after Charles II, the Protestant. Modern scholarship, particularly Louis I. Bredvold's, has shown a logical pattern of development from one poem to the other. But to his
contemporaries, Dryden's motives seemed only too obvious. Brown
attacked with three separate pamphlets[1] and made his reputation in the town. Dryden was already known throughout London
as Mr. Bays, because of the Duke of Buckingham's play, *The
Rehearsal,* which pilloried Dryden as the hack-dramatist. Brown
merely took over the character already established and applied it
to the new situation:

---

[1] *From* The Late Converts Exposed: or the Reasons of Mr. Bay's Changing his
Religion *(1690), the second of three pamphlets, 1688-90.*

Will's Coffee-House in Covent Garden
Crites, Eugenius[1] and Mr. Bays.

Bays. Well Gentlemen, I find you are punctual to the assignation, and now if you please, we'll fall to the business in hand
without any more preface, or ceremony. You know I promised to
make you acquainted in the first place with the motives which obliged me to leave the Church of England, and afterwards to give
you the reasons why I settled in the Romish communion. This
method I design to follow, because it will give us a full view of all
the controverted points between both parties; but I must make
bold to ask you one civil question or two, beforehand, since it is so
material to our present affair; and that is, whether you have seen
a famous poem of mine, called *The Hind and Panther?*

Crites. Seen it, Mr. Bays! Why, I can stir nowhere but it
pursues me; it haunts me worse than a pewter-buttoned sergeant
does a decayed cit. Sometimes I meet it in a band-box when my
laundress brings home my linen, sometimes whether I will or no,
it lights my pipe in a coffee house; sometimes it surprises me in a
trunk-makers shop, and sometimes it refreshes my memory for me
on the backside of a Chancery Lane parcel.—For your comfort
Mr. Bays, I have not only seen it as you may perceive, but have
read it too, and can quote it as freely upon occasion, as a frugal
tradesman can quote that noble treatise, called 'The Worth of a
Penny', to his extravagant prentice that revels in cock ale, stewed
apples, and penny custards.

Bays. Then take it from me, Mr. Crites, you have read the
most exalted, the most sublime piece of poetry, that was ever ex-
tant in the universe. It contains, without vanity I may say it, all
the arguments that can be proposed in behalf of the unerring
guide the Church's infallibility, transubstantiation, tradition, and
the like. So that if this were not an age wherein people were resolved never to trust their faith out of the company of their reason, I should not question to reduce half the kingdom in due time,
only by the sweetness and majesty of my verse. But pray, Mr.
Crites, do me the favour to tell me what the sinful world has said
to this noble offspring of mine.

Crites. Troth Mr. Bays the sinful world, as you call it, is

---

[1] *Crites and Eugenius were two characters Dryden used in his famous dialogue,* Essay of
Dramatic Poesy *(1668). In Dryden's essay, Crites was his brother-in-law, the poet-
dramatist Sir Robert Howard; Eugenius was Charles Sackville, later Earl of Dorset.*

very much divided about the point, and who can help it? Some
persons allow it as little quarter as the Inquisition does a tract of
Lutheran divinity; and others again speak as favourably of the
author, as the Dissenters do of the late immortal Pacqueteer.[1]
Some say you chose a religion, though it were none of the best,
only to confront the world that you had one, like the young prince
in *The Rehearsal,* who was glad to own the fisherman for his
father, rather than lie under the scandal of having none at all.
Some commend your policy for treating your subject in rhyme,
because, as they pretend, the polemic is no more obliged to answer
for the paralogisms of the poet, than the new-made lord is concerned to pay the debts of the private gentleman. Lastly, the more
censorious sort question the sincerity of your conversion, and are
apt to believe, that although you have drawn your pen in the
Church's quarrel, you'd scarce be allowed the humble favour to
stand godfather for a bell, and promise in the bell's name, that
it shall scatter tempests, disperse evil spirits, and disarm thunder
and lightning; for like malicious persons as they are, they observe that you have made the Panther in that noble episode of
the Swallow, tell a better and more pertinent story, than even
your Catholic Hind. In fine, since you'll have all out together,
they say if your own party ever comes to tell noses, that they
must be forced to serve you, and the rest of the new converts,
as the Turkish janizaries do their other foot battalions, place you
in the front, and encompass you round, because you have got
such a damnable trick of running away from your colours, that
you are not to be trusted in the rear.

    Bays. And is the world then so wickedly disposed as to
question the sincerity of my conversion? Oh *tempora & mores*!
I could almost resolve with my own Almanzor,[2] that henceforward
all mankind should walk upon crutches. I can't tell, I gad, what
to offer farther in my own defence, than what I have done already, except only this which comes in my head on the sudden . . .

> Were my commission Hind and Panther so,
> That I could say this hand the Panther's is,
> And this the Hind's—

---

[1] *Likely* Pacquet of Advice from Rome; or, the History of Popery, *an anti-Roman
Catholic journal published weekly from 1680 to 1683.*
[2] *The hero of Dryden's heroic tragedy,* The Conquest of Granada.

Mr. Eugenius for God's sake attend! ...

This is not great satire. Brown has done better. But it was amusing and precisely to the point when Dryden's conversion was the talk of the town. When Dryden died in 1700, Brown did not forget him, and wrote *A Description of Mr. Dryden's Funeral* which, in Brown's oblique way, was not unsympathetic:

A
DESCRIPTION
OF
Mr. Dryden's Funeral.

Of kings renowned and mighty bards I write,
Some slain by whores, and others killed in fight;
Some starving lived, whilst others were preferred;
But all, when dead, are in one place interred. ...
　　A bard there was, who whilome did command,
And held the laurel in his potent hand;
He o'er Parnassus bore imperial sway,
Him all the little tribes of bards obey:
But bards and kings, how e'er approved and great,
Must stoop at last to the decrees of Fate.
Fate bid him for the stroke of Death prepare,
And then removed him to the Lord knows where.
. . . .
　　The day is come, and all the wits must meet
From Covent Garden down to Watling Street;
They all repair to the physicians dome,
There lies the corpse and there the eagles come;
A troop of stationers at first appeared,
And Jacob Tonson[1] Captain of the Guard;
Jacob the muses' midwife, who well knows
To ease a labouring muse of pangs and throws;
He oft has kept the infant poet warm,
Oft licked the unwieldly monster into form;
Oft do they in high flights and raptures swell,
Drunk with the waters of our Jacob's well.

[1] *Dryden's publisher.*

Next these the play-house sparks do take their turn,
With such as under Mercury are born,
As poets, fiddlers, cut-purses, and whores,
Drabs of the play-house, and of common shores;
Pimps, panders, bullies, and eternal beaux,
Famed for short wits, long wigs, and gaudy clothes;
All sons of meter tune the voice in praise,
From lofty strains, to humble ekes and ayes:
The singing men and clerks who charm the soul,
And all the traders in *fa la fa sol:*
All these the funeral obsequies do aid,
As younger brothers of the rhyming trade.
    The tuneful rabble now together come,
They fill with dolesome sighs the sable room;
Some groaned, some sobbed, and some I think there wept,
And some got drunk, lolled down, and snored and slept.
Around the corpse in state they wildly press;
In notes unequal, like Pindaric verse,
Each one does his sad sentiments express.
The player says, My friends, we are undone,
See here the muse's best and darling son,
Is from us to the blest Elysium gone.
What other poet for us will engage
To be the prop of the declining stage?
All other poets are not worth a louse,
There fell the prop of our once glorious house: ...
Not a Crowdero[1] at a bawdy house,
Who used in racy liquors to carouse,
But with sad haste unto the burial ran,
Forgets his tipple, and neglects his can.
With rag-tag, bob-tail was the room full filled,
You'd think another Babel to be built;
Not more confusion at St. Batt's famed fair,
Or at Guildhall at choice of a Lord Mayor.
But stay my muse, the learned Garth[2] appears,
He sighing comes, and is half drowned in tears;

----

[1] *Fiddler.*
[2] *Samuel Garth (1661-1719), a physician and the author of the mock epic poem,* The
Dispensary. *See below, p. 145.*

The famous Garth whom learned poets call
Knight of the order of the urinal.
He of Apollo learnt his wondrous skill,
He taught him how to sing and how to kill;
For all he sends unto the darksome grave,
He honours also with an epitaph. . . .
     Next him the sons of music pass along,
And murder Horace in confounded song;
Whose monument, more durable than brass,
Is now defaced by every chanting ass.
No man at Tyburn, doomed to take a swinging,
Would stay to hear such miserable singing,
Where all the beasts of music try their throats,
And different species use their different notes:
Here the ox bellows, there the satyr howls;
The puppies whine, and the bold mastiff growls;
The magpies chatter, and the night-owls shriek;
The old pigs grunt, and all the young ones squeak:
Yet all together make melodious songs,
As bumpkin trolls to rusty pair of tongs.
     Now, now the time is come, the parson says,
And for their exeunt to the grave he prays:
The way is long, and folk the streets are clogging,
Therefore my friends away, come let's be jogging.

. . . .

     Before the hearse the mourning hautboys go,
And screech a dismal sound of grief and woe;
More dismal notes from bogtrotters may fall,
More dismal plaints at Irish funeral.

. . . .

One pocky spark, one sound as any roach,
One poet and two fiddlers in a coach;
The play-house drab, that beats the beggars bush,
And bawdy talks, would make an old whore blush, . . .
Was e'er immortal poet thus buffooned?
In a long line of coaches thus lampooned?
A man with gout and stone quite wearied,
Would rather live than thus be buried.

Within four years after the first attack on Dryden, from 1688 to 1692, Brown had made five substantial enemies, a creditable achievement considering that Brown only began writing in 1687. Dryden was first. Then Dr. William Sherlock, the leader of the 'non-swearing parsons' who refused to take the oath of allegiance to King William, suddenly began to pray publicly for the new sovereigns and published *The Case of Allegiance* to justify himself. Shortly after, he became Dean of St. Paul's. It seemed to be *The Hind and the Panther* in reverse and Brown responded with another 'reasons' pamphlet, *The Reasons of the New Convert's Taking the Oaths*. Then there was David Jones, the 'mighty bellowing' preacher, the Low Church evangelist who inspired Brown to write for him *The Welsh Levite Toss'd in a Blanket*. Then the poet, Tom Durfey, another example of a convenient switch of principles—he switched from Tory under Charles and James, to Whig under William. To the song writer, Mr. Durfey, in honour of his 'incomparable Ballads, call'd by him Lyrick Odes,' Brown wrote a song himself, of which this was the first verse:

Thou cur, half French, half English breed,
Thou mongrel of Parnassus,
To think tall lines, run up to seed,
Should ever tamely pass us.

Finally there was John Dunton, whom Brown had aroused with his *Lacedemonian Mercury*. It was a busy four years for Brown—one Grub Street battle after another. Except for the incident with Dunton—and even here it was Dunton's pretension that provoked him—Brown had a serious satiric purpose in his attacks. It is surely irrelevant that he had so much fun doing it. But in 1693 the bubble momentarily collapsed and Brown got into the first of a lifetime of difficulties. This was over the marriage of Titus Oates to Margaret Wells, a Muggletonian widow.[1] Titus Oates was the incredible perjurer who created the panic of the Popish Plot and as a proven Whig was therefore pensioned by King William.

To celebrate Oates' marriage, Brown wrote *The Salamanca Wedding*, done with the coarseness for which Brown was famous:

[1] *Muggleton, a tailor, had visions of divinity and gathered around him a group of enthusiasts.*

THE
SALAMANCA WEDDING:[1]
or,
A TRUE ACCOUNT OF A SWEARING DOCTOR'S
MARRIAGE WITH A MUGGLETONIAN WIDOW
IN BREADSTREET.

London, August 18th, 1693.

In a Letter to a Gentleman in the Country.

Sir,

The only news of importance I have to communicate to you at present is that the famous and never-to-be-forgotten Dr. Oates was married the beginning of this week. You know, for a person of his constitution, that always expressed, and perhaps inherited an aversion to the fair sex; and besides, had found out a back door to bestow his kindness and strength elsewhere, to confine himself at last to the insipid duties of matrimony, is as unnatural and unexpected a change as for an old miser to turn prodigal; and this perhaps was the surprising revolution which most of our almanacks both at home and abroad threatened us with in the month of August. . . .

The doctor (as I have been acquainted by several of his intimate friends) had two reasons to incline him to marry in his old age. The first was his great grief and concern to see the noble army of evidences defeated, Bedlow, Dugdale and Dangerfield,[2] sleeping with their fathers; viz. the witnesses that swore against Susanna, and those that stoned St. Stephen. Fuller,[3] who with good management, would have made a clever fellow, buried alive in a prison; Etcaetera Young, his virtuous companion, routed, past all hopes of rallying. Others, at the sight of a pillory, or whipping post, utterly discountenanced, and ashamed of their profession. So the doctor finding the whole hopes of the family of evidences centring in himself, and that if due care were not taken the species would be entirely lost, resolved, as far as in him lay, to prevent its utter extinction, and to raise up seed to the Popish Plot himself.

[1] *Oates pretended to have a doctorate from the University of Salamanca.*
[2] *Fellow conspirators in the Plot.*
[3] *William Fuller. See above, p. 101.*

In the second place, the doctor was touched in conscience for some juvenile gambols that shall be nameless. It seems, though he had quitted the other corruptions of Popery, yet he still fancied cardinalism. Now all the world knows conscience is a sad terrible thing. . . . What says the doctor's friend St. Austin? Why, *conscientia mille testes*, conscience is a thousand witnesses. Is it therefore to be admired if the doctor, who, make the best of him, is but one single witness, and scarce that, found himself forced to yield to a thousand? So then, as I said before, his conscience perpetually alarming and disturbing him, the doctor at last, merely for his own ease and quiet, made a vow to sow his wild oats, and not to hide the talent which God had plentifully given him, in an Italian napkin.

No sooner was this pious resolution communicated to his friends, who were mightily pleased at the news, but they looked out sharp to find him a proper yoke-fellow. It was represented to him that a maid was by no means for his turn, the doctor was fat and pursey, a maidenhead was not to be got without much drudging for't; and besides 'twas now just the dog-days,[1] and who knew but the doctor's reins might receive great damage in case of a violent encounter. At last an independent minister advised him to Mrs. Margaret W—— of Breadstreet (whose former husband was a Muggletonian, and she continued of the same persuasion) urging this argument in her behalf, that in her the doctor might have open and free ingress, egress and regress, as oft as he pleased, that as he might enjoy her without the sweat of, so he might eternally live with her without the least peril of his brows, she being no charmer, and consequently would not equip him with a pair of horns,[2] which he knew the doctor abominated, as being marks of the beast, and altogether Popish. The doctor liked the proposal, and at the first interview, was so extremely smitten with the gravity and goodness of her person, that he could neither eat (which was much) nor drink (which was more) till the business was concluded.

A comical passage happened at the Commons, which I think very well worth the sending to you. The doctor going thither for a licence, two scurvy questions were asked him. The first was,

---

[1] *The time of the rising of the Dog-star, considered the hottest and most unwholesome period of the year.*
[2] *The mark of the cuckold.*

whether he would have a licence to marry a boy or a girl; the second whether he would have a licence for behind or before. At this the doctor lost all patience, held up his cane, and thundered out, You rascal, as thick as hops, till upon the proctor's crying *peccavi,* the sky cleared up again.

The articles of marriage were as follows:

Imprimis, The doctor promises *in verbo sacerdotis,* to keep ne'er a male servant in his house under sixty, and to hang up the picture of the destruction of Sodom in his bedchamber *ad refi-candam memoriam,* and to teach his children to swear as soon as they can speak,

Item, The doctor promises that he will never offer to attack either in bed, or couch, jointstool, or table, the body of the aforesaid Mrs. Margaret W—— *a parte post,* but to comfort, refresh, and relieve her *a parte ante,* giving the aforesaid Mrs. Margaret W—— in case he offends after that manner, full leave to make herself amends before, as she pleases; as also upon a second trespass, to burn his peacemaker. However with this proviso, that whenever the aforesaid Mrs. Margaret W—— happens to be under the dominion of the Moon, that is to say, whenever it is term-time with the aforesaid Mrs. Margaret W—— then the above-mentioned doctor shall have full power, liberty and authority to enter the Westminster half of her body at which door he pleases. This last clause was not obtained till after a stiff dispute on the doctor's part, who threatened to break off if it were denied him. The other articles as less considerable, I pass over, to come to the main business in hand, the marriage.

On the 17th of this present August the doctor was new washed and trimmed, with a large sacerdotal rose in his hat, and all his other clergy equipage, came to the house of an Anabaptist teacher in the city; where in the face of a numerous assembly, consisting of all fores, divisions, and sub-divisions of Protestants, he was married to Mrs. Margaret W——. The doctor was observed to be very merry all dinner time, and the largest part of his face, meaning his chin, moved notably. . . .

Thus the time was agreeably spent till ten, at which time a bell rung to prayers, and afterwards (his spouse, after the laudable custom of England having gone before) the doctor resolutely marched towards the place of execution. There was no sack posset, nor throwing of stockings, both those ceremonies being judged to

E

be superstitious,[1] and things of mere human invention. The bed
continued in a trembling fit most part of the night, which I suppose occasioned the report of an earthquake, which the next neighbours said they felt that unbloody night. . . .

On Tuesday, August 29, 1693, Brown was seized for libel
for having 'printed, composed, written, or caused to be printed
the scandalous and offensive pamphlet without licence or authority.'[2] But after three months, possibly because of Oates' unhealthy
reputation, the case was shelved.

For three years after his arrest we hear very little about
Tom Brown. How he lived in those years we do not know. Benjamin Boyce quotes a pamphlet of 1696, *The Session of the Poets,*
which describes 'T.B.' as head over heels in debt, frequenting
'taverns, tippling-houses, &c., and when the drawer brings up the
reckoning, he sends a porter to his bookseller to redeem him;
makes him great promises that he will make him amends in the
next copy he writes; and by putting these blinds so frequently
upon him, he designs to make the stationer as poor as himself.'
By 1696, it appears, Brown had already acquired the necessary
characteristics of the Grub Street hack. Here is Brown on love:

An EPITAPH upon the charming PEGGY.

Under this marble Peggy lies,
Who did so often spread her thighs,
And made Philander's courage rise.

This morsel of delicious lust,
That kissed with so sincere a gust,
Is now resolved to common dust.

Her hands (forgive me if I am blunt)
Will now no more, as they were wont
Pilot love's sailors to her ——

Her limbs, that used to move so nice,
And taste love's pleasures in a trice,
Are now, alas! as cold as ice.

[1] *As a Dissenter, he would naturally be opposed to most ceremony.*
[2] *Benjamin Boyce,* Tom Brown of Facetious Memory *(1939), p. 48.*

To tell the truth, as short as can be,
She killed herself with drinking brandy,
And all for her dear Jack-a-Dandy.

Thus did our charming nymph expire,
According to her heart's desire,
And as she lived, she died by fire.

Hector,[1] my boy, of thee I beg
Not to forget the illustrious Peg,
But o'er her tomb lift up thy leg.

Then piss such deluges of rain,
In so exuberant a strain,
As shall o'erflow the world again.

This tribute's to her ashes due,
Whose loss ten thousand youths will rue;
And so, immortal Peg, adieu.

He also wrote bottle songs, which reflect another of his interests. The long, arduous, tavern-house hours that Brown kept thoroughly qualified him for the subject. In fact, the number of pieces on ale-houses and taverns, on the chemical reactions of claret, on the delights of being drunk, suggest it was the most popular subject in Grub Street:

The

Claret Drinker's Song;

or,

The Good Fellow's Design, 1684.

A pox of this fooling and plotting of late,
What a pother and stir hath it kept in the state?
Let the rabble run mad with suspicions and fears,
Let 'em scuffle and jar till they fall by the ears;
Their grievances never shall trouble my pate,
So that I can enjoy my dear bottle in quiet.

---

[1] *The name of his Danish dog.*

What coxcombs were those that would father their ease,
And their necks, for a toy, a thin wafe and mass,
At old Tyburn they never had needed to swing,
Had they been true subjects to drink, and their King.
A friend and a bottle is all my design,
It has no room for treason that's top full of wine,
I mind not the Members, nor makers of laws,
Let 'em fit and prorogue as his Majesty please:

. . . .

I'll drink in defiance of gibbet and halter,
This is the profession that never will alter.

For Brown drinking songs did not seem complete without
some salutation to the pox. At least two other poems of his demonstrate this phenomenon:

What a pox do you bellow, and keep such a pother,
And throw candlesticks, bottles, and pipes at each other.
Come—keep the King's peace, leave your damming and
    sinking,
And gravely return to good Christian drinking.
He that flinches his glass, and to drink is not able,
Let him quarrel no more, but knock under the table.

And this:

What a pox d'ye tell me of the Papist's design?
Would to God you'd leave talking, and drink off your wine,
Away with your glass, sir, and drown all debate;
Let's be loyally merry; ne'er think of the State.

. . . .

Another drinking song, 'The Whet', was set to music by
Henry Purcell, the composer. It might help put Brown in perspective to point out here that the great Purcell set to music many
poems that do not fit his dignified image today. For example,
'The Old Fumbler. A Song', which inspired Purcell to music, was
as coarse a piece as ever came out of Grub Street.

THE OLD FUMBLER. A SONG:

Set by Mr. Hen. Purcell.

I.

Smug, rich and fantastic old fumbler was known,
That wedded a juicy brisk girl of the town,
Her face like an angel, fair, plump, and a maid,
Her lute well in tune too, could he but have played;
But lost was his skill let him do what he can,
She finds him in bed a weak silly old man,
He coughs in her ear, 'tis in vain to come on,
Forgive me, my dear, I'm a silly old man.

II.

She laid his dry hand on her snowy soft breast,
And from those white hills gave a glimpse of the best;
But ah! what is age when our youth's but a span,
She found him an infant instead of a man:
Ah! Pardon, he'd cry, that I'm weary so soon,
You have let down my bass, I'm no longer in tune,
Lay by the dear instrument, prithee lie still,
I can play but one lesson and that I play ill.

All these are trivia. But Brown's wit, we have already seen, can be pointed. This satire on the Quakers comes from the same Tory indignation that he demonstrated in the attack on David Jones, the 'mighty bellowing' preacher. The emotional excess of the Dissenters' religion was a stock target of the Tory wits.

Mr. Brown's Sermon at a Quakers Meeting.

Dear Brethren and loving Sisters,

We are met and assembled together, and the end and meaning of our meeting is this, which I shall unfold unto you in as few words, and as clear a sense as the matter itself will bear.

My beloved, our dear brother and fellow-labourer hath gone a little astray, in the opinion of the vulgar and profane; but how far, I say, how far, my brethren, this may be of consequence to the innocent lambs of our flock, shall be the subject of my following discourse. And the matter, as it stands fairly discovered and revealed unto us by undeniable evidence of the Brotherhood, is plainly thus.

Azarius, our dear brother, who, it is well known, lived in good fame and reputation amongst his neighbourhood in the Town of Twittenham,[1] which lieth on the right-hand-side of the River of Thames, as thou goest beyond Brentford. Now this man, our dear brother, as I told you, being obliged to go and his occasions calling him to London, the man arose, took up his staff, and walked. But behold as he was going over the Green which is called Turnham Green, (that unlucky, unfortunate, and scandalous Green) about the north-east corner thereof, as thou turnest towards the south, he met with our sister Ruth, and they twain walked and communed together for some time; and as they were communing together, our sister Ruth cast such obliging glances, with her commanding eyes, on the unfortunate Azarius, and squeezed his hand so sensibly, that the snake peeped from out of the grass, and our dear friend Azarius was forced to obey the all-commanding power of the little unlucky one. Whereupon he said unto her, Dear sister Ruth, the spirit moveth me to lay thee down, that I may fructify upon thee; and she answered him again, and said, Resist not the spirit, for from thence proceedeth no ill. So he took her and laid her down; and when it came to pass that she was down, and laid flat on her back, she took up her coats, even unto the holland-smock which covered her nakedness, and throwing them over her face, said, Whatsoever thou meanest wickedly, Azarius, I will not see. So Azarius let down his breeches, fell with his face downwards on our sister Ruth, and so followed the motions of the spirit.

Now, my beloved, in the meantime, while our brother was exercising his faculties on our sister Ruth, cometh by one of the profane, who being moved and seduced by the instigation of the Devil, hath proclaimed and divulged this abroad with scorn and contempt of our brother, yea also, and of us. But now, my brethren, to expound and explain this matter unto you, and that I may show you how far our brother may be criminal therein, I shall thus proceed:

The casuists have a maxim, and the maxim is extreme

[1] *Twickenham.*

good, and so plain and undeniable, that nobody can gainsay it; and it is this, *ubi intentio bona, actio non mala*; therefore say I, my beloved, *quoad actionem*, our brother is criminal. And, why? Because it was with his carnal part, and all carnality is criminal. And, secondly, as to the place; it was done publicly in an open field, near to the highway-side, whereby he became a scorn and derision unto that profane man, and laid a scandal on the Brotherhood. But then again, *quoad intentionem*, the intent was good, and that appears plainly thus; our brother was moved. And how was he moved? Why, with a fair and tempting object; and when a temptation proceeds from a fair and pleasing object, which is present, who can withstand it? And, secondly, he did not go to it after the ways of the profane, who say G—— damn me, I will do so or so, and by G—— you shall do so or so; but he said unto her, Dear Sister, the spirit moves me. Which brings me in the next place to the intent itself, which was not as the wicked, who do it to satisfy the sensual and carnal appetite with a sort of pleasing delight, but to fructification and edification of a good woman; whereby, my beloved, you may plainly see that his intentions were good, that is, to propagation, fructification, and generation; that he might raise up seed to the Brotherhood, and thereby made that carnal part an agreeable instrument to the continuation of righteous seed in the nation, whereby he hath shown himself a fitting member of this congregation, and by his forward inclination hath laid an eternal obligation upon this kingdom in general, and the Brotherhood in particular, in giving so lively an example for every singular member thereof.

Brown wrote in many genres; he was experimental and inventive. He had to be to keep himself in claret. One of his favourite genres was the letter, which attained enormous popularity in the 17th and 18th centuries and then virtually disappeared as a literary type. The letter was almost a separate para-literature. Dryden wrote literary criticism in dedicatory epistles, Pope wrote poetry in epistle form, Richardson wrote epistolary novels. There were news-letters and, of course, familiar letters, *billets doux*, and letters on almost every conceivable subject that is now expressed in the essay and the more conventional literary forms. Many of Brown's letters were translations from the French and Italian letter writers. But Brown's translations, according to the

manner of the time, were so free and so suffused with Brown's
lively spirit as to be original creations. The following letters, therefore, are presented as entirely his own:

A Letter from Mr. Brickland,

an Oxford Tailor,

to Mr. Thomas Brown; with Mr. Brown's Answer.

Lightning and Destruction, Mr. Brown! what do you
mean? My wife, my man, and I, have been these three days in
pursuit of you, to no purpose. My wife has been at all your old
haunts, from Boccardo to Friar Bacon's study; my man has hunted
all Holywell and St. Giles's, and I myself have been at all the
ale-houses and bawdy-houses in St. Thomas's, St. Towl's, and
St. Ann's, but the devil a word was to be heard of Mr. Brown.
When you have no money, you're easy enough to be found; then
you are to be heard of at Mother Carpenter's, or at Hart's, Hard-
ing's, or some other of your offices, where either you or any of
your comrogues have any credit. What the devil, is the devil in
you, to keep a body out of a body's money, when a body wants
it? Gad's flesh and blood you'd make a body mad. And there's
your two pupils, Heywood and Gosney too, owe me for two suits
and a gown each, and have put me off with their flim-flams for
this five months; but I'll be served so no longer by them, nor you,
nor nobody else. I'll get leave, and one writ will serve you all,
and have you I will, if among the living; and to Boccardo you
go, and there you shall lie till you're as rotten as so many medlars.
'Tis a very hard case, that you'll spend the money you had sent
you, and neither your bedmaker, washerwoman, nor any of your
creditors, of which I am the chief, should have one shilling. This
is the old way; but look you, Sir, your shams shan't always serve
your turn, and I am resolved to be as troublesome and malicious
as I can, unless speedily paid, and then you shall find me your
humble servant, as formerly, to command,

From my House, near   John Brickland.
the May-pole, Sept.
27, being Saturday.

As soon as this letter came to hand [the text continues]
Tom summons a committee to meet at Mother Carpenter's, to

consider what answer was fit to be returned in an affair of so great importance; where 'twas concluded Mr. Brown was the properest person to draw it; which he did in the following manner, and superscribed, to Mr. John Brickland, Tailor, in Oxon.

We the under-written, Simon Heywood, Richard Gosney, John White, Stephen Townsend, and Thomas Brown, having maturely considered the purport of your charge, drawn up from your own house near the May-pole, Sept. the 27th, being Saturday, do think it necessary, in behalf of ourselves, and the rest of your customers, undergraduates of the University of Oxford, to observe to you, that long trust and good manners are the most exemplary qualifications of a tailor, and the surest way for you to preserve your old customers, gain new ones, and recover your debts. But, Sir, we must give you to understand, that if you continue to treat us in this contumelious, enigmatical, and scandalous manner, we shall immediately proceed to such terms of resentment, that will not only oblige you to restrain your wife from such unnecessary pursuits, but likewise consult such other methods, as for the future shall engage both yourself and man to keep yourselves more strictly within the limits of your own jurisdiction. Look you, Mr. Brickland, this is our resolution, that if you should, for the time to come, disturb us any more with your dunning epistles, or attempt to put us under any other difficulties, we shall not only put ourselves upon our guard, and endeavour to repel force with force; but withal unanimously determine not to pay you one shilling for these twelve months next ensuing the date hereof. But if you keep your temper, give good words, and more credit, if we, or any of us shall have any just occasion, then you may depend upon it, when the next returns come, you shall assuredly come in for a snack, according to the true intent and meaning of these presents. Given under our hands this 5th day of October, &c.

A Consolatory Letter to my Lady —— upon the Death of her Husband.

Madam,

I was very much surprised to hear that your Ladyship takes so much to heart the loss of your husband; that your relations should not be able to conquer so obstinate a grief, or that a person of

E*

your good sense and resolution, should be so unfashionable and so weak, as to pay that respect to the ashes of the dead, which well-bred women now-a-days can scarce afford to the living.

I will not pretend to attack your grief in the common forms, I will not represent to you that all flesh is grass, that nothing is exempt from the laws of fate, and that 'tis in vain to regret a loss, which it was not in our power to prevent; these threadbare topics I shall leave to divines and philosophers, and shall content myself, to oppose your lamentations with arguments better suited to your present condition.

'Tis true, Madam, you have lost a husband, and what of that? Have not thousands done so before you? But then consider, that this death makes room for a new election. A widow ought no more to afflict herself for the death of her husband, than a country corporation is obliged to go into mourning for the death of the member that represented them in Parliament; for, without staying for a writ from the Clerk of the Crown, she may proceed to a new choice as soon as she sees convenient. Your husband, God be thanked, has neither carried your youth with him into the other world, not your jointure; could he have robbed you of either of those blessings, you might have just reason to complain; but I think a woman's condition is not very desperate, when her two surest friends, her beaux and her wealth stick close to her.

As you have charms, and money enough to procure you store of lovers, so in my opinion, it must needs be an agreeable diversion to you in your present sorrow, (for I will allow you, Madam, to keep up the appearance of it) to observe the different address and language of your admirers.

One will tell you, that he adores the perfections of your soul, exclusive of all worldly considerations; but, Madam, have a care of these Platonics, for a man that makes vigorous court to the body, is worth a thousand coxcombs, that pretend I know not what mighty kindness to the soul.

Another will tell you, that he is ready to hang or drown for your sake, and desires you to choose what sort of death for him you think fit, if you deny him that blessing, wherein his life can be only happy. Be governed by me, Madam, and take such a lover at his word; if he decently dispatch himself you may take it from me, that he loved in earnest, but if he fails to give you this testimony of his affection, you may conclude he was a hypocrite, and consequently not worth the saving.

A third perhaps will boast of his acres, and tell you what a large settlement he will make you; whatever you do, pray take care of these Smithfield gentlemen, these land and tenement panders, for not one in a thousand is honest at bottom, and if he can but join your estate to his, never troubles his head about the more comfortable conjunction of persons and affections.

It will be a pleasant amusement for you, to manage these humble servants so artificially, as to make all of 'em hope; yet, at the same time jealous of one another, to steal a kind glance sometimes at one, and bestow a gracious nod sometimes upon another, to see them languish at your feet, and hear the different turns of their rhetoric; then after you have thoroughly examined their several merits and qualifications, 'twill be high time to proceed in your choice. But whenever you go about that, Madam, let me advise you to observe the same policy, as the cardinals do at the election of a Pope, and pitch upon one who, in all probability, is soonest like to make a *sede vacante.* . . .

A Love-Letter to an Old LADY

By Mr. Smith.

Madam,

Paying a visit yesterday to Mrs. —— I was informed of your Ladyship's displeasure. What should occasion your indignation, I cannot well apprehend. I do assure you, no man living has a greater veneration for your Ladyship, or has been readier upon all occasions to testify it to the world. To convince you of the truth of what I say, I will relate to you what happened last Saturday; by which it will appear, that I have been so far from ridiculing your Ladyship, which is the accusation you fasten upon me, that no one could have given greater demonstration of his respect. For being in company where mention was made of your Ladyship, not so honourable indeed, as I could have wished, or your quality and character might have required, I took occasion to do justice to your merit. Gentlemen, said I, you do my lady wrong; for my own part I must profess, I think her a very agreeable woman. You cannot be serious sure, replies a certain gentleman, who had more malice than wit; in my whole life, I never saw so hideous a complexion. Sir, said I, 'tis unjustly done to find fault with a complexion, which is none of her own; if her face displeases you, blame her woman who made it. But I hope, returned he, you will not deny, but that she is red-haired. With submission, Sir, I do, to my certain knowledge she has not one hair on her head. But then her teeth, all the world must allow are execrable. I deny it, Sir, for she has but one that is bad. But you must grant me her chin is too long by three inches. But do you apprehend the reason? 'Tis because her neck is too short by two. I see, Sir, said he, with some little heat, you are obstinately bent to oppose the power of truth; but I hope you are not so far prejudiced, as to maintain her breath to be sweet? That infirmity. Sir, replied I, is the effect of the foulness of her lungs, and not of her mouth; and if her lungs are rotten, is it her ladyship's fault, or Nature's? And then her gait, says he, is the most disagreeable in the world. You have betrayed at once, Sir, said I, both your malice and ignorance; if you had the least acquaintance with her ladyship, you must have known better; Alas! poor lady! She has not walked without crutches these ten years. But then her conduct, I hope you will not undertake to justify that; how does it become old Eve, think you, to patch and paint, intrigue, read romances, and love verses, talk smuttily, look amorously, dress youthfully; insomuch, that if it were not for her looks, you could not distinguish her from her daughter. Under favour, Sir, you mistake, 'tis her granddaughter you mean. And then to keep a young fellow of five and twenty to satisfy her brutal lust. 'Tis false, I have heard Mr. —— affirm a thousand times she was insatiable.

He would have proceeded in his defamations, but I desired him to omit all farther discourse on that subject, for that I could not, with patience, support, that a woman of your Ladyship's merit, and virtue, and a woman for whom I had so particular an honour, should be so impudently vilified and blasphemed to my face.

I hope by this time you are made sensible, Madam, that I am quite another person than you apprehend me to be, and that I am so far from having any disrespectful thoughts of your Ladyship, that no one of your grand-children, the nearest relation you have remaining, could have gone farther in your vindication. But I would not have you attribute my defence of your Ladyship altogether to respect; give it a tenderer, and truer name, and call it love. I say love, for let me die, Madam, if I have not a violent passion for your Ladyship. I know you may very well suspect the truth of what I say; for love in me, you will tell me, ought to imply beauty in you. But love, you know very well, creates beauty no less frequently, than beauty does love. And if by the help of imagination, I can find out charms in you, which nobody else can discover, I think I have reasonable foundation enough for my passion; there is something, I know not where to fix it, 'tis not in your face or shape, or mien, or air or any part of your body; much less in your mind; but something that is so very agreeable; something I know not what, nor where, so bewitching, that 'tis not in my power to defend my heart against you. Perhaps the malicious world will say you are old; but we know old wine intoxicates more than new; and an aged oak is stronger than a young one. 'Tis with your Ladyship's beauty, as with old buildings when they fall, it destroys with its ruins. As I profess myself an admirer of antiquity, by consequence I should have no small passion for your Ladyship. For I must tell you, Madam, there are finer fragments of antiquity in your face, than any Greece or Italy can boast of; and more beauty lies buried in one wrinkle of yours, than in the ruins of the most stately arches, or most magnificent temples. You cannot therefore question the sincerity of my proposal. . . .

The liveliest years of Brown's life were from 1697 to 1700. They began with his meeting William Pittis, 'drunken Pittis',[1] who had just left Oxford to begin his Grub Street career. William Pittis's life in some respects was a pocket version of Brown's. He never achieved the stature of Brown, but he probably consumed more wine, made almost as much noise, and got into as much trouble. He became a close friend of Brown's, though he still felt free to lampoon him when some profitable occasion arose. He began his career auspiciously with a short-lived journal called *Miscellanies over Claret* (1697), which meant virtually what it said, and to which Brown was a contributor. By 1699 he had already acquainted himself with the sponging-house and debtor's prison. The following bit of doggerel shows his Grub Street bravado in financial matters:

---

[1] *See above, pp. 47 ff. for one of Brown's escapades with Pittis. See also pp. 112 ff.*

Landlady, seeing nothing come,
Takes out a writ, and sees a bum [bailiff],
And, to make good the pay of quarters,
Calls in the assistance of the Tartars;
And at my chamber-door, confound her!
Places a four and twenty pounder.
. . . .
Sir, it's at the suit of one you know well,
Your landlady, old Mrs. Powel,
A trifling action, cries the varlet,
For one, like you, in stockings scarlet,
Who makes so noble an appearance;
I could have wished she'd had forbearance;
But four and twenty pound, said Bum, Sir;—
An inconsiderable sum, sir:
When in comes B——, of house the mistress,
And thus addresses man in distress,
Sir, it is in vain to stand here prating,
Pay for your lodging and for eating;
Money's the thing I want, for words
They signify no more than turds,
Your mother's rich, your brother preaches,
In Lombard Street among the riches,
They'll lay down what's your debt, or bail you;
Sure such relations will not fail you!
I, who knew better, said no more,
But dressed myself, and damned the whore
Put nicest periwig and phiz on,
And off I marched with bum to prison.

Despite their insouciance, the Grub Street hacks were always serious about their politics. As a Tory extremist, Pittis was arrested seven times for his political writing, was fined, sent to the pillory, sent to prison and on one occasion managed to escape arrest because the authorities were unable to prove his authorship.[1]

As for Brown, in these years, 1697 to 1700, he gave his already spicy reputation a pornographic lift that carried him

---

[1] *See below, pp. 252-3.*

through the rest of his days. For the most part, this was achieved by one book which was translated into French—his one foreign translation. Boyce explains that the translators were compelled by 'le bon gout & la pudeur' to moderate the original somewhat.[1] The title of the book is itself a Grub Street masterpiece: '*Marriage Ceremonies; as now Used in all Parts of the World*. Very diverting, especially to the Ladies, Written Originally in Italian, by Seignoir Gaya.... To which are added, Large Animadversions, and some Remarks upon Marriage. As also, a Looking-Glass for Married People: or, The Fantastick Adventures of Sir E—— H—— with his seven wives. Written by himself in the time of his Confinement.' Ironically, except for a few pornographic passages and a touch of Brown's characteristic obscenity, much of the book is moralizing and dull. If his readers were angry, it was probably from frustration, because the title promised more than the text delivered. But that is in the best Grub Street tradition.

In this period Brown also wrote his *Satyr upon the French King* (1697), which involved him with the courts for half of 1698. From 1699 to 1700 he was in the centre of four battles on Grub Street: The Dispensary Quarrel, the battle against the wits, the baiting of the astrologer, Partridge, which extended several years beyond 1700, and the Kingston-Smith-Roper affair, which has already been described. All of these fights seemed to be going on at the same time. These Grub Street wars seem trivial now, but the issues were serious, and behind some of them can be heard the rumblings of a social revolution which led to the gradual submerging of a dissolute, elegant society by the middle-class elements of London with their middle-class respectability and moral values.

A string of 'societies for the reformation of manners' sprang up. 'Reformation of manners' became their slogan. In literature the attack was directed against the 'wits', both of the theatre and the printed page. The theatre was the more vulnerable. It was no longer under court protection after the reign of Charles II and it swiftly became the main target for the moral reformers. In 1696 the Lord Chancellor ordered all plays to be fully licensed, and in 1697 he restricted lewd expression on stage. By 1698 the way was prepared for the explosive book of Jeremy Collier, 'a non-swear-

[1] Op. cit., *p. 56.*

ing parson', *A Short view of the Immorality and Profaneness of the English Stage,* a short view of some 300 pages. After Collier's attack the theatre was no longer the same. In fact, every aspect of literature seemed affected. 'Wit' became a dirty word. It suggested the licentious verbalisms of the Restoration stage and the clever obscenities of Grub Street. But for Sir Richard Blackmore, a physician and poet and the main figure in the attack on the wits, it suggested one man above all, Tom Brown.

The Dispensary Quarrel can be traced back to 1687, when some public-spirited members of the College of Physicians tried to establish a dispensary for the 'sick poor', who were being squeezed by the apothecaries. Naturally the apothecaries objected, and they naturally were supported by those physicians who had a more than therapeutic interest in the apothecaries' high prices. There was an angry exchange of pamphlets that went on sporadically for a dozen years. Brown did not make his first contribution until 1697 and then with a skit so dull that he promptly disowned it in an advertisement in the *Post-Boy*. It was entitled *'Physick lies a Bleeding, or the Apothecary turned Doctor. A Comedy Acted every Day in most Apothecaries Shops in London.'* Here is one of its bright spots:

Trueman. Come in, come in, we were no sooner talking of rogues but enter an apothecary. Prithee, Tom, where hast been that thou comest with the accoutrements of thy profession thus?

Tom Gallypot. Truly, Sir, I have been at your house; your lady was not very well today, and she sent for me to—to—to—cannonade her posteriors. You know by my instrument what I have been doing. And now I have done that, I have prescribed a specific bolus for her to take after it.

Tr. A pox of your specific bolus, and you. My wife is never well but when she's taking physic, I think. Prithee, Mr. Gallypot, what will be the charges of this morning's work?

Gallyp. O, Sir, but little, you never stand upon that I am sure for your lady's good; she must also have a pearl julep, and an anodyne draught: and then I hope she'll be very speedily well again.

Tr. A pox had you with your cramp names. Tell me what all this will cost? I am sure I left her well not above an hour ago.

Gallyp. [Starts back.] Good Sir, be not so unreasonably

passionate, and I'll tell you. Sir, the pearl julep will be six shillings eight pence; pearls being dear since our clipped money was current. The specific bolus 4s. and 6d. I never reckon less; my master in Leadenhall Street never set down less, be it what it would. The antihysteric glyster, 3s. and 6d. (a common one is but 2s. 6d.) and the anodyne draught 3s. 4d. That's all, Sir, a small matter and please you, Sir, for your lady. My fee is what you please Sir. All the bill is but eighteen shillings.

Tr. Very fine, in faith, d'ye make a *but* at it? I do suppose to be genteel, I must give you a crown.

Gallyp. If your worship please; I take it to be a fair, and an honest bill.

Tr. Do you so indeed? But I wish you had called a doctor, perhaps he would have advised her to have forbore taking anything, as yet at least, so I had saved 13s. in my pocket.

Gallyp. O Sir, call a doctor; we never do that, at least very rarely till we have done all we can with the patients. And when we can't tell what to do with 'em, then we oblige a doctor and call him in.

By 1699, when Dr. Samuel Garth wrote the mock epic poem, 'The Dispensary', attacking the apothecaries, the quarrel had become entangled with the battle between the wits and the anti-wits. The connection was simple. Garth had ridiculed the physician, Blackmore for supporting the apothecaries. That was provocation enough. But Garth also ridiculed Blackmore's literary pretensions, particularly his epic poem, *Prince Arthur*, a wonderfully tedious piece that Blackmore had written in 1695. And so the two quarrels became one.

Blackmore's reply to Garth was not immediate, but when it came a few months later it was weighted with the whole middle-class reaction against the alleged licentiousness of literature and the stage. Any writer who had no taste for Blackmore's poetry, presumably, had no taste for morality—he was a wit. Along with Garth, this seemed to include almost every major writer of the age, because Blackmore put them all in his monumental *Satyr Against Wit*.[1] Their captain, he said, was Tom Brown.

Blackmore did not leave out very much in his attack. He

[1] *See* R. C. Boys, *'Sir Richard Blackmore and the Wits'*, Contributions in Modern Philology, *No. 13 (1949).*

included not only Garth and the Dispensary Quarrel, but even the Ancients in the Ancients-Moderns controversy. It was a brave and heady thing to attack all the wits of one of the wittiest ages in English literature, and in 1700 came the first reply, a collection of squibs by Sir Charles Sedley, Richard Steele, Garth, Dr. James Drake, the Countess of Sandwich and many more, including Tom Brown, entitled, *Commendatory Verses, on the Author of the Two Arthurs, and the Satyr against wit; By some of his particular friends.* Interestingly enough, Brown's was the most effective of a dull lot. His main poem was an extensive parody of Blackmore's satire, 'An Epitome of a Poem, truly call'd, *A Satyr Against Wit*; done for the undeceiving of some readers, who have mistaken the Panegyrick in that immortal Work for the Satyr, and the Satyr for the Panegyrick.' Another of his poems was entitled, 'Upon seeing a man light a Pipe of Tobacco in a Coffee-House with a Leaf of *King Arthur*' [the second of Blackmore's epic *Arthur* poems]. As a creator of long epic poems, without a shred of talent, Blackmore was a heaven-sent target for the wits. Richard Steele made the obvious point in one of his squibs, 'To the Mirror of British Knighthood, the worthy Author of the Satire against Wit. . . .' (Blackmore had been knighted for some obscure political reason. Brown suggested it was for his poem, *King Arthur*.)

> Well may'st thou think an useless talent wit;
> Thou, who without it, has three poems writ.

Brown carried the point one step further in 'An Epigram, occasion'd by the News that Sir R——d B——e's Paraphrase upon Job was in the Press':

> When Job contending with the devil I saw,
> It did my wonder, but not pity, draw;
> For I concluded, that, without some trick,
> A saint at any time could match old Nick.
> Next came a fiercer fiend upon his back,
> I mean his spouse, stunning him with her clack;
> But still I could not pity him, as knowing
> A crabtree-cudgel soon would send her going.

But when the quack[1] engag'd with Job I 'spy'd,
The Lord have mercy on poor Job I cry'd.
What spouse and Satan did attempt in vain,
The *quack* will compass with his murdering pen,
And on a dunghill leave poor Job again.
With impious doggerel he'll pollute his theme,
And make the saint against his will blaspheme.

The war between the two factions went on sporadically for some time. Blackmore replied to the *Commendatory Verses* with his *Discommendatory Verses on those which are truly Commendatory, undoubtedly getting assistance from a number of allies.* It systematically parodied every verse of the *Commendatory Verses*, sometimes very effectively. For example, Tom Brown's 'Upon seeing a Man light a Pipe of Tobacco ... with a Leaf of *King Arthur*' became, in *Discommendatory Verses*, 'Upon seeing a Man wipe his A——se with T.B.'s *Satyr Against the French King*,' ending with the lines :

When mortal is buried, then the word
Is *dust to dust,* but here it's Turd to Turd.

Brown delighted in attacking Blackmore on almost every conceivable occasion, whether or not it was relevant. Even in his *Amusements*, at the beginning of a description of debtors' prisons, Blackmore is dragged in: 'Having taken a sound nap, by preparing my person with the invincible opiates of a glass of good wine, and the lecture of some pages in Sir Richard Blackmore's *Eliza.* . . .' As for Blackmore, he was so infuriated by Brown that he was still attacking him (in 'The Kit-Kats') four years after Brown died.

In the middle of these controversies Brown found time for yet another battle and turned a corner of his mind to Partridge, the astrologer. Brown was the first of a long line of wits to bait Partridge, writing a parody of Partridge's *Merlinus* entitled *Prophecies out of Merlin's Carmen* as early as 1690. But his main attack came in 1700. It is useful, by way of a long digression, to see what Brown was attacking. This, in turn, will lead us into another Grub Street battle, the battle of the astrologers.

John Partridge and his astrological almanac, *Merlinus Lib-*

---

[1] *The physician Blackmore.*

the 17th century. He was a cobbler until middle age, manufactured a medical degree from the University of Leyden and accordingly was qualified to sell pills with his astrology, which he advertised at the end of his almanacs. He had a genius for making his prophecies so equivocal that he could always claim after the event that this was exactly what he foretold. From 1690 to 1700 his popularity was immense, despite the persistent attacks of two rivals, Parker and Gadbury—or perhaps because of them. Who could resist fascinating titles like Gadbury's *The Ungrateful Demon Dispossessed,* referring to Partridge, and Partridge's *The Black Life of John Gadbury,* in the pamphlet war with Gadbury that resulted?

Partridge's battle with George Parker was on a larger scale and had a political dimension, because Parker was a Jacobite Tory and Partridge a Dissenting Whig. Here Partridge offers a few candid comments on his rival's character:

Flagitiosus Mercurius Flagellatus:

or the

Whipper Whipp'd:

Being an Answer to a Scurrilous Invective Written by George Parker in his Almanack for MDCXCVII.
In such Language and base Expressions that none but a Bended Mechanick would be seen to own; and this without any Provocation given by me.

The pretended ground of this quarrel is to inform us, that he is able to show in all cases the beginning of a direction's operation to a few days; and this in opposition to what I say of the lady's direction in 1696. But by the management of the whole, there is something else at the bottom, and therefore take it right. The truth of all is, to be plain both with you and him; he is poor and infamous, despicable in his person, ill-natured and saucy in his conversation, unjust in his dealings, immoral in his behaviour, weak in his understanding, ignorant in his professions; and wanting parts, prudence, virtue and honesty, finds he hath no other way to recommend himself to the world to be taken notice of, by quarrelling with somebody or other, no matter whether they give him any occasion or not. And knowing this to be the truth of the case, I will certainly give him a cast of my office, and do the most and best I can to make my hard-faced adversary famous. . . .

Parker was not a man to turn the other cheek:

J. Partridge's Scurrilous Reflections in his Almanack for the
Year 1699, Answered.

Of all the knavish bloodthirsty villains that is to be found, it will be difficult to find one to parallel J. Partridge, for he makes it no matter of consequence to be brewing his hands in the blood of men, as appears by the foregoing depositions; and of lesser moment to be ruining a man's reputation, which is a sort of murder too; for if by that means a person be deprived of an honest method of getting his bread, he must inevitably starve. And this he has and does endeavour, by all the ways and strata-gems he can invent, to bring me to, (as appears by his almanack for this year), and this without any provocation, except what is before related. . . .

The battle between the astrologers even went to the courts. In the *Post-Boy*, May 7-9, 1700, this notice appeared:

This week commences a trial at Guild-Hall, between Part-ridge the Almanac-Maker and Parker, the Astrologer; the first is the plaintiff. He brings action for £1000 against the other, for printing in his *Ephemeris* this year, that he's a rebel in his prin-ciples; an enemy to monarchy; ungrateful to his friends; a scoun-drel in his conversation; a malignant in his writings; a liar in his almanac; and a fool of an astrologer. Though they are great men in the way of predictions, they can't tell how the cause will go. We hear the polite gypsies, alias judicial fortune tellers, lay great wagers on both sides.

The trial was the joke of the day. Ned Ward gave a full account of it in his *London Spy*, from which we take the verdict:

The plaintiff, however his stars favoured him, obtaining a verdict, the compassionate jury, not knowing but some time or other it may be their own case, gave him five pounds damage for the great abuses he had honestly deserved by a just provocation.

The decision of this controversy proved very unlucky to both enemies, for they were neither of them well satisfied with the justice done to both parties, the plaintiff being very angry his damage was no more, and the defendant very much displeased they had given him so much; so that the jury would have had a very hard task to have pleased both, since they were so unfortunate in their concurrence that they could content neither.

As late as 1708 the astrologers were still at it, as we see in this excerpt from Parker's *Ephemeris for the Year of our Lord, 1708*:

To Johannodion the Magotmatical Astrologer, who teaches Errors.

The person here treated of, has more confidence than an old carted bawd, for whenever she is brought to justice, there is some side turns to obstruct the view of her face, and that people when they see her again, may not know, that she is the person that has rendered herself so remarkably infamous. But it is otherwise with Johannodion, he writes predictions year after year, which never come to pass. He foretells storms and tempests with great exactness, which shall happen in *Terra Incognita*, or in *Lubber-Land*, where none but himself has the privilege to have any sensible knowledge of 'em. So likewise he has killed the French King too, more than 100 times over, *cum multis aliis*, and yet he never blushes at any of his disappointments, no remorse of conscience for these his lying predictions, but goes on still in the same method, notwithstanding the admonitions that have been frequently given him. Such cant, such stuff, is really obnoxious to all persons, except the Silitonians of the same stamp with himself, who are his only admirers.

I gave him a large catalogue of his ridiculous predictions the last year, wherein I limited myself to inspect his observations on the year preceding only, viz. 1706; and at this present time, shall take notice of what he imposed upon the world in the year 1707, now expiring; and we shall find that he is no changeling, but Johannodion still. The same face, the same impertinence, all things exactly of the same hue and cut, with the former.

The first thing he presents the world with in his *January*

observations, is to acquaint them how Augustus King of Poland, and the King of Sweden, manage the tack; and because these two potentates were at war, and the latter having possessed himself of the other's country, at that time when he was writing his book, he therefore declares abundance of unhappiness to attend Augustus, and it was to be by fighting; for such news was to come in February from the North, and in June of his being beat. But alas! Johannodion's stars had turned the dice upon him. These two kings deceived this addle-brained predictor, having concluded a peace between themselves, before Johannodian's book could get from the press: so little is his judgement in these matters. . . .

Parker discovered Partridge in some very elementary errors:

Merlinus Hewson, or Johannodion's Ignorance in Trigonometry Exposed.

In the foregoing pages I have taken some pains to show his ignorance in mundane astrology, that the kingdom may be sensible how much he is beside the matter he pretends to in those affairs; and therein I hope it can't be said that I have lost my labour. That being done, I will proceed now to show his parts in trigonometrical performances, whereby it will appear without any contradiction, that he is a mere lump of ignorance; and that the stigma of Johannodion, which I have bestowed upon him, is the most proper appellation that could be given him.

This Johannodion, in the year 1694, brought to light his book *Mopus Reformatus*, and therein (that he might be thought somebody) publishes a direction that is not frequently heard of, for to initiate a fit of sickness that had befell a certain person. The thing being novel, it caused much admiration by some, and Johannodion hugged himself mightily upon it, as being a wonderful discovery in the art of directions in nativities. The thing pased for some time without anyone replying to it, or perhaps any taking notice of it with that intent, till myself being provoked by his scurrilities, did in the year 1699, by mathematical demonstration, undeniably prove that there was no such thing to be directed to, which he had so impudently affirmed.

By that means I gave him so fair a turn upon his back, that I never expected to hear of him again upon that score; 'tis true, I must have his nose to the grindstone some time or other, before I have done with him about *pars fortunae*; but that is not the thing designed now, so then I will omit it for a time.

But contrary to my expectations, in the year 1704, this Johannodion produces a puzzling triangle (as he would have it thought), and so indeed it will appear, when it comes to be considered, though in a quite different method from his apprehension; for what he affirms is not directed true by the great mathematical astrologers, he will presently find to fall upon his own noddle, and old Argol, Regiomentanus, and the rest of the ancient sage fathers, whom he has basely insulted, in taking them in an unmannerly method by the beards, will be cleared from his fullsome charge, and the title of ignorant fop will be fixed upon himself.

And that the air and vanity of this Johannodion may the better be known, I will transcribe what he writ in his own words.

I have made, (says he) some peculiar enquiry into directions, do find among the rest, that the ascendant, (which every novice says he can direct to a minute) is not by our great mathematical masters directed true, by the tables of oblique ascension, and yet they very well satisfied so long as nobody knows better. To prove this, I would direct the ascendant in 10 deg. of γ, to no deg. no min. of π, and I find it gives under the Pole 52.25 deg. 37 min. which is too much by a degree and a half, and will make some difference in the exact correction of a nativity (if I understand it).

This parenthesis and question is well placed. For he had good reason to suspect it. But he goes on. . . .

I think here's as much insolence and conceitedness, as can be expressed in so many words, and since he is willing to stand the test, and be trigonometrically tried, I'll join issue with him, and try the cause. And because I will do fairly by him, I will insert the triangle with the same letters he put to it, that it may be the readier understood.

. . . In this triangle (says he) the work being first prepared, the angles are all known; so is everything when they are found; the angle at A is 14 deg. 45 min., the angle at C is 16 deg. 51 min., and the angle at B 151 deg. 25. The two last positions I deny, and challenge any man to make it appear as he says; but to proceed.

Then having the sides A B and A C, he proceeds, and calculates by the signs of opposite sides and angles, and so determines the side A C, to be 24 deg, 6 minutes; all which is erroneous, and to prove it I proceed thus.

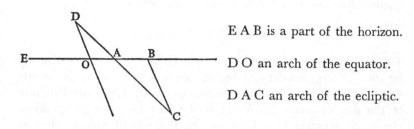

E A B is a part of the horizon.

D O an arch of the equator.

D A C an arch of the ecliptic.

Then B C is a line parallel to the equator D O, consequently B C is a lesser circle of the sphere, and not to be applied to be determined by numbers; in like manner, his angles A B C and B C A are false, and there is no truth in what he has alleged; so that 'tis plain, that Johannodion's query, if he but understood it, was very properly suggested, though he was not aware of his ignorance.

. . . Thus, Johannodion, a mathematical astrologer has taken your request into consideration, and once more turned your inside outward, and exposed your emptiness to the world.

On October 16, 1700, Tom Brown began to issue his own almanac, *The Infallible Astrologer.* He called himself Silvester Partridge, out-Partridging John with the infallible accuracy of his day-to-day predictions and the infinite claims of his all-purpose pills. It ran for eighteen issues, but Brown dropped out, probably after Number Eight, and the almanac was continued by Ned Ward. Here are some of Brown's predictions for Wednesday, October 16:

'Cloudy foggy weather at *Garraway's* and *Jonathan's,* and most coffee-houses, at and about twelve. . . . Afternoon noisy and bloody at His Majesty's Bear Garden in Hockley-in-the-hole. . . . If rainy, few night-walkers in Cheapside and Fleet Street.' For October 17: 'Excellent pease porridge and tripe in *Baldwin's* Gardens at Twelve. At night much fornication all over Covent Garden, and five miles round it.' For Sunday, October 20: 'Great jangling of bells all over the city from eight to nine. . . . Vast consumption of roast beef and pudding at one. Afternoon sleepy in most churches.'

Like Partridge, Tom Brown advertised his skills and his medicines at the end of each issue of his almanac. The advertisements below are from the first and second issues:

ADVERTISEMENT

Women, whether with child or no; children, whether male or female. Young maidens, whether they will have their sweethearts; and lovers, whether able and constant. The critical minute of the day to marry in. What is the best hour for procreation. Husbands, whether long lived or no. The second match, whether happy or unhappy. What part of the town best for a sempstress to thrive in. What the most fortunate signs for a shopkeeper, and under what planet to be set up. With other like questions, fully and satisfactorily resolved, by me Silvester Partridge, student in physic and astrology, near the Gun in Moorfields.

ADVERTISEMENT [from the second issue]

The best time to cut hair. How moles and dreams to be interpreted. When most proper to bleed. Under what aspect of the moon, best to draw teeth, and cut corns. Paring of nails, on what days unlucky. What the kindest sign to graft or inoculate in; to open beehives, and kill swine. How to get twins. And how many hours boiling, my Lady Kent's pudding requires: With other notable questions, fully and faithfully resolved, by me Silvester Partridge, student in physic and astrology, near the Gun in Moorfields.

Of whom likewise may be had, at reasonable rates, trusses, antidotes, elixirs, love powders, washes for freckles, plumpers, glass eyes, false calves and noses, ivory jaws, styptic drops to contract the parts. A new receipt to turn red hair into black; as likewise, the famous *annulus anti-cornatus,* or a ring to prevent cuckoldom, very useful for all married persons. 'Tis a hair ring, of a bright beautiful red within, and is of that wonderful efficacy and virtue, that so long as a man keeps it on his finger, he may defy all the devils in hell, nay, what's more, the wife of his bosom to cuckold him, though she has never so great a mind to it.

But to show the extent of his astrological skill in medicine, Brown devotes the entire issue of November 20 to November 27:[1]

From Nov. 20 to Nov. 27.

Gentlemen,

I promised in my last to give you an account of my pills and other medicaments, so deservedly famous for curing all manner of distempers, and am now as good as my word. I confess it goes somewhat against the grain to display myself thus in print, since so many ignorant quacks have made the method infamous; and indeed nothing but my great regard for the public, to which, as St. Austin says, every honest man ought to sacrifice all private considerations, could have induced me to appear in a paper in this nature: But if a thing is to be totally laid aside for the abuse of it, goodnight to the law and the Gospel; we must e'en turn our pulpits into powdering-tubs, and Westminster Hall into a meal-market. So much by way of introduction.

I have been often grieved to see the noble art of physic so run down and despised and invaded as it has been of late; but to say the truth, the professors may thank themselves for it. They are eternally jangling and quarrelling at the College, and persecuting one another, while they ought to lay their heads together, and unite to baffle those undermining enemies of mankind, called diseases. This would be an employment worthy of their most serious thoughts, and recommend them to the good opinion of the world; but, as affairs are managed at present, they don't so much endeavour to restore people to their health, as to make a vain ostentation of their learning. The first thing they think of, is to set up an hypothesis, as they call it, even before they think of setting up a coach; and as they make all the shifts in the world to set up the latter; so 'tis to keep up their beloved hypothesis, they strain every phenomenon in nature to make it bear that way. 'Tis a melancholy, but true observation, that as our number of physicians has increased, so the weekly bills have done the same.

Gentlemen, I was born with a natural antipathy to all diseases whatever, as some people are to cheese and onions. I hate diseases, and diseases hate me; by the same token they fly

---

[1] *The whole of Brown's part of* The Infallible Astrologer *was republished as* A Comical View of London and Westminster.

from my presence, as 'twas observed in the last great plague, that the dogs by natural instinct ran away from the city dog killer: neither can I blame 'em for it, for I make it my constant business to destroy 'em root and branch wherever I meet 'em. But gentlemen, don't misunderstand me; though I kill the disease, I do the man no harm, like lightning that melts the sword, and never injures the scabbard.

To qualify myself for this noble profession, I never troubled my head with reading Hippocrates, Dioscorides, Celsus, Galen, and other reverend blockheads of antiquity, neither did I think it worth my while to lose any time in perusing the modern coxcombs, for so I may justly call them. No, gentlemen, I went a wiser way to work; instead of turning over old musty pagan volumes, I have walked over every mountain in England, Scotland, and Wales: I have enquired into the nature of every plant and vegetable; examined every moss, grass, and flower, and by virtue of thirty years observation and upwards, have forced them to confess their respective virtues and qualities.

Nor was this all; for ever since I have been able to write I have kept a constant correspondence with all the knowing experienced men in our faculty from London to Japan; I don't mean those nonsensical hobby-horses, the virtuosos of Holland, Spain, Italy and Germany, that value themselves so much upon their philosophy, and the lord knows what unintelligible stuff. I only concerned myself with men that read the great folio of nature, and instructed themselves out of that. I have maintained a monthly commerce these twenty years with the famous Demetrius Basilowiski, Physician to the present Czar of Muscovy, with the industrious Abrahim Alibanali, who serves the Grand Signior in the same capacity, with the courteous Achmet Ben Ishmael, Doctor to the Sophy of Persia, with the inquisitive Ibin Hasna Muladezar, who constantly attends the person of the Great Mogul, and the infallible Kara Shu, who resides in the Palace of the Emperor of China; not to mention the physicians belonging to the powerful monarchs of Tonquin, Malabar, Mingrelia, Bisnagar, Golconda, Gurgistan, Pegu, Siam, Sumatra, Palemban, and the rest; from whose observations, to be most friendly communicated, as likewise my own experience, I have arrived to a greater knowledge than any physician before me, as will appear.

First, by my *pillula intentionalis*; or, my intentional pill.

I defy any physician in the king's dominions to show me the like. It never works but when the recipient would have it, and therefore is of singular use for all persons who may be obliged to take physic, and yet by reason of their employments and business cannot confine themselves to their chambers. I dare engage that a man may take it upon a journey, and never be incommoded by it. Last Easter Term, I gave it to a Yorkshire attorney, the very morning he went out of town, who had no occasion to evacuate till he came to Leeds. But what is more surprising, one Ezechiel Tar, Boatswain to the Sampson, took three of them at Deptford, upon April 16, 1699, and intended they should never work with him till he came under the equinoctial, and accordingly so it fell out, and then he had a stool, that any prince in Christendom would have been glad of, as he informed me in a letter, dated from Fort St. George, Nov. 22. In short, a man that takes it, may adjourn and prorogue his backside, as long as he pleases; and this, as I take it, can be said of no pill now known in Christendom.

Secondly, my *pillula divulgatoria*, or my divulgatory pill: the great excellency of this pill lies in extorting secrets from whoever takes it: very proper consequently for married men in Cheapside, Cornhill, or any part of England, to know how their respective wives stand affected to them; for as 'tis no bigger than a pin's head, so if the party dextrously slips it into a glass of ale, or wine, or any such vehicle, and gives it his wife, it will make her tell all the secrets of her heart in her sleep; as for instance, whether she has actually cuckolded her husband, or has only intended it; as likewise who is the person she most admires.

Thirdly, my *pillula otiosa*; or my idle pill. This is the strangest pill of 'em all, for 'tis neither diaphoretic, nor diuretic, nor hedrotic, nor hypnotic, nor yet emetic; that is to say, it neither operates by stool, nor urine, nor sleep, nor vomit; and yet makes a shift to do its business by doing nothing at all, as some lawyers do theirs by being bribed to hold their tongues.

Fourthly, my *pillula anti-moabitica*; or, my anti-moabite pill. A man that takes one of these pills before he stirs out of his lodgings, though he owes as much money as the two late sheriffs were worth, yet may go and whet his knife safely and securely at the counter-gate, and the devil of a sergeant dares meddle with him, by reason of some wonderful effluviums it sends out of the thorax: very useful for breaking tradesmen, disbanded officers, and others in the same predicament. In fine, 'tis infinitely better and cheaper than a protection from a L——d or a P——t—man. Though I constantly keep sixty operators at work, yet I can hardly serve the town for their occasions. I would say more of it, but an ancient gentlewoman, who has buried four husbands, and is in hopes to bury the fifth, stays for me below in the parlour, to have her fortune told. So, gentlemen, adieu till next Wednesday.

From the Globe and Urinal   Yours, &c.
  in Moorfields, next   Silvester Partridge.
  Door to the Gun.

For eight more years after *The Infallible Astrologer* the wits continued to bait Partridge. But even in 1706 Partridge was still popular enough for the publisher Benjamin Harris and his astrologer son to pirate his almanac. Harris's piracy was complete. He merely reprinted Partridge's almanac, made a few additions, called it by the same name, *Merlinus Liberatus*, and faithfully signed it, J. Partridge. 'I have been abused and the country also,' Partridge wrote, 'by a supplement added to my almanac, forged and contrived by Benj. Harris and his son, though I knew nothing of it till it was printed.' Partridge then had a *hand* printed at the end of his almanac and warned that anything printed after the hand 'is a cheat and he is a knave that did it.' Harris obligingly inserted his additions in the body of the almanac. In the 1707 *Merlinus Liberatus*, Partridge wrote:

If there is anything added to this Almanac by B. Harris, either in the middle or the end of it, besides these sheets, it is a piece of knavery and not mine. Likewise, if there is anything in my name, called a prophecy or prediction, it is done by a pack of rascals, contrary to my will or knowledge.[1]

This was the least of the problems vexing Partridge by this time. The wits were on the attack and Swift was soon to give Partridge the *coup de grâce* with the 'Bickerstaff Papers'. But it took the combined talent of Brown, Ward, Rowe, Steele, Addison, Prior, Congreve, Yalden and finally Swift, some of the greatest satiric talent of English literature, to annihilate Partridge.

[1] *The quotations and other details of the Harris-Partridge affair are from J. G. Muddiman,* The King's Jornalist *(1923), pp. 249-250.*

If there can be glorious years in the life of a hack, for Brown they were 1699 and 1700. He was the hub around which most of the literary controversies seemed to revolve, and at the same time he wrote his best work, *Amusements, Serious and Comical.* The *Amusements* is a translation of Dufresny's *Amusements Sérieux et Comiques* (1698), but translated in Brown's free manner, with many additions, so that it became his own creation. Together with Ned Ward's *London Spy,* Brown's comment on the London scene is one of the forerunners of a tradition of low-style realism which includes Defoe and Dickens.

In the following excerpts from the *Amusements,* it is interesting to notice that, Grub Street hack or not, Brown has a serious satiric purpose:[1]

Some carry, others are carried. 'Make way there,' says a gouty-legged chairman, that is carrying a punk of quality to a morning's exercise; or a Bartholomew baby-beau, newly launched out of a chocolate-house, with his pockets as empty as his brains. 'Make room there,' says another fellow, driving a wheelbarrow of nuts, that spoil the lungs of the city 'prentices and make them wheeze over their mistresses as bad as the phlegmatic cuckolds, their masters, do when called to family duty. One draws, another drives. 'Stand up there, you blind dog,' says a carman, 'will you have the cart squeeze your guts out?' One tinker knocks, another bawls, 'Have you brass-pot, iron-pot, kettle, skillet or a frying-pan to mend?' Another son of a whore yelps louder than Homer's Stentor, 'Two a groat, and four for sixpence, mackerel.' One draws his mouth up to his ears and howls out, 'Buy my flounders,' and is followed by an old burly drab that screams out the sale of her 'maids' and her 'soul' at the same instant.

Here a sooty chimney-sweeper takes the wall of a grave alderman, and a broom-man jostles the parson of the parish. There a fat greasy porter runs a trunk full-butt upon you, while another salutes your antlers with a basket of eggs and butter. 'Turn out there, you country putt,' says a bully with a sword two yards long jarring at his heels, and throws him into the kennel. By and by comes a christening, with the reader screwing up his mouth to deliver the service *à la mode de Paris,* and afterwards

[1] *From* Amusement III, *'London.'*

talks immoderately nice and dull with the gossips, the midwife strutting in the front with young original sin as fine as fippence; followed with the vocal music of 'Kitchen-stuff ha' you maids,' and a damned trumpeter calling in the rabble to see a calf with six legs and a top-knot. There goes a funeral with the men of rosemary after it, licking their lips after three hits of white sack and claret at the house of mourning, and the sexton walking before, as big and bluff as a beefeater at a coronation. Here a poet scampers for't as fast as his legs will carry him, and at his heels a brace of bandog bailiffs, with open mouths ready to devour him and all the nine muses; and there an informer ready to spew up his false oaths at the sight of the common executioner. . . .

There stalks a sergeant and his mace, smelling at the merchants' backsides, like a hungry dog for a dinner. There walks a public notary tied to an inkhorn, like an ape to a clog, to put off his Heathen-Greek commodities, bills of store, and charter-parties.

That wheezing, sickly show, with his breeches full of the prices of male and female commodities, projects, complaints, and all mismanagements from Dan to Beersheba, is the Devil's broker, and may be spoken with every Sunday, from eleven in the morning till four in the afternoon, at the Quakers' meeting, or his lodging, and not after; for the rest of his time on that day he employs in adjusting his accompts, and playing at back-gammon with his principal. There goes a rat-catcher in state, brandishing his banner, like a black-moor in a pageant on the execution-day of roast-beef, greasy-geese, and custards [Lord Mayor's Day]. . . .

Here is the notice of a ship to be sold, with all her tackle and lading. There are virtuous maidens that are willing to be transported with William Penn into Maryland, for the propagation of Quakerism. In another is a tutor to be hired, to instruct any gentleman's or merchant's children in their own families; and under that an advertisement of a milch-ass, to be sold at the nightman's, in Whitechapel. In another column, in a gilded frame, was a chamber-maid that wanted a service; and over her an older bachelor that wanted a housekeeper. On the sides of these were two less papers, one containing an advertisement of a red-headed monkey lost from a seed-shop in the Strand, with two guineas reward to him or her that shall bring him home again with his

The Poet's Condition

Of the several Fetters, Irons, & Ingines of Torture that were taken from the Marshalsea Prison, with their exact Weight. The Draughts of the Sick Mens Ward in the Marshalsea, also the Strong Room in the Fleet in which Mr. Arne Dyed, The manner of wearing the Collar, the Scull Cap, the Sheers &c. with a particular explanation of the whole. Prayer to be bound with Reports of the honourable the Committee of the House of Commons.
Report on Marshalsea Prison to Ho. of C. 14 May 1729.

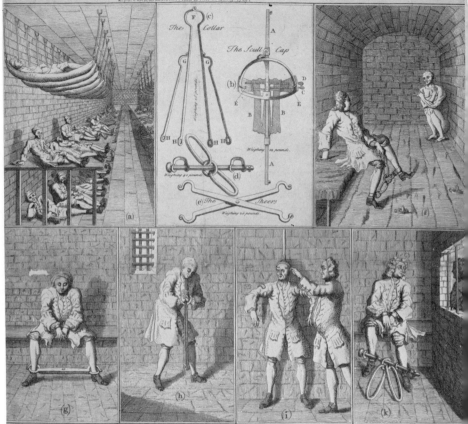

The first Draught (a) exhibited on this Plate, is a view of the Sick Mens Ward in the Marshalsea Prison, as in Page 4 in the last Report of ye Committee. In this small Place the Sick Men were crowded in a very affecting & melancholy condition, one Tire of them being disposed on ye Floor under a Press, a second Tire over them upon ye Press, and a Third Tire in Hammocks.――――The Draught (b) is the Iron Scull Cap, reported by the Ho. Committee in ye 8th Page of the last Report AA. is an Iron fastned at Top & Bottom to the walls, upon which the Scull Cap BB Slides higher or lower according to the height of the Man to be Tortured with it, C. the Screw which fixes the Cap, D is another Screw which presses the Parts EE on the Temples. It was with this Hellish Engine that The Bliss a Carpenter was tortured till the Blood started out of his Ears & Nose, the Draught (i) represents the manner it was fixed on him. His Thumbs were also put into Thumb screws which were screw'd so tight that the Blood started out of them.――――
The Draught (c) is mentioned in ye 8th Page of ye last Report, &b call'd the Collar, F is ye Part that goes round the Neck, G G the Cuffs for ye Wrists, H H are holes through which a piece of Iron passing screws the Instruments close, as represented figure (h) where Acton is shewn with ye Collar fixed on him. He being a lusty Man, was pressed to such a degree by this Collar, that his Eyes were ready to start out of his head, the Blood gushed out of his Ears & Nose, he foam'd at the Mouth, the slaver ran down, & he was not able to speak. After he had been tortured in this manner, he was for many days confined in the strong Room, loaded with heavy Irons call'd ye Sheers, the manner of using which will easily appear by viewing the Draught (g).――――(d) Are a sort of heavy fetters brought from the Marshalsea Prison, and used as in (k).――――(f) Is a view of the Strong Room in the Fleet Prison in which Jacob Mendes Solas, Capt. Sinclair, Sr. Wm. Rich & others have been confined, & in which Mr. Arne the Upholster, the Melancholy acct. of this Place may be read Page 10 of the first Report of ye Hon. Comittee Cap.n.――――M――― a Merchant of considerable Estate but a Prisoner by an extent, from ye Crown on acct of some securities he was formerly engaged for, Makes the following Relation. Viz that on ye 25 of June 1729 about 3 in ye Morning, a Spectre appeared to him & told him his Name was Arne, that he had been most inhumanely Starved to Death in that Place, & required him to send for one Mr. Gore, to converse with him about ye matter, & Justice might be done. The unhappy Gentleman says, this could be no delusion because he did not at that time know that any one had dy'd in ye Strong Room, nor did he ever hear Mr. Arne's Name before then. The aforesaid Mr. Gore was a Prisoner & an acquaintance of Arne's & on the Capn. speaking with him, did Affirm that Arne dyed in that place, & did believe his confinement there was the cause of his Death. NB. while the Capn. was in the Strong Room he was obliged to burn several Candles to take of the Dampness occasioned by the Common Shore running under it.――――May 1729.

183

The Representations
See p. 295

tail and collar on; the other side was a large folio, filled with wet and dry nurses, and houses to be let, and parrots, canary-birds, and setting-dogs to be sold.

Having no occasion for wet-nurses, etc., since my children sit by other folks' fires, and being desirous to give my Indian[1] a sight of the most remarkable things my time would allow me, we squeezed out of a throng of cuckolds, and went to make a visit to the madmen in Moorfields.

Bedlam[2] is a pleasant place, that it is, and abounds with amusements. The first is the building so stately a fabric for persons wholly insensible of the beauty and use of it; the outside is a perfect mockery to the inside, and admits of two amusing queries, whether the persons that ordered the building of it, or those that inhabit it, were the maddest? But what need I wonder at that, since the whole is but one entire amusement? Some were preaching, and others in full cry a-hunting; some were praying, others cursing and swearing; some were dancing, others groaning; some singing, others crying; and all in perfect confusion. A sad representation of the greater chimerical world! Only in this there's no whoring, cheating, or fleecing, unless after the Platonic mode, in thought, for want of action. However, any gentleman that is disposed for a touch of the times, may take his choice for the price of one penny, which is Cerberus's fee at the entry; or any lady that has got the *prurigo copulandi* has a spark at her service to be found walking here any time of the day. Is your wife or your daughter mad, for something that shall be nameless? Send 'em hither to be made sober. Or has any one a relation, male or female, that's over-bashful? Let not either him or her despair of a cure, for here are guests enough to teach 'em to part with their modesty.

As the buildings took their magnificence from a palace at Paris, so the company that resort to make assignations within 'em[3] very often bring off the Parisian distemper from the bottled ale and cheesecakes which are eaten after they are coupled and gone out of 'em; and if, in giving Bedlam the resemblance of the

[1] *The satiric device Brown used: the innocent stranger from another civilization who observes with astonishment the tortuous, mad complexities of sophisticated society.*
[2] *Hospital of St. Mary of Bethlehem, converted to asylum for insane in 1547. It was one of the public diversions of the time to visit the hospital and tease the inmates—admission, one penny.*
[3] *Bedlam was a popular place of business for the London whores.*

F

Louvre, we have been witty upon the French, they have been
even with us by making a present of a disease to us, which may
be bargained for with no more difficulty than half a turn in the
Long-Gallery.

Here were persons confined that having no money nor
friends, and but a small stock of confidence run mad for want
of preferment; a poet that, for want of wit and sense, ran mad
for want of victuals; and a hard-favoured citizen's wife, that lost
her wits because her husband had so little as to let her know that
he kept a handsome mistress. In this apartment was a common
lawyer pleading; in another a civilian sighing; a third enclosed
a Jacobite, ranting against the Revolution; and a fourth, a morose,
melancholy Whig, bemoaning his want of an office and complain-
ing against abuses at court, and mismanagements. A fifth had a
comical sort of a fellow, that was laughing at his physician,
Doctor Tyson, for his great skill in taciturnity; and a sixth had
a Cantabrigian organist for his tenant, that had left sonnet and
madrigal for philosophy, and had lost his senses while he was in
pursuit of knowledge. 'How now!' said I, 'honest friend, what
dost think of *materia prima*, and the rest of the pretended en-
tities?' 'I think,' said he, 'if you thought of 'em at all, you would
ask a more pertinent question; for I am mad because I know nothing of the matter, but thou art so much in love with ignorance
that thou wouldst have lost thy wits if thou hadst.'

I expected not such a home reply from a Bedlamite, and
without any more to do with such a touchy spark, left him railing
against the sin of murdering lice, and showing his detestation
against eating good roast-mutton, as a cruelty to the creatures,
and went to take a sight of a young fellow quite dumbfounded
with love. Poor lad! His mother and two sisters, that are milliners
in Oxford, I dare swear, will never keep him company; for they
know a trick worth two of his, and have often experimented,
that if one won't, another will. Here was Bishop the Quaker
preaching, and an audience of modest women peeping through
their fingers to see whether his notes were written in legible characters or no; and there was a shopkeeper's wife retailing out the
sight of the best in Christendom, for a half-penny a head, to young
Templers, Moorfields sharpers, and old citizens that had taken
the opportunity of their wives being abroad; and being ready to

run mad themselves, were come to divert themselves with the sight of those that were actually so.

Missing many others whom I thought deserved a lodging among their brethren, I made inquiry after them, and was told by the keeper that they had many other houses of the same foundation in the city, where they were disposed till they grew tamer, and were qualified to be admitted members of this soberer society. The projectors,[1] who are generally broken citizens, were cooped up in the Compters and Ludgate; the beaux and rakes, and common mad jilts, that labour under a *furor uteri*, in Bridewell, and Justice Long's powdering-tub; and the virtuosi[2] were confined to Gresham-College.[3] 'Those,' continued he, 'in whose constitutions folly has the ascendant over frenzy, are permitted to reside and be smoked in coffee-houses; and those that by the governors of this hospital are thought utterly incurable, are shut up in the Inns of Court and Chancery with a pair of foils, a fiddle, and a pipe; and when their fire and spirits are exhausted, and they begin to dote, they are removed by Habeas Corpus into a certain hospital built for that purpose near Amen-Corner.'...[4]

THE PLAYHOUSE[5]

The Playhouse is an enchanted island, where nothing appears in reality what it is nor what it should be. 'Tis frequented by persons of all degrees and qualities whatsoever, that have a great deal of idle time lying upon their hands and can't tell how to employ it worse. Here lords come to laugh, and to be laughed at for being there and seeing their qualities ridiculed by every worthless poet. Knights come hither to learn the amorous smirk, the *alamode* grin, the antic bow, the new-fashioned cringe, and how to adjust their phiz to make themselves as ridiculous by art as they are by nature.

Hither come the country gentlemen to shew their shapes, and trouble the pit with irrelevancies about hawking, hunting, their handsome wives and their housewifery. There sits a beau

[1] *Speculators or cheats.*
[2] *Experimenters engaged in scientific projects. The word had overtones of the absurdly speculative.*
[3] *The meeting-place of the Royal Society until 1710.*
[4] *The Royal College of Physicians.*
[5] *From* Amusement IV.

like a fool in a frame, that dares not stir his head nor move his body for fear of incommoding his wig, ruffling his cravat, or putting his eyes or mouth out of the order his *maître de dance* set it in; whilst a bully beau comes drunk into the pit, screaming out, 'Damn me, Jack, 'tis a confounded play, let's to a whore, and spend our time better.'

Here the ladies come to shew their clothes, which are often the only things to be admired in or about 'em; some of them having scabbed or pimpled faces wear a thousand patches to hide them, and those that have none, scandalize their faces by a foolish imitation. Here they shew their courage by being unconcerned at a husband being poisoned, a hero being killed, or a passionate lover being jilted; and shew their modesties by blushing at a bawdy song or naked, obscene figure. . . .

That beau there is known by the decent management of his sword-knot and snuff-box; a poet, by his empty pockets; a citizen, by his horns and gold-hatband; a whore, by a vizor-mask and a multitude of ribbons about her breast; and a fool by talking to her. A Playhouse wit is distinguished by wanting understanding; and a judge of wit, by nodding and sleeping till the fall of the curtain and the crowding to get out again, awake him.

I have told you already, that the Playhouse was the land of enchantment, the country of Metamorphoses, performed with the greatest speed imaginable. Here, in the twinkling of an eye, you shall see men transformed into demi-gods, and goddesses made as true flesh and blood as our common women, here fools, by sleight of hand, are converted into wits, honest-women into arrant whores, and, which is most miraculous, cowards into valiant heroes, and rank coquets and jilts into as chaste and virtuous mistresses as a man would desire to put his knife into. . . .

PHYSIC[1]

. . . Here[2] were also chirurgeons in great numbers, talking hard words to their patients, as solution of continuity, dislocations, fractures, amputation, phlebotomy, and spoke Greek words without understanding the English of them. One of the gravest among them propounded this question to the rest. 'Suppose a man

[1] *From* Amusement XI.
[2] *The Royal College of Physicians, which was in Warwick Lane from 1674 to 1825.*

falls from the main-yard, and lies all bruised upon the deck, pray what is the first intention in that case?' A brisk fellow answers, 'You must give him Irish slate *quantum sufficit*, and embrocate the parts affected *secundum artem*.' At which I seeming to smile, another reprimands me, saying 'What do you laugh at, Sir? the man's i'th' right on't.' To whom I replied, 'With reverence to your age and understanding, Sir, I think he's in the wrong; for if a man falls from the main-yard, the first intention is, To take him up again.'

Among all these people everything is made a mystery to detain their patients in ignorance, and keep up the market of Physic; but were not the very terms of art and names of their medicines sufficient to fright away any distempers, 'tis to be feared their remedies would prove worse than the disease.

That nothing might be wanting in this famous college, there were others, as corn-cutters and tooth-drawers, that like porters and plasterers stood ready to be hired. The first will make you halt before the best friend you have, and if you do but yawn, the other knaves will be examining your grinders, depopulate your mouth, and make you old before your time; taking as much for drawing out an old tooth as would buy a set of new ones.

An ugly accident happened while we were viewing the curiosities of this college. A boy had swallowed a knife, and the members of the college being sitting, he was brought among them to be cured, if it were possible. The chirurgeons claimed the patient as belonging to their fraternity, and one of 'em would have been poking a crane's bill down his throat to pluck it up again, but the doctors would not suffer him.

After a long consultation, one of these two remedies was agreed on, viz. that the patient should swallow as much *aqua fortis* as would dissolve the knife into minute particles, and bring it away by siege; but the other remedy was more philosophical, and therefore better approved, and that was to apply a loadstone to his arse, and so draw it out by magnetic attraction. But which of the two was put in practice I know not, for I did not stay to see the noble experiment, though my particular friend, Dr. W——d[1] was the first that proposed that remedy, and he is no quack, I assure you.

[1] *Dr. John Woodward, Professor of Physics at Gresham College.*

Not but that there are some quacks as honest fellows as you would desire to piss upon. This foreigner here, for instance, is a man of conscience, that will ask you but half a crown a bottle for as good Lamb's-Conduit water as ever was in the world. He pretends it has an occult quality that cures all distempers. He swears it, since this very individual water has cured him of poverty, which comprehends all diseases.

'Tis with physicians in London, as with almanacs, the newest are the most consulted; but then their reign, like that of an almanac, concludes with the year.

When a sick man leaves all for nature to do, he hazards much; when he leaves all for the doctor to do, he hazards more; and since there is a hazard both ways, I would much sooner choose to rely upon nature. For this, at least, we may be sure of, that she acts as honestly as she can, and that she does not find her account in prolonging the disease....

Compared with his year of glory, 1700, the last years of Brown's life were uneventful, though exciting enough for any normal existence. There were still a few minor controversies to struggle over, a few more pieces to write. The famous *Letters from the Dead to the Living* were written then, and his *Adventures of Lindamira*, a form of epistolary novel, as well as the usual stint of translations. Translations were the bread and butter of Brown's life—he was, in fact, one of the best-known translators of the day, along with Dryden, L'Estrange and Peter Motteux. His translation, entire or in part, of the *Colloquies of Erasmus* from the Latin, *The Works of Scarron* from the French, and *Don Quixote* from the Spanish, are still readable and in some respects superior to the many translations since. But after all the wars and the glory and the gallons of claret, Brown's last years were wretched. His reckless habits of living got him deeper into debt and much of his time was spent in the sponging house, where he was forced to write continually to keep from going to prison. Boyce[1] quotes an interesting passage from Alexander Smith's *The Comical and Tragical History of the Lives ... of the Most Noted Bayliffs in and About London*, about the bailiff Jacob Broad,

[who kept his customers] close to their business, particularly Tom

[1] Op cit., *p. 173*.

Brown the poet, who being once very remiss in writing a book for Hartley the Bookseller.[1] ... Jacob goes to Tom's lodging, where he acquainted his landlord and landlady he had an action against him at the suit of the aforesaid Hartley, but knowing his circumstances to be but mean, he would not willingly take him, unless he came full—but in his way; however, he advised them to tell Tom, to make the matter up with the plaintiff as soon as he could, for fear worse should come of it. This so much frightened Tom out of his wits, that he kept as close in his garret as a broken shopkeeper in a privileged place, and he writes like a d——l, till he had wrought his redemption out of his adversary's hands.

Brown, however, did not escape prison, as we see from his poem, 'The Mourning Poet'; and in his last years his dissolute life had caught up with him. His health had failed, he had become bitter and melancholy. But there is still a certain defiance even in his last poems.

'The Poet's Condition' is mere doggerel—Brown has done better. It is not autobiographical; Brown never married, nor to one's knowledge supported four children. Yet the poet's condition, in many respects, was Brown's condition in the last years of his life. It reflects his mood.

The Poet's Condition

Without formal petition
Thus stands my condition:
I am closely blocked up in a garret,
Where I scribble and smoke,
And sadly invoke
The powerful assistance of claret.
Four children and a wife,
'Tis hard on my life,
Beside myself and a muse,
To be all clothed and fed,
Now the times are so dead,
By my scribbling of doggerel and news.

[1] *John Hartley published in Holborn and Fleet Street. He was the publisher of many important books, including Bentley's* Dissertation upon the Epistles of Phalaris *(1709)* *(Plomer).*

And what I shall do,
I'm a wretch if I know,
So hard is the fate of a poet;
I must either turn rogue,
Or, what's as bad, pedagogue,
And so drudge like a thing that has no wit.
My levee's all duns,
Attended by bums,
And my landlady too she's a teaser,
At least four times a day
She warns me away,
And what can a man do to please her?
Here's the victualler and vintner,
The cook and the printer,
With their myrmidons hovering about, sir:
The tailor and draper,
With the cur that sells paper,
That, in short, I dare not stir out, sir,
But my books sure may go,
My master Ovid's did so,
And tell how doleful the case is;
If it don't move your pity,
To make short of my ditty,
'Twill serve you to wipe your arses.

'Farewell to Poor England' was written just before he died:

Farewell to Poor England;

Farewell false friends, farewell ill wine,
Farewell all women with design;
Farewell all pocky cheating punks,
Farewell lotteries, farewell banks;
And England, I'm leaving thee,
May say, farewell to poverty:
 Adieu, where e're I go, I'm sure to find,
 Nothing so ill, as that I leave behind.

Farewell nation without sense,
Farewell exchequer without pence;

Farewell Army with bare feet;
Farewell navy without meat;
Farewell wrighting fighting beauxs,
And farewell useless plenipoes.
  Adieu, &c.

Farewell you *Good Old Cause*, promoters,
Farewell bribed artillery voters;
Farewell to all attainting bills,
And record which for witness kills;
Farewell to laymen's villainy,
And farewell church-men's perjury;
  Adieu, &c.

Instead of one king, farewell nine,
And all who associating sign;
Farewell you gulled unthinking fops,
Poor broken merchants empty shops;
Farewell packed judges, culled for blood,
With eight years war for England's good;
  Adieu, &c.

Farewell you judges, who dispense,
With perjured cut-throat evidence;
Farewell thou haughty little mouse,
With those that choose thee for the house;
Farewell long—and spiteful looks,
With Reverend Oates, and all his books
  Adieu, &c.

Adieu once more, Britannia fare thee well,
And if all this wont mend thee,
May the D—— triumph in your spoil,
May beggary run throughout your isle,
And no one think it worth his while
To take up to defend thee.

NED WARD

After Tom Brown, the other major Grub Street figure is Ned Ward. Ward was not born a gentleman, as Brown was, he did not attend university, his style is less subtle, more coarse. In fact, it is one of the most raucous on Grub Street, and the liveliest. Not being a university man, he lived more circumspectly than Brown, though he had his share of poverty and claret. He ended up a well-fed tavern-keeper.

Ward began his professional life in the traditional Grub Street manner, as we see from this bit of doggerel, written in 1691, which he claims to be autobiographical:

The Author's Lamentation.

A shirt I have on, little better than none,
   In colour much like to a cinder,
So thin and so fine, it is my design,
   To present it the muses for tinder.

My blue fustian breeches, so fall'n are in stitches,
   You may see what my legs have between 'em,
My pockets all four, I'm a son of a whore,
   If the devil a penny be in 'em.

A hat I have on, which so greasy is grown,
   It remarkable is for its shining,
One side is stitched up, 'stead of button and loop,
   But the devil a bit of a lining.

My coat it is turned, with the lappets piss-burned,
   So out at the arm-pits and elbows,
That I look as absurd, as a seaman on board,
   That has lain half a year in the Bilboes.

I have stockens 'tis true, but the devil a shoe,
   I am forced to wear boots all weathers,
Till I've broke my spur-rowls, and damned my boot soles,
   And confounded my upper leathers.

My beard is grown long, as hogs bristles and strong,
   Which the wenches so woundily stare-at,
The colour is whey, mixed with orange and grey,
   With a little small spice of the carrot.

I have a long sword, you may tak't on my word,
   For the blade is a Toledo trusty,
The handle is bound, with a black ribbon round,
   And the basket-hilt damnable rusty.

O had you but seen, the sad state I was in,
   You'd not find such a poet in twenty,
I'd nothing that's full, but my shirt and my skull,
   For my guts and my pockets are empty.

As true as I live, I have but one sleeve,
   Which I wear in the room of a cravat,
In this plight I wait, to get an estate,
   But the devil knows when I shall have it.

The legacy which he had expected never materialized, and he arrived in London with only his wits, a lively talent and an empty stomach. Those first years from 1691 to 1698 could not have been encouraging. He obviously was writing, but his name does not appear in the title-pages or in the gossip of the day. There was evidently no money in putting the name Ned Ward on a title page even if he was published. There is one title we can attribute to him, however, *Female Policy Detected, or the Arts of a Designing Woman laid Open,* published in 1695. This seems to be a set piece, unabashed hack work, to milk the current demand for books on women. The role of women had been changing in the 17th century. The first rumblings of emancipation were being heard and men were getting alarmed. But alarm is the element from which sales are made and Grub Street accordingly poured out a large number of publications on the subject of women, how women should be educated, what they should talk about and do with themselves, their strengths and weaknesses, their virtues and vices. Few of those pamphlets were intended to be taken seriously—they were commodities for sale. Women were admonished, flattered, patronized, and almost always pandered to, because they now had become readers. Ward's book appealed by provocation, taking the orthodox line that women were a sly lot, a constant threat to a young man's virtue. Luckily, Ward had provided the men with just the guidance they needed to defend themselves:

THE
EPISTLE DEDICATORY
TO THE
Apprentices of LONDON.

As there is nothing tends more to the destruction of youth, or renders 'em the more incapable of considering their own welfare than the conversation of intriguing women, I thought, young men, I could not do a better service in this age, where to tempt cunningly, and deceive slyly, are the study of the female sex, than present you with a pocket-piece, which shall serve as armour to defend you from the darts thrown by wanton and designing women.

When one considers the coarseness of Ward's writing, its carefree obscenity, the heavy moralizing of 'Female Policy Detected'[1] makes amusing reading. It is the pure spirit of hack writing, refined of any trace of sincerity, dedicated to the simple principle of earning a living:

Of the Allurements of WOMEN.

Of all vices, an unlawful freedom with the female sex, is the most predominant; and of all sins hath the most powerful temptations and many allurements to betray and draw men into this folly. The inducements of the fair sex are so prevailing, a propensity in nature so forcible, it is hard to stand unmoved, when tempted forward by the charms of a subtle woman, and drove by the frail desires of an unbounded lust.

But as there is no passion too strong to be conquered, or temptation too great to be refitted; so if you will observe the maxims I shall give you in this little treatise, you'll be armed against beauty;

[1] *From* Female Policy Detected, *published 1695.*

Be careful how you conceive too good an opinion of a woman at first sight, for you see not the woman truly, but her ornaments. Paint, patches and fine dresses are to hide defects; for beauty, like truth is always best when plainest.

Many in rich ornaments look inviting whose beauty, when they undress, flies away with their apparel, and leaves you (as Juno did Ixion) nothing but a cloudy mistress to embrace.

If you like a woman, and would discover if she be in nature, what she may seem by art, surprise her in a morning undress, and it is ten to one, but you will find your goddess hath shifted of her divinity, and the angel you so much admired turned into a Magmillion.

Be always jealous of a maid who extols her own virtue; a wife who exclaims against her own husband in his absence and a widow that courts your company; for when a woman praises her virtues 'tis as a shopkeeper does a commodity, desiring to be rid of it; and she that sticks not to lay open the failings of her husband to another, will to the same man, lay open herself, whenever he shall require it of her, and when a widow seems fond of your conversation, be sure 'tis through design, and if you are not careful she will bury you alive.

Be not tempted to pick up any woman in the street, but if you should, be sure you have an eye before, and another behind; for wheresoever lust leads, danger follows. . . .

He that serves the lust of a woman, makes himself her monkey, for she admires him no longer than while he is playing with his tail.

Be careful how you live upon a whore as how you keep one; for by the former you will get nothing, and by the latter lose everything you have got. . . .

Think not every woman rich that wears gay apparel, for many forfeit their virtue to maintain their pride. . . .

Covet therefore no woman's love, but whom you will be diligent to oblige, for small neglect is taken by them as a great ingratitude.

Deal with a revengeful woman as with a hand-granado, which you cast from you as soon as the fuse is lighted, lest it burn to the prejudice of him that fired it.

Have no familiarity with her you have highly disobliged, lest bee-like, she stings you with her tail. . . .

Take not always a woman's frowns as slights, nor her smiles as a sure argument of her love; for every time the sun is clouded, it does not predict foul weather, and when it shines out, a storm may be near at hand. Women can dissemble their passions, and change their looks, as a scorpion can its colour.

A woman's love is like to vinegar, which can never be reduced to its primitive goodness, but will always remain sour till it's dead....

Evidently Ward felt that he was on to a good thing, because there was a sequel:

THE SECOND-BOOK,

A Pleasant and Profitable

DISCOURSE

In Defence of

MARRIED-MEN,

Against Peevish, Fretful,

SCOLDING-WIVES,

With Several Notable Examples of the
Mischiefs and Miseries which have Attended
Their Lust and Pride.

Having in the foregoing book laid down proper rules and maxims for the avoiding the arts of a designing woman I shall now to deter men from running headlong upon a marriage-state, without consideration, entertain them with a discourse of their other most shameful and abominable vices, and that somewhat longer than the former, whereby they may see what vanity, misery, mischief and ruin attends an implacable, noisy, scolding wife....

There is no question that Ward pandered to public taste. That was his *métier*. Like any craftsman, he was conscious of his techniques: 'If anybody should wonder why I couched some of the poems under such surprising titles, I must needs tell them, I borrowed my method from our Moorfields conjurors, who use their utmost art to put on a terrible countenance, that everybody that gazes on their outsides may think the devil is in them; and they undoubtedly find it a very useful policy; for I have commonly observed, that he thrives the best, and has his door most crowded, that can look most frightful.'[1] And behind the title-page in Ward's mature writings was the same artistic concern about catching the reader's interest and holding it. Troyer quotes this advertisement from Ward's bookseller: 'Here's pleasant poetry for the youthful, that love the jingling of rhyme, and merry prose for the graver Christian readers. . . . Here are amorous intrigues to oblige the ladies; tales, jests, flirts, puns, and conundrums, to tickle the fancies of the witty; also rambles, drunken frolics, squabbles, wrangles, and rencounters, to please nocturnal tiplers.' This is a fairly accurate description of Ward's writings. He was continually conscious of a changing public taste. When *trips* were popular, he produced *trips*. When the *character* was popular he produced *characters,* playing the variations in every conceivable way, with an ingenuity that kept him one step ahead of his rivals. When the market was brisk for articles on women, Ned Ward wrote on women:

THE
BATCHELOR'S ESTIMATE
of the
EXPENCES OF A MARRIAGE L I F E, &c.[2]

Sir,

To the proposal you made me (for which I acknowledge the obligation, because I am sure it proceeded from your good opinion of me) I return the following answer.

You propose I should marry your relation, who is worth £2000 down, which is indeed a handsome fortune, and such that I have the modesty to think I do not deserve, yet at present cannot accept of the proposal, because the following necessary expenses arise so frequently, and so openly to my view, that I must own, whenever I have thought of matrimony, they have (contrary to thy real inclination) deterred me from entering into that agreeable state.

---

[1] *Quoted from Howard W. Troyer,* Ned Ward of Grub Street, *Cambridge, Mass., 1946, p. 122.*
[2] *Published 1725.*

I now live in chambers, which cost me £12 10s. a year, as soon as married I must take a house, which I cannot have suitable to me and my business under £50 so that there will be a yearly increase in house-rent only.

	£	s.	d.
	37	10	0

Church, window and poor's taxes, payments to Rector Reader and Lecturer, Water, trophy-money, militia, lamp, scavenger, watch, constable, etc. which I am now free from, must be paid, which cannot amount to less than

	£	s.	d.
	9	0	0

Expenses of tea, coffee, chocolate, sugar, spirits, and fresh supply of China yearly

	£	s.	d.
	12	0	0

To my bed maker, I pay about 50s. a year, when married I must keep two maid servants and a man, whose wages, and the man's livery, must at least come to £20 a year, so that here is an extraordinary expense of

	£	s.	d.
	17	10	0

Coach, and chair-hire, for my wife to make visits, take the air, to see plays, etc. as a reasonable and yearly computation.

	£	s.	d.
	3	10	0
Her expenses at those diversions	3	10	0

I now seldom go to see above a play in a year. I must in complaisance to my wife sometimes wait on her and partake of those entertainments (for it is not proper she should go alone) which I will moderately compute at

	£	s.	d.
	1	10	0

It costs me now about 40s. a year in coals, I am sure it must then cost me £10 so that here is another yearly increase of expense.

	£	s.	d.
	8	0	0
The same of candles in proportion	5	0	0
My wife's necessary wearing apparel.	30	0	0
	127	10	0

Having a family of my own, I shall diminish little or nothing else out of the expenses of my dinners, as to the evening expenses, you know married men go abroad as often at that time as bachelors, and I won't promise to be more uxorious than my neighbours, so instead of £25 a year at the most it now costs me in dinners, I shall have the following bills to pay yearly, viz.

	£	s.	d.
From the former calculation	127	10	0
The Butcher	35	0	0
Poulterer	10	0	0
Fishmonger	6	0	0
Herb-woman	7	0	0
Oilman	5	0	0
Baker	8	0	0
Brewer	10	0	0
Grocer	6	0	0
Confectioner	2	0	0
Cheesemonger	4	0	0
Wine, Cider, &c. at a moderate computation	30	0	0
Fruiterer	1	10	0
Milk-woman	1	0	0
Salt, Small coal, Rotten-stone, Brick-dust, Sand, Oat-meal, Whiteing, and many other little ingredients in housekeeping I am ignorant of	2	0	0
	255	0	0

So that deducting thereout the £25 being the charge of my dinners, there will be a necessary additional expense of

	£	s.	d.
	230	0	0

If my wife pleases me, as I do not doubt but your relation will, (I know my own temper so well in that respect, that) I shall be often making her presents of either rings, jewels, snuff-boxes, watch, tweezers, some knick-knacks, and things of that nature, in which, one year with another, I am sure I shall expend

5	0	0
Brought forward 235	0	0

Then comes an article I least wish for, but happens in most families, which is, the expenses of doctor and apothecary, and though it is accidental, yet one year with another cannot come short of

£	s.	d.
5	0	0
240	0	0

As for children, I dare say, our attempts in that respect will not prove fruitless, and that we may reasonably expect one in every two years, if not oftener, but it shall not be my fault if it does not.

The expense of lying-inn, childbed-linen, midwife, nurses, cawdles, possets, cradle, christenings &c. must at least be £30 so that if it should happen once in two years, it may be reckoned a yearly expense of

15	0	0

Nursing, maintaining, education, clothes, schooling of our children even in their infancy, and which must be increased as they advance in years, besides their fortunes (which must be saved or got) at a random calculation, and vastly less than I am satisfied it will be

	30	0	0
Pew in the Church	2	0	0
Washing my wife's and the family linen,	8	0	0
Repairs of furniture, new brooms, mops,			
brushes, and rubbers	2	0	0
	297	0	0

The furniture of my house, and table-linen, cannot come short of £300 which with £50 for plate (without which, being so moderate a quantity, I dare say my wife, nor indeed should I myself be satisfied) will lie dead, daily decrease in its value, and bring me in no income, I must therefore reckon my wife's fortune (in point of its bringing me in a yearly income) at no more than £1650.

Now, Sir, as you have been a housekeeper, and married these several years, pray tell me, if any one article, I have charged too much? Whether if I have not under charged them, and omitted several? That I, not being acquainted with these sort of things, can have no knowledge of.

If therefore it is a moderate computation, and necessary supposing interest to continue at five per cent. (which is unlikely) the produce of £1650 is only £82 10s. and if it should fall to four per cent. is only £66. In the one case, I must necessarily expend on my wife £231 10s. in the other £215 above the income of the fortune she brings, besides the hazard and want of certainty for the money, which ought to be considered, and though it be necessary, yet how reasonable it is I submit to you.

These things considered (and he that marries without previous consideration acts very indiscreetly) I do not see how I can marry a woman with the fortune you propose, or that I should better myself at all by it, and in prudence, people should do so, or let it alone, (not that I propose or think to have more) I must therefore live single, though with some regret that I cannot do otherwise, and increase my own fortune, which happens to be sufficient for my own maintenance (till if I may so call it) I can afford matrimony.

I wish the lady all happiness and a better husband, and if it be for her satisfaction one who has thought less of the matter, not but that I have very good opinion of matrimony, and think of it with pleasure, hoping at one time or other to enter into its list but I now wait with patience, till my circumstances or thoughts vary.

One thing I would not have you mistaken in, is that I do not mean that your relation will be thus expensive to me, more than any other, only that whenever I marry, let her be who she will, I must necessary (if she has no more fortune than you propose) expend considerably more than £200 a year on her, above the income of her fortune, and at present I cannot persuade myself to be at so great an expense, for the value of trying a dangerous experiment, whether the pleasures of matrimony are yearly worth that sum? All which is submitted to your consideration by

Sir, Your most obliged humble Servant.

The supreme advantage of this cash-resgister attitude to marriage is that it demands an answer. It reeks of a masculine arrogance that must have infuriated Ward's female readers and creates a provocative issue where none had existed. This is sound journalistic practice. So Ned Ward, having played the reluctant bachelor, can now play the irate father and give the bachelor the answer he deserves, thus extracting two articles from the one idea. The answer was entitled: THE WOMAN'S ADVOCATE/or the /BAUDY BATCHELOR/Out in his/CALCULATION/Being the Genuine/ANSWER/Paragraph by Paragraph,/To the/BATCHE-LOR'S ESTIMATE/Plainly proving/That MARRIAGE is to a Man of Sense and/Economy, both a Happier and Less Charge-able/STATE, than a Single LIFE./Written for the Honour of the Good WIVES and pretty GIRLS of Old England. The father not only questions the bachelor's calculations but denies that he ever made the proposal; he would not have such a man for his daughter's hand even if he were willing. By adding a dash of soap opera to his championing of the cause of women, Ward is able to create a very marketable product.

Another feature of the times was the provocative use of titles. Here is an example of a Ned Ward title:

Nuptial

DIALOGUES AND DEBATES:

OR, AN

USEFUL PROSPECT

OF THE

FELICITIES AND DISCOMFORTS

OF A

MARRY'D LIFE,

Incident to all Degrees, from the Throne

to the COTTAGE,

Containing

Many great Examples of Love, Piety, Prudence, Justice, and all
the excellent virtues that largely contribute to the true happiness of Wedlock. Drawn from the Lives of our own Princes,
Nobility, and other Quality, in Prosperity and Adversity.

Also the fantastical Humours of all Fops, Coquets, Bullies, Jilts,
fond Fools, and Wantons: old fumblers, barren Ladies, Misers,
parsimonious Wives, Ninnies, Sluts and Termagants; drunken
Husbands, toping gossips, schismatical precisians, and devout
Hypocrites of all sorts.

Digested into serious, merry, and satyrical Poems, wherein both
Sexes, in all Stations, are reminded of their Duty, and taught
how to be happy in a Matrimonial State.

Titles like this, juicy with expectation, were a Ward speci-
alty, even if what followed did not always fulfil the expectation.
For example, 'The Insinuating Bawd: and the Repenting Harlot.
Written by a Whore at Tunbridge, and Dedicated to a Bawd
at the Bath', turns out to be a poem on how Little Nell goes
wrong:

> Ladies beware, let miserable me.
> The sad example of a harlot be:
> Let not loose women tempt you to the hook,
> With which themselves unwarily were took;
> For if you're once betrayed, you'll surely find,
> You're cursed from the first moment you are kind.

Ned Ward served a long Grub Street apprenticeship. In
1698 he got into debt again and this time had to flee to Jamaica.
But it was the beginning of his success. He returned in a short
time, bitter about the conditions he discovered there, and published anonymously a pamphlet entitled, *A Trip to Jamaica.*
Within a year it had gone through six editions. Here is an excerpt:

A Character of JAMAICA

The dunghill of the universe, the refuse of the whole creation, the clippings of the elements, a shapeless pile of rubbish con-

fusedly jumbled into an emblem of the chaos, neglected by omnipotence when he formed the world into its admirable order. The
nursery of heaven's judgements, where the malignant seeds of all
pestilence were first gathered and scattered through the regions
of the earth, to punish mankind for their offences. The place
where Pandora filled her box, where Vulcan forged Jove's thun-
der-bolts, and that Phaeton, by his rash misguidance of the sun,
scorched into a cinder. The receptacle of vagabonds, the sanc-
tuary of bankrupts, and a close-stool for the purges of our prisons.
As sickly as a hospital, as dangerous as the plague, as hot as hell,
and as wicked as the devil. Subject to tornadoes, hurricanes and
earthquakes, as if the island, like the people, were troubled with
the dry belly-ache. . . .

Of Port-Royal.

It is an island distinct from the main of Jamaica, though
before the earthquake, it joined by a neck of land to the Palisados,
but was separated by the violence of an inundation (through God's
mercy) to prevent the wickedness of their metropolis diffusing
itself by communication, over all the parts of the country, and
so call that judgement upon the whole, which fell more particularly upon the sinfulest part.

From a spacious fine built town (according to report) it is
now reduced, by the encroachments of the sea, to a little above a
quarter of a mile in length, and about half so much the breadth,
having so few remains left of its former splendour, I could think
no otherwise, but that every traveller who had given its description, made large use of his licence. The houses are low, little, and
irregular; and if I compare the best of their streets in Port-Royal,
to the fag-end of Kent Street, where the broom-men live, I do
them more than justice.

About ten a clock in the morning, their nostrils are saluted
with a land breeze, which blowing o'er the island, searches the
bowels of the mountains, (being always cracked and full of vents,
by reason of excessive heat) bringing along with it such sulphurous
vapours, that I have feared the whole island would have burst
out into a flaming Etna, or have stifled us with suffocating fumes,
like that of melted mineral and brimstone.

In the afternoon, about four a clock, they might have the

refreshment of a sea breeze, but suffering the negroes to carry all their nastiness to windward of the town, that the nauseous effluvias which arise from their stinking dunghills, are blown in upon them; thus what they might enjoy as a blessing, they ungratefully pervert by their own ill management.

They have a church, 'tis true, but built rather like a market house; and when the flock were in their pens and the pastor exalted to overlook his sheep, I took a survey round me, and saw more variety of scarecrows than ever was seen at the Feast of Ugly-faces.

Everything is very dear, and an ingenious or an honest man may meet with this encouragement, to spend a hundred pounds before he shall get a penny. Madeira wine and bottle beer are fifteen pence the bottle; nasty claret, half a crown; Rhenish, five shillings; and their best Canary, ten bits, or six and three pence. They have this pleasure in drinking, that what they put into their bellies, they may soon stroke out of their fingers' ends; for instead of exonerating, they fart; and sweat instead of pissing.

Since 'trips' were saleable, a few months later Ward wrote *A Trip to New England, with a Character of the Country and People, both English and Indians*.[1] There is no evidence that Ward even took the trip. He had discovered the technique of writing 'trips' without having to make them. And the *Trip to New England* sold because it was written 'By the Author of the *Trip to Jamaica*'. His name had become worthy of a title-page.

A
TRIP
to
New England, &c.

Bishops, bailiffs, and bastards, were the three terrible persecutions which chiefly drove our unhappy brethren to seek their fortunes in our foreign colonies. One of these bugbears, I confess, frighted me from the blessings of my own dear native country; and forced me to the fatigue of a long voyage, to escape a scouring.

[1] *Published 1699.*

But whether zeal, debt, or the sweet sin of procreation, begot in my conscience those fears, which hurried me a great many leagues beyond my senses, I am as unwilling to declare to the world as a Romish damsel that has lost her maidenhead is to confess her frailty to the priest.

For many years my mind sat as easy in my breast as an alderman in an elbow-chair, till the Devil envying my felicity, flung so many crosses and losses in my way, that every step I took in my occupation, I was timorous of tumbling.

I thought it then high time to seek for balm, but finding none in Gilead, I was moved by the spirit of necessity, to forsake ungodly London, for religious Boston in New England; hoping to purify myself by the way in an ocean of brine, that when I got thither, I might find my condition, as well as my conscience, in a tolerable pickle, fitted for the conversation of the saints in so holy a land.

I packed up my alls in order for my voyage; and embarked the ship the *Prudent Sarah,* at Gravesend, who was weighing anchor, with a fair wind for The Downs, that I had no leisure to step back to London to satisfy my creditors; but, like a girl that's ravished, was forced, with a very good will, to do that which I intended.

Every stranger is unavoidably forced to take this notice, that in Boston, there are more religious zealots than honest men, more parsons than churches, and more churches than parishes: for the town, unlike the people, is subject to no division.

The inhabitants seem very religious, showing many outward and visible signs of an inward and spiritual grace. But though they wear in their faces the innocence of doves, you will find them in their dealings, as subtle as serpents. Interest is their faith, money their god, and large possessions the only heaven they covet.

Election, commencement, and training days, are their only holy days; they keep no saints days, nor will they allow the Apostles to be Saints, yet they assume that sacred dignity to themselves; and say, in the title page of their Psalm Book, 'Printed for the Edification of the Saints in Old and New England'.

They have been very severe against adultery, which they punished with death; yet, notwithstanding the harshness of their law, the women are of such noble souls, and undaunted resolutions, that they will run the hazard of being hanged, rather than not be revenged on matrimony, or forbear to discover the corruption of their own natures.

If you kiss a woman in public, though offered as a courteous salutation, if any information is given to the Select Members, both shall be whipped or fined. It's an excellent law to make lovers in private make much of their time, since open lip-lechery is so dearly purchased. But the good humoured lasses, to make you amends, will kiss the kinder in a corner.

Public kissing, and single fornication are both of a price; for which reason the women wisely consider, the latter may be done with more safety than the former; and if they chance to be detected, and are forced to pay the fine, they are sure beforehand of something for their money.

A captain of a ship who had been a long voyage, happened to meet his wife, and kissed her in the street; for which he was fined ten shillings, and forced to pay the money. What a happiness, thought I, do we enjoy in Old England, that can not only kiss our own wives, but other men's too without the danger of such a penalty.

Another inhabitant of the town was fined ten shillings for kissing his own wife in his garden; and obstinately refusing to pay the money, endured twenty lashes at the gun: who, in revenge of his punishment, swore he would never kiss her again, either in public or private. And at this rate, one of the delightfulest customs in the world, will in time be quite thrown out of fashion, to the old folk's satisfaction, but to the young ones' lamentation, who love it as well in New England, as we do in the Old. . . .

The women here, are not at all inferior in beauty to the ladies of London, having rather the advantage of a better complexion; but as for the men, they are generally meagre; and have got the hypocritical knack, like our English Jews, of screwing their faces into such puritanical postures that you would think they were always praying to themselves, or running melancholy mad about some mystery in the Revelations: so that it is rare to see a handsome man in the country, for they have all one cast, but of what tribe I know not.

A woman that has lost her reputation, hath lost her portion; her virginity is all her treasure : and yet the merry lasses esteem it but a trifle, for they had rather, by far, lose that than their teeming-time.

The gravity and piety of their looks, are of great service to these American Christians: it makes strangers that come amongst them, give credit to their words. And it is a proverb with those that know them, 'Whosoever believes a New England saint, shall be sure to be cheated; and he that knows how to deal with their traders, may deal with the devil and fear no craft.'. . .

Trips were now selling briskly on the Grub Street market and Ward reached for every conceivable variation to stretch out a good thing. His next 'trips' were closer to home, for example, *A Frolick to Horn-Fair*,[1] which is coarse stuff, even for Ward :

A
FROLICK
to
Horn-Fair.

. . . When the happy morning came, and nothing but cuckold-makers, cuckoldom, cuckolds, and Horn-Fair, were the common discourses of every sober citizen to his next neighbour, as soon as the shops were opened, I getting up an hour before my time, had recourse to the barber's, that my face and periwig might not want the advantages of his nice management, but have all the effeminate improvement of powder, washball and perfume, that I might be as fragrant to my mistress' nostrils, as a Bermuda breeze, and smell as odoriferous as any sweet-bag. When I was thus washed, curled, and combed, like any lady's lapdog; and after I had spent as much time in dressing, as a merchant's wife on a Sunday before churchtime, I did at last judge by my glass I was a very complete figure to make an amour, though to a squeamish lady. My shoes were as black as Spanish balls could make 'em, and shone like a physician's ebony cane new rubbed upon a visit to an alderman. My stockings were gartered up as tight as a boot upon a last, and stuck as close to my calves as a bag to a boiled pudding. My garters being as hard girted as a

---

[1] A Frolick to Horn-Fair, *with a walk from Cuckold's Point thro' Deptford and Greenwich (1699).*

fillet bound for bleeding, that I did more penance than a man half throttled to be pricked in the jugular. My knees hooped round with rolls, turned up with that exactness, that a wedding ring upon a citizen's wife's thumb, could no ways fit more precisely regular. My breeches stuck so close to the ignoblest of my flesh, that I durst not stride an inch beyond the given bounds of my tailor, without the danger of a rent; and when I came to a broad kennel I was forced to wade through, because I could not venture to step over without damage. My coat was cut all-amode a Paree, with skirts not much longer than those of a waterman's jacket. My linen was made by an Inns-of-Court sempstress, and was digitized with her handle-bauble fingers, into as much formality as a lady's headdress. My wig, like the rest of the fools, was so woundily bepowdered, that whenever the wind sat in my face, it endangered the eyes of him that walked behind me. Which procured me as many curses in a day, as a good man has prayers for his charity. My hat was in the mathematical cock, with the brims tucked up to the crown, into an exact triangle. My gloves were right cordivant, and stank so of Muscovy cat's turd, that persons subject to vapours started from me as I walked (like a beau from a chimney-sweeper) for fear of being suffocated. Thus equipped according to the nice rules of foppery and courtship, I went along, cursing the rudeness of the wind, that at every street's corner ruffled the curls of my wig into some disorder, being forced to give as many strokes to each bushy side as a milk woman does to a cow's teat at a meal, to reduce the straggling hairs into their proper places: till at last, with a panting heart, like a dispirited lover, I came to the place appointed; where, with as much courage as I could summon together, I asked for my lady, who was not yet come. I thinking it my duty to wait, rather than hers, it made me careful to be something earlier than the time prefixed, to manifest my diligence, as well as the eager desires I had to her dear company. I bid 'em show me a room, and then called for a pint of canary, as the most amorous cordial I could think on, over which, I sat near half an hour, sometimes disheartening myself with the thoughts of being jilted, then comforting myself up with the assurance of her sincerity, from some little knowledge I had of her person. At last, to remove my doubts and jealousies, in steps my lady, dressed up with as much art, as if all the tirewomen in both Exchanges had been her chambermaids. But, to tell you the truth on't, finding her no more afraid of tumbling her pinners, than I was of rumpling my cravat, our greeting was so mutually kind and satisfactory, that it would have made the reader's heart go pit-a-pat to have seen our loving salutation. She begging pardon for her presumption, and desiring my good construction of the freedom she had taken. I answering her in a familiar dialect, that her company was the only happiness I had long coveted; and had not the conjugal obligations she lay under frighted me from discovering my love, she long before now should have received sufficient testimonies of my inextinguishable affections; or had I in the least known the just reasons she had to withdraw her friendship, and alienate that beauty and delight remaining in her dear self from her marriage bed, no addresses and importunities should have been wanting from her humble servant, to have happily supplied those impotencies, which, according to the laws both divine and humane, she might modestly complain of. . . .

Citizens and their mates, swarm now to the waterside, in order to take boat for the horn-headed rendezvous at Charlton: and nothing being heard beneath our window, but the wrangling of watermen about their fares, and the noisy mouthing acclamations of 'Greenwich, Greenwich Ho!' that had we been seated at the Hockly Hole Theatre, when the blind bear had been let loose, our ears could not have been terrified with more discording outcries. Upon which we arose from our seats, and moved to the window, to divert ourselves a little with seeing the bachelor cuckold-makers and the citizens' wives; also city cuckolds, and their maiden-looking mistresses, stow themselves as close in a boat together, as they do in a Cheapside balcony, at my Lord Mayor's Show, to gaze like a drove of bullocks, between one another's horns, at the triumphs of the city. . . .

Having thus pretty well secured our bodies from the coldness of the water [by a flask of wine] we took boat at Billingsgate stairs, and away for Cuckold's Point; but we were no sooner put off from the shore, but we were got into such an innumerable fleet of oars, skullers, barges, cock-boats, bum-boats, pinnaces and yawls; some going, some coming, and all attacking each other with such volleys of hard words, that I thought Billingsgate market had been kept upon the Thames, and all the fish whores in the town, had been scolding for a plate, given 'em by some rich oyster woman, to encourage the industry of the tongue; calling my poor lady and I, so often by the opprobrious names of whore and rogue, that for my part, I thought they were witches, and had known what we had been doing; tossing ladlefuls of water into one another's boats, till the passengers were many of 'em as wet as a turbulent woman just taken out of the ducking-stool. At last an unlucky rogue, with Bridewell-looks and a ladle in his hand, fishes up a floating Sir-reverence[1] in his wooden vehicle, and gives it an unfortunate toss upon my lady's bubbies. She crying out to me her protector, to do the office of a scavenger, and take away the beastliness, she being herself so very squeamish, that she could no more endure to touch it with her fingers, than a monkey does a mouse, it being lodged in the cavity, between her breasts and her stays, she could not shake it off, but I was forced to lend a hand to remove the poisonous pellet from her snowy temptations, giving on't a toss into another boat, with the like success, wounding an old cuckoldy waterman just in the forehead, and so bedunged his brow antlers, that I make no question but they spread and flourished, being thus manured like the horns of an ox after well greasing, which put the grisly churl (who I'll warrant, by his grey hairs, had at least served nine prenticeships to the Thames) into such a wonderful passion, that he began to roar out his aquatic scurrility at us, with as much indignation and revenge, as a she-mumper when bilked of her crib, or an alley-scold when called barren bitch, by her neighbour, clawing the unsavoury birdlime off his face, snapping on't, as a barber does suds from the ends of his fingers; saluting my mistress, and I, in the height of his fury, after the following manner. 'You shitten-skulled son of a t——d, that has spat your brains in my face, who was begotten in buggery, born in a house of office,[2] and delivered at the fundament, fit for nothing but to be cast into a goldfinder's ditch, there lie till you're rotten, and then be sold out to gardeners, for a hot bed, to raise pumpkins to feed the Devil withall. And as for you, you brandy-faced, bottle-nosed, bawdy, brimstone whore, every time you conjobble together, may he beget your belly full of live crabs and crawfish, that as you strive to pluck 'em out, they may hang by the sides of your toquoque, and make you squeak nine times louder than a woman frighted into labour a month before her reckoning.'

[1] *A piece of dung.*
[2] *Privy.*

This, and such sort of waterbred language, he pelted at our ears, till we were out of hearing: being both as glad when we had out-rowed his impudence, as a man that has outrun a bailiff; for if ever anybody was under an ill tongue, we thought ourselves at that time in the same condition.

Every boat that came by had a pelt at my poor mistress and I, who being but two, besides watermen, were most lamentably mauled by other boats, who being better manned, were quite too many for us, and rattled us into silence with a broadside of Billingsgate language, which was thrown on all sides so thick upon us, that we found it but a vain attempt to endeavour to be heard amidst this shower of ill words. We jogged gently on, as fast as our neighbouring enemies would give us leave, who lay ahead of us, upon our bow, broadside, quarters, and stern, that we could not turn our heads any way out of tongueshot, but either rogue, or whore, pimp, cuckold, or tailor, hit us a box of the ear, that almost deafened us. 'Dear heart,' says my mistress, 'I wonder the magistrates of the city do not take some care to prevent these sad abuses upon the water; for 'tis a shameful thing that civil people should be called thus out of their names.' 'Prithee,' said I, 'never mind 'em; for if my Lord M—— were here himself, they'd be as ready to call him cuckold as they would anybody else; and he would not know which way to help himself, but must put it up as we do. There's no remedy.'

After we had spent about half an hour upon the water in this misery, we arrived at our intended port, Cuckold's Point, where we landed in a crowd, with as much difficulty as a man crosses the Change at two o'clock, or squeezes into Paul's choir on a Sunday, whilst they are singing of an anthem. Having discharged our watermen, we went into the house, where the troop of merry cuckolds used to rendezvous armed with shovel, spade, or pickaxe; their heads adorned with horned helmets; and from thence to march, in order, for Horn-Fair, levelling the way as they go, according to the command of their leaders, that their wives might come after with their gallants, without spoiling their laced shoes, or draggling their holiday petticoats. . . .

When we had warmed and refreshed our chilled carcasses, we set forward for Deptford, and having heard great commendation of that serviceable projection, the New Dock, I had a great desire to take a view of that by the way, and so shaped my course accordingly. After we had passed by a long range of little cottages, at the doors of which sat abundance of Dutch-buttocked lasses, with sea handkerchiefs about their pouting bubbies, which were swelled with much handling, so far beyond their natural proportion, that their breast and their bellies, like Mother Shipton's nose and chin, met one with the other; some knitting, some spinning, and others picking okum; but all, as I suppose, ready enough to quit their several exercises and betake themselves to a pleasanter pastime, if anybody will hire 'em. . . .

From hence we proceeded till we came to Deptford, where I think the first house in the town, like many others, is accounted a convenience for his Majesty's Waterrats, when residing upon land, to cool their tails in; when we came a little further into the town, we might easily discern, by the build of the houses, what amphibious sort of creatures chiefly inhabited this part of the kingdom; their dens were chiefly wood, all of one form, as if they were obliged by Act of Parliament, to all build after the same model; here a pretty woman or two at a door, there another or two at a window, all looking as melancholy as old maids and widows, for want of male conversation; gazing upon each man that passed 'em, with as much earnestness and desire, as ever our great grandmother did upon the forbidden fruit. The ladies that chiefly inhabit these cabins, were the wives of mariners, whose husbands were some gone to the East Indies, and some to the West, some Northward, some Southward, leaving their disconsolate spouses to make trial of their virtue, and live upon public credit till their return, who if it were not for the benevolence of a well-disposed neighbouring knight, and a few more charitable worthy gentlemen, they might, though married, grow sullen, like the Negro women, for want of husbands, and pine away because nature is not supplied with due accommodation. Many shops we observed open in the streets, but a brandy-bottle, and a quartern, a butcher mending of a canvas doublet, a few apples in a cabbage-net, a peelful of Deptford cheesecakes, an old waistcoat, a thrum cap, and a pair of yarn mittens, were the chief shows that they made of their commodities, every house being distinguished by either the sign of the Ship, the Anchor, the Three Mariners, Boatswain and Call, or something relating to the sea: for as I suppose, if they should hang up any other, the salt water novices would be as much puzzled to know what the figure represented, as the Irishman was, when he called the Globe the golden case-body, and the unicorn the white horse with a barber's pole in his forehead.

The women we chiefly met in the streets, were accoutred most commonly like the meanest of our oyster women, in ragged gowns, daggled petticoats, blue aprons, speckled handkerchiefs about their necks, and their heads adorned with flat caps; those that we met coupled, had generally short squat well-trussed fellows by their sides, in new coarse cloth coats, speckled breeches, grey stockings, round-toed shoes, picked heels, stitched round the quarters, tied on with scarlet tape instead of buckles, with mittens on his hands, a fur cap on his head, armed with an oak cudgel, with a head as big as a four pounder. I observed they all, Spaniard-like, kept up to one fashion, so that the same description would serve any I saw, with a very slender variation. Now and then, 'tis true, we met a bluff blade, who looked as burly as if he had fed his whole lifetime upon peas and swine's flesh, with a campaign wig on, the hairs of which, for want of combing once in a month, hung in as many tangle locks, as if he had been flying, and a sword tied on as high as the waistband of his breeches, and had no more motion when he walked, than a two-foot rule, stuck into the apronstrings of a carpenter: these sort of sea monsters, I observed the mumpers saluted with the title of noble captain, and had the right knack of coaxing these quarter-deck blunderbusses out of their farthings and halfpence, with the taking and insinuating cant of honour and worship, as fast as a horse mountebank gulls the mob out of their twopence, by calling of them gentlemen; his noble worship looking round him as big, after he had paid the beggar a penny for his title, as an old cozening curmudgeon, who has built an almshouse, or a rich citizen that has got a poor brother's child into the Bluecoat Hospital.

We walked on till we came to the upper end of the town, where stood some very pretty houses, whose gates for ostentation's sake, were made with bars, that each passenger might delight his eyes, with an external prospect of these their most creditable and beautiful habitations: in this row stood a most famous hospital, erected for the entertainment of thirty-one decayed masters of vessels, or their widows, depending on the Trinity House; the masters of which, having the care thereof; to the relief and sup-

Dunton's Whipping-Post:

OR, A

SATYR upon Every Body.

To which is added,

A Panegyrick on the most deserving Gentlemen and Ladies in the Three Kingdoms.

With the

WHORING-PACQUET:

OR,

News of the St——ns and Kept M——s's.

VOL. I.

To which is added,

The LIVING ELEGY:

OR,

Dunton's Letter to his Few Creditors.

With the

𝕮𝖍𝖆𝖗𝖆𝖈𝖙𝖊𝖗 𝖔𝖋 𝖆 𝕾𝖚𝖒𝖒𝖊𝖗=𝖋𝖗𝖎𝖊𝖓𝖉.

ALSO,

The Secret History of the Weekly Writers,

𝕴𝖓 𝖆 𝖉𝖎𝖘𝖙𝖎𝖓𝖈𝖙 𝕮𝖍𝖆𝖑𝖑𝖊𝖓𝖌𝖊 𝖙𝖔 𝖊𝖆𝖈𝖍 𝖔𝖋 𝖙𝖍𝖊𝖒.

To the Interloping Whipsters.

You do not Jerk the Times; are like the Fleas,
You bite the Skin, but leap from the Disease.

LONDON: Printed, and are to be Sold by B.
Bragg, at the *Black Raven* in *Pater-noster-Rowe.* 1706

Dunton's *Whipping-Post*: title-page

Why Satan, you have beaten all this Turf (or rather Temp-
ted the Humane Race) but to purchase your self a Whipping.
Like some Travellers who measure so many Acres Abroad, but
return Home Block-heads: For, I have several Weighty
Things to lay to your Charge: And in the First Place I
shall strive to un——Wickedness in the Original, The Source and
Fountain of all Mischief. All the Instances of Extravagance which happen in our nether Climate, are but distant
Streams, and Participations of your Primitive Irregularity.
To represent your Effigies, wou'd put Nature into a Fright,
and turn the Poles Topsy turvy. However, that I may give
the World a rude Sketch of your Deformity, I shall
Expose to Publick View Two of your most Daring,
tho' Diminutive Lineaments; that from the Foot they
may be able to find out the Hercules ——

Now the spiritual Parts which I at present design to
Whip, are your Two Beloved Members, Envy and Ambition: Envy at the greater Happiness of your Maker,
and Ambition to put your self into the same Circumstance.

That Member which I shall first Whip, is your Envy.
You had the Forehead to be displeas'd at the Felicities of your Creator: You sicken'd at the Sight of your
Maker's Happiness: You were angry that He who gave
you Being Gratis, shou'd continue to exist; and were
vex'd that *He* who could not but be, was. You were the
first of Atheists; and like the rest of your Successors,
not so much an Atheist in Principle, as in Desire:
Tho' you might have liv'd like an Angel, yet because
you were not suffer'd to Top the Omnipotent, you
resolved to be Nothing: Because you cou'd not strip
Suits with your Maker, make Merchandise of your
Identity, and run out of your own Being into his, (like
an Errant Metaphysical Devil as you was) you wou'd
needs be making Faces against his Beauty, and for the
Time to come have nothing to do with Him.

The other Prospect of your Character I shall set to
the Spectators, is the Landscape of your *Ambition.* And
here I see you Enterprising Infinite Designs, and going
about Daring Atchievements. You endeavour'd to over-
turn

---

turn the Eternal State of Things, to dispossess the Omnipotent of his Ancient Throne, and laying close Siege
to the Kingdoms of Eternity, you were resolv'd to make
the best of your Way into the Throne; to turn him out
like another Satan, and to make new Promotions according to your Pleasure. And thus (which your Hellish Majesty can't but own.)

The Golden Age was first, when Man yet new,
No Rule, but uncorrupted Reason, knew:
And with a Native Bent did Good pursue,
Unforc'd by Punishment, unaw'd by Fear,
His Words were simple, and his Soul sincere:
Needless was written Law, where none oppress'd,
The Law of Man was written in his Breast.
No suppliant Crowds before the Judge appear'd,
No Court Erected yet, nor Cause was heard,
But all was safe, for Conscience was their Guard.
No MINE nor THINE did then Mens Hearts infest,
For Chimery Courts were kept in every Breast.
The Mountain Trees in distant Prospect, please,
Ere yet the Pine descended to the Seas:
Ere Sails were spread new Oceans to explore,
And happy Mortals, unconcern'd for more,
Confin'd their Wishes to their Native Shore.
No Walls were yet, nor Fence, nor Mote, nor Mound,
Nor Drum was heard, nor Trumpet's angry Sound;
Nor Swords were forg'd; but void of Care and Crime,
The soft Creation slept away their Time:
The Teeming Earth yet guiltless of the Plow,
And unprovok'd did Fruitful Stores allow,
Content with Food which Nature freely bred,
On Wildings and on Strawberrys they fed,
Kernels and Bramble Berrys gave the rest,
And falling Acorns furnish'd out a Feast;
The Flow'rs unsown in Fields and Meadows Reign'd,
And Western Winds Immortal Spring maintain'd:
But when good Saturn banish'd from Above,
Was driven to Hell, the World was under Jove.
Succeeding Times a Silver Age behold,
Excelling Brass, but more excell'd by Gold.

D 2   *Then*

Then Summer, Autum, Winter did appear,
And Spring was but one Season of the Year;
The Sun his Annual Course obliquely made,
Good Days contracted, and enlarg'd the Bad:
Then Air with sultry Heats began to glow,
The Wings of Winds were clog'd with Ice and Snow;
And shiv'ring Mortals into Houses driv'n,
Sought Shelter from the Inclemency of Heav'n.
To this came next in Course the Brazen Age,
A Warlike Offspring prompt to Bloody Rage.

——————   *Hard Steel succeeded then,*
And stuborn as the Metal were the Men;
Truth, Modesty and Shame the World forsook,
Fraud, Avarice and Force their Places took.
Then Sails were spread to ev'ry Wind that blew,
Raw were the Sailors, and the Depths were new.
Trees rudely hollow'd did the Waves sustain,
E're Ships in Triumph plow'd the Watry Main.
Then Land-Marks limited to each his Right,
For all before was common as the Light:
Nor was the Ground alone requir'd to bear
Her Annual Income to the crooked Share;
But greedy Mortals rummaging her Store,
Dig'd from her Entrails first the precious Ore;
(Which next to Hell the prudent Gods had laid,)
And that alluring Ill to Sight display'd:
Thus cursed Steel, and more accursed Gold,
Gave Mischief Birth, and made that Mischief bold,
And double Death did wretched Man invade,
By Steel assaulted, and by Gold betray'd.
Now, Brandish'd Weapons glitt'ring in their Hands,
Mankind is broken loose from Moral Bands.
No Rights of Hospitality remain,
The Guest, by him who harbour'd him, is slain.
The Son-in-Law pursues the Father's Life;
The Wife her Husband murthers, He the Wife:
The Step-dame Poyson for her Son prepares;
The Son enquires into his Father's Years:

Faith

Faith flies, and Piety in Exile mourns,
And Justice, here oppress'd, to Heav'n returns.

And ever since this Apostacy (I mean ever since the
Devil turn'd Rebel, and tempted *Eve*) he has gone about
seeking whom he may devour, and so will continue to do
to the End of the World.

And now Ambitious, spiteful Devil, having Expos'd your
Character, and that of your Children, to open View, I shall
proceed (in the Second Place) to let down your Spiritual Breeches, Erect the Whipping-Post, and
tye up your Crimes to the Machine of Castigation.

And in the First Place, I shall bring your Envy to the
Stake. Now, the Place which I have Assign'd for the
Whipping of this Viper, shall be the Test and Standard of Universal Excellence. The Stake, or Post I shall
bind you to, is General Success, the Conquests of Religion, the Bloomings of Paradise, the Victories of Religion, the Bloomings of Paradise, the Victories of Religion, and the Blessings of Providence, &c. After this you
shall take a Turn with me in the Gardens of Nature,
examine the Variety and Curiosity of their Productions; and Scan over all the Agreeableness of the Creation. Behold these Plants, in what Comely and Beautiful
Order they are Ranged! See the Delicacy of their Structure!
And what Art hath been employ'd in spreading forth their
Branches! ———— Methinks you don't seem Transported
with the Prospect! But if you examin'd the Admirable
Virtues of their Leaves, the Harmony of their Lineaments, and the Exquisite Prettiness of their various
Tincture, you wou'd soon change your Countenance,
look as sleek as a Cherub, and smile upon them, at least
from the Inclination of Sympathy. What? Can nothing
give you Pleasure? I thought you wou'd almost have been
Transport'd to Madness, and that you cou'd not but have
admir'd the Omnipotence of your Maker; But I find (on
the Review) Envy is not so much of Kin to Enthusiasm; it can slumber on the Bosom of Beauty without Ravishment; Rolls thro' the Curiosities of the Creation without Wonder, and turn over Nature's Great
Poem

Four pages of Dunton's Whipping-Post

port of which charitable design, every ship at her clearing, pays according to her burden so much money. Our curiosity led us to take a turn into it, which we found very pleasant and commodious, as to the building and situation; but when I enquired into the allowance, I found it so very small, that it might rather be called Pinch-Gut-College, than a hospital for poor pensioners; who with much difficulty gaining admittance into these starving confines, have no more allowed 'em, to find meat, drink, washing, fire, clothes, and all necessaries of life, than twelve shillings per month; and four months in the year are set at five weeks, to take in the odd month; most that are there having paid more money towards it, before they came into it, than ever their allowance would amount to, if they were to live fifty years in the hospital; to which many great legacies have been left, but the number of pensioners never increased, nor their pensions advanced; so that how it is sunk, or embezzled, or to what use converted, nobody knows, but those persons who have the discretionary power, as 'tis supposed, of laying it safe up in their own pockets. An East India captain, some few years since, dying, bequeathed thirteen hundred pounds to this hospital; out of which money, it never received any other apparent advantage, than the statue of the benefactor set up in the garden, for the pensioners to feast their eyes, instead of their bellies, withall. The members of this society of tarpaulin paupers, are only during the pleasure of the masters of the Trinity, and are liable to be turned out, upon very slender misbehaviours. There is another such hospital by the church, originally founded by Queen Elizabeth, but for twenty-one poor masters, or their widows; and except in number, is equal in every particular, with the former; so that by all the observations I could make, in so short a passage through the town, I could not but think it very well deserved this following character: the town's without necessaries, they've butchers without meat, alehouses without drink, houses without furniture, and shops without trade; captains without commission, wives without husbands, whores without smocks, a church without religion, and hospitals without charity. . . .

Two of his most delightful 'trips' are *A Step to Stir-Bitch* [*Sturbridge*] *Fair* and *A Step to the Bath*, both published in 1700:

G

A

Step to STIR-BITCH-FAIR

with

Remarks upon the UNIVERSITY

of

CAMBRIDGE.

... We came to a small village called Trumpington, a mile on this side Cambridge. This town is not a little famous for two great conveniences it affords the young scholars of the University; for here the free men first learn to be good companions, and afterwards, when in orders, practise to be good preachers; for here they commonly drink their first merry cup with their friends after their initiation, and generally deliver their first sermon, when qualified by the Bishop for the ministerial function. As we passed through Trumpington, where the scholars at their leisure hours are some or other of them usually refreshing themselves; we saw several black gowns pop in and out of the little country hovels, like so many black rabbits in a warren, bolting out of their coney burrows; I have some reason to be jealous, the name of this place was originally given it for no good, but rather from some wild scholars, who being libidinously given, had usual recourse thither, and kissed the wenches till they farted again, from whence, as some sages conjecture, in process of time, it gained the name of Trumping-Town. ...

The next place we arrived at, was our journey's end, Cambridge; where black and purple gowns were strolling about town, like parsons in a country metropolis, during the Bishop's visitation; some looking with as meagre countenances, as if in search of the Philosopher's Stone, they had studied themselves into a hypochondriac melancholy; others seeming so profoundly thoughtful, as if in pursuance of Agrippa's notions they were studying how to raise sparagrafs out of ram's horns, or to produce a homunculus as gardeners do pumpkins; by burying the sermon in a dunghill; some looking as plump and as jolly as a painted Bacchus bestriding a Canary butt; smiling as he passed by, at his own soliloquies, as if he was muttering over to himself some Bacchanalian ode, he had conceived in praise of good claret; others seeming as sottishly sorrowful as if they were maudlin fuddled, and lamenting the

misfortune of poor Anacreon, who choked himself with a grape
stone; some strutting along about eighteen years of age, in new
gown and cassock, as if they had received orders about two hours
before, and were the next morning to have institution and induc-
tion, to become the hopeful guide of a whole parish, and here
and there one appearing so rakishly thoughtless, as if nature, by
his empty looks, had designed him to grind mustard or pick mush-
rooms for some nobleman's kitchen; though his parents, in opposition to his destiny, resolved to make him a scholar. As for the
town itself, it was so abominably dirty, that Old Street in the
middle of a winter's thaw, or Bartholomew Fair, after a shower
of rain, could not have more occasion for a scavenger, than the
miry street of this famous corporation; and most of them so
very narrow, that should two wheelbarrows meet in the largest of
their thoroughfares, they are enough to make a stop for half an
hour before they can well clear themselves of one another, to
make room for passengers.

After the coach had set me down, and I had taken a fair
leave of my fellow-travellers, I walked about, to take a more complete survey of the town and University. The buildings in many
parts of the town were so little and so low, that they looked more
like huts for pygmies, than houses for men; and their shopkeepers
seemed to me to be so well-sized to their habitations, that they
appeared like so many monkeys, in their diminutive shops,
mimicking the trade of London. Amongst the rest of the pomps
and vanities of this wicked Corporation, there is one very famous
inn, distinguished by the sign of the Devil's Lapdog in Petty-
Cury; here I went to refresh myself with a glass or two of Canary;
where I found an old grizzly curmudgeon, corniferously wedded
to a plump, young, brisk, black, beautiful, good landlady; who,
I afterwards heard, had so great a kindness for the University,
that she had rather see two or three gownmen come into her
house, than a cuckoldy crew of aldermen in all their pontificali-
busses: and indeed, I had reason to believe there was no love lost,
for the scholars crept in as fast, and as slyly, for either a kiss, a
kind look, or a cup of comfort; as hogs into an orchard after a
high wind, or flies into pig sauce, for the sake of the sugar; I liked
my pretty hostess so wonderfully well, and was so greatly delighted
with the pleasant conversation I met with in the house, that I
determined with myself to make this my place of residence, dur-

ing my continuance in the town; so bespeaking a bed, I afterwards
took a walk in order to view the University, of which I shall proceed to give you a sober and concise description.

The colleges stand outside the town, which, in plain terms,
is a corporation of ignorance, hemmed round with arts and
sciences, a nest of fools, that dwell on the superfluities of the
learned, an ungrateful soil where the seeds of generosity are daily
scattered, but produce nothing in return, but the wicked weed of
unthankfulness and ingratitude. Of learned societies there are in all
sixteen, twelve colleges, and four halls, the most magnificent of
which, being that of Trinity, whose spacious quadrangle, and commodious library, remain without comparison. The scholars of this
foundation are distinctly habited in purple gowns; the rest of the
University wearing black, agree in one and the same mode. The
next piece of building more particularly remarkable is King's
College Chapel, founded by Henry the Sixth, and is greatly famed
by all men of judgment for its admirable architecture, much after
the manner of Henry the Seventh's chapel at Westminster, if not
finer and larger. The rest of the colleges, except St. John's (which
has been beautified and enlarged of late years) wear the faces of
great antiquity, and though they are not so fine as those which
have had the advantage of a modern improvement, yet the rust
of the aged walls, and obsoleteness of their structure, procure
veneration from all spectators, and seemed to me more noble in
their ancient uniformity, than others disagreeable enlarged with
additional novelties. In short, the colleges are so splendid, the
government so regular, the orders so strict, the ceremonies so
decorous, and the preferments so honourable, that in all Europe,
it is not excelled by any university, except Oxford.

Having thus feasted my eyes with a general view of the
colleges, I retired to my inn, where I reposed myself, after a good
supper, till the next morning, which proving fine and pleasant,
I took a walk to Stir-Bitch Fair, though for the expense of threepence I might have been accommodated with the convenience
of a London hackney, who at this season bring passengers from
London, and ply there for the fortnight, carrying tag, rag, and
bobtail, for the aforesaid price, provided they have as many as
will fill their coach; but for eighteenpence a scholar and his mistress may have a running bawdy house to themselves, draw up
their tin sashes, pinked like the bottom of a colander, and hug

one another as private as they please, obscured from the wandering eyes of all observing passengers.

I had not walked above half a mile from Cambridge towards the Fair, but I came to a renowned village, which, by all reports, very deservedly has gained the ignominious epithet of Bawdy-Barnell, so called from the numerous brothel houses it contains for the health, ease, and pleasure, of the learned vicinity, and has had so ancient a reputation for sacrificing its female offspring, through many ages, to the use and service of the neighbouring societies, that there has not been a maidenhead known in the town, at eighteen years of age, since the time of King Henry the First, in whose reign Cambridge was new modelled into a university. Besides the women of this place have such a love for the scholars, and hatred for the townsmen, that a Bachelor of Arts shall have more favour for a distich of English verses, in praise of simple fornication, than the best tradesman throughout the corporation shall find for an ounce of sterling.

From thence I marched forward till I came to the Fair, where I beheld such a number of wooden edifices, and such a multitude of gentry, scholars, tradesmen, whores, hawkers, pedlars, and pickpockets, that it seemed to me like an abstract of all sorts of mankind, drawn into a lesser body, to show the world in epitomy: at first I came to the proctor's booth, wherein he keeps an arbitrary court to punish, as the learned divan shall think fit, all misdemeanours touching the scholars, from whence there can be no appeal; and near to this is held another wooden court of justice on the behalf of the corporation, where his Worshipful Bulkiness, the Mayor, sits to determine all such matters as concerns his authority, assisted with the cornuted elders of the town, who are ready to lend a horn upon occasion, to help the head of their superior in all cases of difficulty. . . .

From thence I turned to the left, by the riverside, where my nostrils were saluted with such a saline savoury whiff, as if I had been walking in a dry fishmonger's shop in Thames Street. At last I came into a Dutch market of red and pickled herrings, salt fish, oysters, pitch, tar, soap, &c. Next these a parcel of wooden trumpery, ranged in as much order, as a cupboard of plate, where Bacchanalian students may furnish themselves with punchbowls, agreeably sized to their own consciences; sots supply themselves with cans, modelled to their own humours, and the beggars accomodate themselves with spoons and porridge dishes of any dimension, suitable to their own appetites. Adjoining to this place, stand about a dozen of sutlers boozing kens, distinguished by the name of the Lyn Booths, the good people that keep 'em being inhabitants of that town, and have so fair a reputation for the foul practice of venery, that their sinful hovels have always maintained the character of being notorious bawdy houses; the scholars, to encourage the old trade of basket-making, have great resort to these uptail academies, where they are often presented with a Lyn fairing, which brings 'em to thin jaws, and a month or two's spare diet, as a penance for a minute's titillation, giving many of 'em reason to say with a scholar under the same affliction, who, being at chapel, whispered to his chamberfellow, Chum, chum, though I have the word of God in my mouth, to tell thee the truth on't, I have a Lyn devil in my breeches.

From these booths I went straight up a hill, and came into a very handsome street called Garlic Row, where slit deal tenements were occupied by sempstresses, perfumers, milliners, toymen, and cabinet-makers; and is chiefly frequented by powdered beaux, bushy-wigged blockheads, country belsas, and beautiful Bury ladies, the latter of which being as commendable for their good nature, as remarkable for their prettiness, are attended with such crowds of Duchified fops, with their hats under their arms, and their hands in their pockets, bowing and cringing with such flexible submission to each proud enchantress, as if their backs were made of whalebone; which brought into my mind the following distich of my Lord Rochester's, in which if I alter one word, for decency's sake, I hope the reader will excuse it.

So a proud minx does lead about,
Of humble curs the amorous rout.

This terminates in a place called originally Cook's Row, but now more properly Cuckold's Row, from the great number of booksellers that are now crept into possession of their greasinesses' division; this learned part of the Fair is the scholars' chief rendezvous, where some that have money come to buy books, whilst others, who want it, take 'em slyly up, upon condition to pay if they're caught, and think it a pious piece of generosity, to give St. Austin, or St. Gregory, protection in a gown sleeve, till they can better provide for 'em. Here the most famous auctioneer of all Great as well as Little Britain, sells books by the hammer, and gives the scholars as merry an entertainment, as a mountebank and his Andrew. 'Here's an old author for you, Gentlemen, you may judge his antiquity by the fashion of his leather jacket; herein is contained, for the benefit of you scholars, the knowledge of everything; written by that famous author, who through his profound wisdom, very luckily discovered that he knew nothing. For your encouragement, Gentlemen, I'll put him up at two shillings, advance three pence; two shillings once: what nobody bid? The bidder advances threepence, two and threepence, once: Gentlemen, fie, for shame, why sure men of your parts and learning will never suffer the works of so famous an author to be thus undervalued: if you'll believe me, gentlemen, he's worth more to a powder monkey to make cartridges of, than what's bid: two and threepence, twice? What nobody amongst you gentlemen of the black robe, that has so much respect for the wisdom of our ancestors, as to advance t'other threepence? Well sir, I find you must have him for two and threepence, knock, and now you've bought him, sir, I must tell you, you'll find learning enough within him to puzzle both Universities: and thus much, I promise you further sir, when you have read him seven years, if you don't like him, bring him to me again, in Little Britain, and I'll help you to a man shall give you a shilling for him to cover bandboxes.' At this sort of rate he bantered the young students; and whatever they purchased, gave 'em a jest into the bargain.

From thence I passed into a great street called Cheapside, where on one side were a considerable number of wholesale tradesmen, as linen drapers, silk men, ironmongers, leather-sellers, tobacconists, &c. who swelled in their shops, and looked as big above the rest of the petty dealers, as the bluff well-fed senior fellows of a college do above the lean thin-gutted poor sizers. On the opposite side are sutlers booths, much frequented by the London citizens, who are easily to be known by their thin calves' leather boots, and the bloodiness of their spurs, whose rowels had been often buried in the sides of their hackneys. Their pretence is, coming down to meet their customers; though it's plain by their loitering they have little else to do but to drink, smoke, and whore, and to help support the Fair in its ancient custom of debauchery; cozening themselves of their time, their families of their money, and their dear wives of their company. Their whips they wear under their arms, as a beau does his hat; and tie up the ends of their bob wigs in black rags with a ridiculous hope of being thought gentlemen.

Behind these booths is a place called the Duddery, encompassed round with salesmen, and people that sell Norwich stuffs, and in the middle, abundance of packs of that deceitful commodity Yorkshire cloth: the salesmen ply at their booth doors as they do in Long Lane; and lug and tug the poor country folk into their mercenary wardrobes, as if they had power to arrest 'em; who are surely cheated if they buy, and almost worried if they don't. In the centre of this place stands an old weatherbeaten pulpit, where on Sunday a sermon is delivered, for the edification of the strolling sinners, who give open attention, as in a field conventicle. . . .

On the other side the river there's a little town, called Chesterton, in which there is the sign of the Black Bull, where the country chapmen generally lodge that come to the Fair, for the sake of rare strong humming ale, for which 'tis famous; over which they get drunk, quarrel, and make bargains, till the fox brings 'em to sleep; and sleep, by the next morning, to a sober repentance.

The chief entertainment of the Fair, is stubble geese, and apple sauce; fat pig, and fly sauce; bad sack, and good walnuts; the last of which the citizens send as fairings to their wives, to divert 'em behind the counter, in their husbands' absence.

At night, when their booths are shut up, which is only by skewering two haircloths together, then all that are freshmen are fought for by their acquaintance in order to be christened: the manner of which is thus, two or three contrive to decoy him, or her into a sutler's booth, under pretence of somebody being there to speak with them about business; and then privately send for an old fellow dignified with the title of Lord Tap, from his going armed all over with spiggots and fossets, like a porcupine with his quills, or looking rather like a fowl wrapped up in a pound of sausages; who when he comes, rings his bell over the head of the party, repeating these bombast words with an audible voice:

Over thy head I ring this bell,
Because thou art an infidel;

And I have found thee out by th' smell.
With a hoxius doxious call upon him,
That no vengeance my light on him.

Then the party christened chooses two of the company to
be his godfathers, who generally give him some very bawdy
name; then they swear him upon the horns, as at Highgate, make
him give Tap sixpence, and spend four or five shillings to treat
the company, and then for ever after he's free of Stir-Bitch Fair;
of which, having given myself the satisfaction of a general survey, I went back to Cambridge, took a place in the stage-coach,
and returned to London.

A

S T E P

to the

B A T H

... The first we went to, is called the King's; and to it
joins the Queen's, both running in one; and the most famous for
cures. In this Bath was at least fifty of both sexes, with a score
or two of guides, who by their scorbutick carcasses, and lacquered
hides, you would think they had lain pickling a century of years
in the Stygian Lake. Some had those infernal emissaries to support their impotent limbs, others to scrub their putrified carcasses
like a racehorse. In one corner was an old fornicator hanging by
the rings, loaded with rotten humidity; hard by him was a buxom
dame, cleansing her *nunquam satis* from mercurial dregs, and the
remains of Roman vitriol. Another, half covered with searcloth,
had more sores than Lazarus, doing penance for the sins of her
youth: at her elbow was a young hero, supported by a couple of
guides, racked with aches and intolerable pains, cursing of Middle-
sex court, and Beveridges dancing school, as heartily as Job the
day of his birth. At the pump was several drenching their gullets,
and gormandizing the reeking liquor by wholesale.

From thence we went to the Cross Bath, where most of the
quality resorts, more famed for pleasure than cures, though they
pretend it hath wrought miracles on barren soil, and wonderfully
helps conception. Not long since, a gentleman of quality was be-

G*

holden to it for an heir, as he reported; but his lady is of a contrary opinion; yet I know not what operation such tempting objects may have by causing titillation, and heightening imagination, to procure an immediate conjunction. Here is performed all the wanton dalliancies imaginable; celebrated beauties, panting breasts, and curious shapes, almost exposed to public view; languishing eyes, darting killing glances, tempting amorous postures, attended by soft music, enough to provoke a vestal to forbidden pleasure, captivate a saint, and charm a Jove. Here was also different sexes, from quality to the honourable knights, country put, and city madams. Nay, the circumcised Jew, could bathe in delight, swim in pleasure with the Gentile, and outvie a courtier in splendour, though they crucified his God; and dispense with Christian's flesh, though not with swine's. The ladies with their floating Japan bowls, freighted with confectionary knick-knacks, essences, and perfumes, wade about, like Neptune's courtiers, suppling their industrious joints. The vigorous sparks, presenting them with several antic postures, as sailing on their backs, then embracing the element, sink in a rapture, and by accidental design, thrust a stretched arm; but where the water concealed, so ought my pen.

The spectators in the galleries, pleasing their roving fancies with this lady's face, another's eyes, a third's heaving breasts, and profound air. In one corner stood an old lecher, whose years spoke him no less than threescore and ten, making love to a young lady, not exceeding fourteen. The usual time being come to forsake that fickle element, half-tub chairs, lined with blankets, plied as thick as coaches at the playhouse, or carts at the Custom house.

Bathing being over for that day, we went to walk in the grove, a very pleasant place for diversion; there is the Royal Oak and several raffling shops. In one of the walks, is several sets of ninepins, and attendants to wait on you; tipping all nine for a guinea, is as common there, as two farthings for a porringer of barley broth, at the hospital gate in Smithfield. On several of the trees was hung a lampoon on the marriage of one Mr. S—— a drugmonger, and the famous Madam S—— an old B—— of London.

Having almost tired ourselves with walking, we took to a bench to ease our weary pedestals. Now, said my friend, I'll give you an impartial account of the perfections, qualities and functions, of a few particular persons that are among this amphibious crowd. For notwithstanding I have been here not above a fortnight, I am as well acquainted with the town and its intrigues, as old Justice P—— with Moorfields and Drury Lane bawdy houses.

Those two ladies with the gentleman in blue, are sisters, live near the church that is dedicated to a saint who expired on a gridiron; they are amorous dames. The gentleman is a broken officer, and lives better on their allowances, than he could on his pay. This gentlewoman in the white damask gown, is a sea captain's lady; who, while her corniferous mate is plowing the ocean, takes care to manure his pasture, that he may have a fruitful crop this harvest. That foppish beau in scarlet stockings, whose hilt of his sword bears a bob with his calves, and his jubilee hatband lies stitched cross the crown, was a petticoat pensioner to Madam C—— near Bucklersbury; but being lately discarded, is come down here for promotion. That young lady with the gold orice petticoat, was a great fortune, and not long since was married to a flannel waistcoat, and a double nightcap of the same stuff; but now by reason of her husband's imbecility, is forced to have recourse to the Bath. That tall gentleman attended by three liveries, is something of quality, a right courtier, for he abhors the citizens' wives as much as the swordbearer does custard. That broadpiece doctor, in the diminutive band, makes a purchase every year by the wickedness of the age; and vindicates w——ing more than even G. K—— wrote against the Quakers. That pert young gentlewoman with the two silver fringes, was compelled by her friends to marry a slovenly stockjobber, and now is surfeited with his embraces; and came to the Bath to mend his breed. That crafty priest, that son of Levi, is as fickle as a weathercock, and would sooner discard a good conscience, than a fat benefice. This ton of iniquity, in the crimson gown with Monsieur at her elbow, two devils behind her, Aetna in her face, all the water in the Severn is not able to quench her desires; she is a second Messalina, will tire, but ne'er be satisfied; she hath already quartered a troop of French dragoons, a regiment of Dutchmen, and now is come to exercise a battalion of Britons. That powdered lobster in the edged hat, is the spawn of a broker; from thence evapulated to a bully, now shams an officer, sets up for a stallion of the first rank, and pretends he receives several favours from a qualitificated lady. That spark with his hat under his arm, is a limb of

the law, but hath studied Chamberlin's midwifery, more than
Cook's reports. That dowdy minx in the scarlet topping, and
pinked scarf, is the relic of a broken grocer; an industrious woman,
for her head's no sooner laid, but her breech is at work. In short,
for fops, beaus, and belsas, this place exceeds Gray's Inn Walks on
a Sunday evening; and consists of greater variety of persons, remarkable for some vice or folly, than there are ingredients in a
Lombard pie for a city feast; to give you a particular description of each of 'em, will require a week's time at least. Come therefore let's go to some tippling mansion, and carouse till we have
exhilarated our drouthy souls: to which I readily agreed. About
five in the evening, we went to see a great match at bowling;
there was quality, and reverend doctors of both professions, topping merchants, broken bankers, noted mercers, Inn's of Court
rakes, city beaus, strayed prentices, and dancing masters in abundance. Fly, fly, fly, fly; said one: Rub, rub, rub, rub, cried another.
Ten guineas to five, I uncover the jack, says a third. Damn those
nice fingers of mine, cried my lord, I slipped my bowl, and mistook the bias. Another swearing he knew the ground to an inch,
and would hold five pounds his bowl came in. But in short, the
citizens won the courtiers' money, and the courtiers swore to be
revenged on their wives, and daughters.

From hence we went to the groom porter's, where they
were labouring like so many anchor-smiths, at the oak, back-
gammon, tick-tack, Irish, basset, and throwing of mains. There was
palming, lodging, loaded dice, levant, and gammoning, with all
the speed imaginable; but the Cornish rook was too hard for them
all. The Bristol Fair sparks had but a very bad bargain of it; and
little occasion for returns. Bank bills, and exchequer notes, were
as plenty, as fops at the chocolate houses, or Paternoster Row.
Having satisfied our curiosity here we left them as busy shaking
their elbows, as the apply women in Stocksmarket, walnuts in
October. . . .

A *Letter from Tunbridge* is not an actual 'trip', but it has
the same lively journalistic description:

A Letter from Tunbridge to a
Friend in London; being a
Character of the WELLS
and Company there.

By Mr. Ward, Author of the London SPY.

Dear Friend,

You are sensible that the reasons that induced me to make
my appearance at this general rendezvous, Tunbridge, were neither
the air nor waters, but purely the curiosity of seeing the people;
to which, till now I was as great a stranger as yourself: and since
I promised to transmit to you a character of this country parade,
I have here undertaken to discharge my duty; I shall therefore
proceed to give you first a description of the Wells, and next of
the company.

It is situated upon the side of a heath, so barren and so
poor, that had it not produced a Well, it would have yielded nothing: much pains I perceive have been taken to improve the walks,
though to little purpose; for new Tunbridge Wells at Islington as
much exceeds the old for pleasure, as a girl of fifteen a woman
of fifty, for a bedfellow. The fiddlers are as saucy as bum bailiffs
at a sessionshouse, and tug you by the sleeve for half-a-crown the
very first time of your appearance. The chief diversion at the
Wells, is to stare one at another; and he or she that is best dressed,
is the greatest subject of the morning's tittle-tattle. The chiefest
compliment among the women is I hope the waters pass well with
your ladyship, which is in plain English, I hope, madam, you
p——ss well: the sons and daughters of fortune thrive here so
mightily, it is hard to know the lady from the jilt, or the lord
from the sharper, all higgledy-piggledy mixed one among another,
like skulls in a charnelhouse, or knaves and cuckolds at my Lord
Mayor's Show. A glass of Rhenish is here prescribed as the only
cordial with the waters; and a handful of comfits esteemed the
best breakfast. Physicians swarm here like pickpockets at a fair;
and quality neither eat, drink, or exonerate without the advice
of a doctor. The chief lechery of the beaux is to watch the ladies
into their private apartments, and if their ears are but blessed
with a whiz when a belsa opens her sluice, they think themselves
as happy in their own fancies, as an old lecher that peeps through

a hole and sees a nymph in her bathing tub. Bachelors and their mistresses come hither in pairs; but married people come down single, men without their wives, and women without their husbands; so that I suppose, whilst one part are here pleasing their palates with a new dish, the other may be gone to the Bath to feast their appetites with a fresh dainty. The chief virtue ascribed to the waters are the following two: they very often cure the green sickness in maids, and cause fruitfulness in married women, provided they are but properly administered by a young vigorous physician: the old grizzly Galenists have but little business here; the youngest doctor by the female sex, is esteemed the ablest, and runs away with the most practice; for which reason I believe the women come hither to be kissed for health's sake, much rather than be physicked; and when the patient is so bad that neither lip nor belly-salve will do her good, she may be honestly given over as past cure. Some fools indeed, through their great opinion of the waters, have made their bodies such perpetual aqueducts, that they have washed themselves into mere skeletons, and go creeping about like West Indian Creolians troubled with the dry bellyache. It's a rare place for a beau to be jilted in a wife, for many set up to be great fortunes, who feed their mouths with their tails, and cover their backs with their bellies. Maidenheads here bear an extravagant price, for a great lover of priority, gave fifty guineas for one at secondhand, though he bought it for span new, but unhappily heard soon after, it had been sold for a hundred a fortnight before; and when he found himself cheated by his commodity broker, was forced to undergo the lash of the old proverb, A fool and his money were soon parted. Handsome men come here to a good market, they may sell themselves for what money they please, if they will but turn slaves to pampered lechery: here are a great many goldmines to be found under the petticoat, where an able workman may line his pockets at the trouble of digging. Here are many parts acted worth a wise man's observation; gentlemen play the fool, ladies play with their squirrels, poor whores play the jilt, sharpers play the knave, the beaus play the bubble, the old women the bawd, the servants the pimp, and the fiddlers play like devils.

Their chiefest pastimes, next the old trade of basket-making, are the following four: bowling at Rust Hall, where fools lose their money, and knaves win it; dancing upon Southborough

Green, where he that has another man's wife by the hand o'er night, often makes him a cuckold before morning; walking in the grove where the ringdoves coo above, whilst the lovers bill below, and project all things in order to make themselves happy at their next merry meeting; and gaming at the groom porter's, where everyone strives to win, whilst the box runs away with the money.

Lodgings are so dear and so scarce, that a beau is sometimes glad of a barn, and a lady of honour content to lie in a garret: the horses being commonly put to grass, for the servants to lie in the stable. My landlord was a farmer, and his very outhouses were so full, that having sheared some sheep, he abated me half a crown a week, to let the wool lie in my bedchamber; by which means a tick one night had buried himself so far in my belly, that I was forced next morning to borrow a shoemaker's pincers to pluck the bloodthirsty vermin out of his nest by the arse, before I could get rid of him, for he had filled his belly so full, and stuck so close by the strength of his new diet, that he held his hold like a bulldog; for which offence I punished him blood for blood, according to the old law.

The most noble of their provisions is a packsaddle of mutton, and a wheat-ear pie, which is accounted here a feast for a Heliogabalus; and is indeed so costly a banquet, that a man may go over to Amsterdam, treat half a dozen friends with a fish dinner, and bring 'em back again into their own country, almost as cheap as you can give yourself and your mistress a true Tunbridge entertainment. The liquors chiefly produced by this part of the country are beer made of wood-dried malt, and wine drawn out of a birch tree; the first is infected with such a smokey tang, that you would think it was brewed in a chimney; and every pint you drink, instead of quenching your drought, begets a thirst after a gallon; the latter, as 'tis ordered, drinks almost like mead, and makes a man's mouth smell of honey, as if he had a beehive in his guts, and is so abominable windy, that the breath of a man's breech, after drinking of a bottle, is strong enough to sound a trumpet. Here's claret good at a great price, but at the common rate not drinkable: we have rattleheaded vintners, and drunken drawers; and the rooms we are forced to sit in, are sometimes as unfurnished as the garrets of a sponging house, being hung with plaisterer's tapestry, bordered round with black, like an old whore's pin-up petticoat, furnished with a Spanish table, that stands as

ticklish as the nose of an old fluxed strumpet, round which are
three or four crazy turkeywork conveniencies, which, by often
carrying double, are over-occupied into such a weakness, that
they squeak when they're sat in, like a litter of suckling pigs in
the sow's absence: though I must confess, for the reputation of
the place, in the greater taverns you have better usage, but you
must pay as dear for it, as a country squire does at Moll Quarles's,
for tickling his rump with a pair of whore's kidneys.

Therefore, if the truths I've told you, will encourage you
to follow me, pray let your pockets be well furnished, for if here
you either want money, or spend it sparingly, you'll be as little
looked upon as a man would amongst a parcel of beaus, that
should pluck out an oval watch, or a pump snuffbox. In your
next, let me hear what you have determined to do, as to your
coming or not, and you will oblige

your friend and servant,

——— ———

Ward is remembered now for only one book, *The London
Spy*. It was written as a periodical, with eighteen numbers between November, 1698 and May, 1700. In a sense, it is another
'trip', but this time through London, moving about town from
one popular spot to another on a continuous journey that his
readers could follow. As always with Ward, the 'trip' was not the
main subject-matter. It was Ned Ward, reporter, commentator,
columnist, but first and last entertainer. The whole pulsing life of
the city flowed through his veins and into his detailed, subjective
descriptions of the social trivia of the day. He kept his readers'
interest from one issue to another by the simple device of showing them the city they knew in a continuous narrative that made
them eager to know what was going to happen next. He tan-
talized his readers by breaking off his narrative in the middle—
'to be continued next month'. *The London Spy* became one
of the few successful periodicals of the town, and made Ward's
reputation. After this, his title-pages carried the words, 'By the
author of *The London Spy*'. Here is his description of London
traffic, on the roads and on the river:

Our Stratford tub, by the assistance of its carrionly tits

of different colours, outran the smoothness of the road and entered upon London's cobble stones with as frightful a rumbling as
an empty haycart. It had no more sway than a funeral hearse,
or a country wagon, so that we were jumbled about like so many
peas in a child's rattle, running a great hazard of dislocation
at every kennel jolt. This we endured till we were brought within
Whitechapel Bars, where we lighted from our stubborn caravan,
with our elbows and shoulders as black and blue as a rural Joan
that has been under the pinches of an angry fairy. Our weary
limbs, rather more tired than refreshed by the thumps and tosses
of our ill-contrived engine, were as unfit to move upon a rugged
pavement as a gouty sinner is to halt o'er London Bridge with his
boots on.

'For my part,' said I, 'if this be the pleasure of riding in a
coach through London streets, may those that like it enjoy it, for
it has loosened my joints in so short a passage, that I shall scarce
recover my former strength this fortnight. I would rather choose
to cry mouse-traps for a livelihood, than be obliged every day to
be dragged about town under such uneasiness, and if the coaches
of the quality are as troublesome as this, I would not be bound
to do their penance for their estates.' 'You must consider,' says my
friend, 'you have not the right knack of humouring the coach's
motion, for there is as much art in sitting in a coach finely, as
there is in riding the great horse, and many a younger brother
has got a good fortune by his graceful lolling in his chariot, and
his genteel way of stepping in and out when he pays a visit to her
ladyship. There are a great many such qualifications amongst our
true French-bred gentlemen, that are admired amongst our nicer
ladies nowadays, besides the smooth dancing of the minuet, the
making of a love song, the neat carving up a fowl, or the thin
paring of an apple.'

'Pray, friend,' said I, 'don't let us trouble ourselves how
the ladies choose their husbands, or what they do with their gallants, but consider how we shall get to the other end of the town,
for my pedestals are so crippled with our whimsical peregrination
that I totter like a foundered horse.'

My friend answered, 'You have expressed such a dislike to
a coach that I know not which way to get you thither if you
cannot walk it, except you can make your supporters carry you
down to the bridge, and there we may take water at the Old

Swan and land at Salisbury Court. Then we shall be properly placed to proceed further in our ramble.'

I submitted accordingly to my friend's advice and hobbled down to the waterside with as much uneasiness as a bear walks downhill. There a jolly grizzle-pated Charon handed us into his wherry, whipped off his short-skirted doublet, whereon was a badge to show whose fool he was, then fixed his stretcher, bid us trim the boat, and away he rowed us. But we had not swum above the length of a west country barge before a scoundrel crew of Lambeth gardeners attacked us with such a volley of saucy nonsense that it made my eyes stare, my head ache, my tongue run, and my ears tingle.

One of them began with us after this manner: 'You couple of treacherous sons of Bridewell b——s, who are pimps to your own mothers, stallions to your sisters, and cock-bawds to the rest of your relations! You were begot by huffling, spewed up, and not born, and christened out of a chamberpot! How dare you show your ugly faces upon the river Thames and fright the Queen's swans from holding their heads above water?'

To this our well-fed pilot, after he had cleared his voice with a hem, most manfully replied, 'You lousy starved crew of worm-pickers and snail-catchers! You offspring of a dunghill and brothers to a pumpkin, who can't afford butter to your cabbage, or bacon to your sprouts! Who was he that sent the gardener to cut a hundred of asparagus and dug twice in his wife's parsley bed before the good man came back again? Hold your tongues, you nitty radishmongers, or I'll whet my needle upon my a——s and sew your lips together.'

This verbal engagement was no sooner over, but another squabbling met us, being most women, who, as they passed us, gave us another salutation: 'You tailors, who pawned the gentleman's cloak to buy a wedding dinner, and afterwards sold his wife's clothes for money to fetch it out again? Here, Timothy, fetch your mistress and I three hap'worth of boiled beef. See first they make good weight, then stand hard for a bit of carrot.' To which our orator, after a puff and a pull-up, being well skilled in the water dialect, made this return: 'You dirty brood of night-walkers and shoplifters! Which of you was it that tied her apron about her neck because she would be kissed in a nightrail, and reckoned her gallant a shilling for fouling of linen, when she had never a smock on? Have a care of your cheeks, you whores; we shall have you branded next sessions so that the world may see your trade in your faces. You are lately come from the hemp and hammer[1]. . . .'

Here we took our leaves of the Lady Thames, wondering she should have so sweet a breath, considering how many stinking pills she swallows in a day. For each neighbouring tail, in contempt of her pride, defiles her peaceful surface, which unsavoury droppings the courteous dame with patience wears to adorn her smooth countenance instead of patches.

Being now landed upon *terra firma*, we steered our course to Salisbury Court, where every two or three steps we met some old figure or another that looked as if the devil had robbed 'em of all their natural beauty, and infused his own infernal spirit into their corrupt carcasses, for nothing could be read but devilism in every feature. Theft, whoredom, homicide, and blasphemy, peeped out at the very windows of their souls. Lying, perjury, fraud, impudence and misery, were the only graces of their countenance.

One with slip shoes, without stockings, and a dirty smock (visible through a crepe petticoat) was stepping from the alehouse to her lodgings with a parcel of pipes in one hand, and a gallon pot of guzzle in the other, yet her head was dressed up to as much advantage as if the members of her body were sacrificed to all wickedness to keep her ill-looked face in a little finery. Another, I suppose taken from the oyster tub and put into whore's allurements, made a more cleanly appearance but became her ornaments as a sow a hunting saddle. Every now and then a fellow would bolt out and whip nimbly cross the way, being equally fearful, as I imagine, of both constable and sergeant, and looked as if the dread of the gallows had drawn its picture in his countenance.

Said I to my friend, 'What can these people be, who are so stigmatized in their looks that they may be known as well from the rest of mankind as Jews from Christians? They seem to be so unlike God's creatures, that I cannot but fancy them a colony of hell-cats planted here by the devil as a mischief to mankind.' 'Why truly,' says my friend, 'they are such an abominable race of degenerate reprobates that they admit of no comparison on this side Hell's dominions. All this part, quite up to the square,

[1] *Making rope, the occupation at Bridewell prison for women.*

is a corporation of whores, coiners, highwaymen, pickpockets, and housebreakers. Like bats and owls they skulk in obscure holes by daylight, but wander in the night in search of opportunities wherein to exercise their villainy.'

When we had taken a gentle walk through this abominable Sodom, where all the sins invented since the fall of Lucifer are daily practised, we came into Fleet Street, where the rattling of coaches loud as the cataracts of the Nile robbed me of my hearing, and put my head into as much disorder as the untunable holloas of a rural mob at a country bull-baiting.

'Now,' says my friend, 'we have a rare opportunity of replenishing our boxes with a pipe of fine tobacco; for the greatest retailer of that commodity in England lives the other side of the way, and if you dare run the hazard of crossing the kennel, we'll take a pipe in the shop, where we are likely to find something worth our observation.'

'Indeed,' said I, 'you may well style it a hazard, for whenever I have occasion to go on the wrong side of the post I find myself in as much dread of having my bones broke by some of these conveniences for the lame and lazy as an unlucky 'prentice to a crabbed master is of a sound beating after a stolen holiday.' However, when we had waited with patience for a seasonable minute to perform this dangerous service, we at last ventured to shoot ourselves through a vacancy between two coaches, and so entered the smoky premises of the famous fumigator. There a parcel of ancient worshippers of the wicked weed were seated, wrapped up in Irish blankets to defend their withered carcasses from the malicious winds that only blow upon old age and infirmity, every one having fortified the great gate of life with English guns well charged with Indian gunpowder.

Their meagre jaws, shrivelled looks, and thoughtful countenances, might render them philosophers; their bodies seemed very dry and light, as if they had been as hard-baked in an oven as a sea-biscuit, or cured in a chimney like a flitch of bacon. They fumbled so very often at a pan of small coal that I thought they had acquired a salamander's nature, and were sucking fire through a quill for their nourishment. They behaved themselves like such true lovers of this prevailing weed that, I dare engage, custom had made their bodies incapable of supporting life by any other breath than smoke.

There was no talking amongst 'em but that puff was the period of every sentence, and what they said was as short as possible, for fear of losing the pleasure of a whiff, as 'How d'ye do?' Puff. 'Thank ye.' Puff. 'Is the weed good?' Puff. 'Excellent.' Puff. 'It's fine weather.' Puff. 'G—d be thanked.' Puff. 'What's o'clock?' Puff, &c. . . .

And, finally, here is a description of John Dryden's funeral, and the end of an era. It is interesting to compare this description with Tom Brown's poem on Dryden's funeral:

A deeper concern has scarce been known to affect in general the minds of grateful and ingenious men, than the melancholy surprise of the worthy Mr. Dryden's death [May 1, 1700] has occasioned through the whole town, as well as in all other parts of the kingdom, where persons of wit, and learning have taken up their residence. Wheresoever his incomparable writings have been scattered by the hands of travellers into foreign nations, the loss of so great a man must needs be lamented amongst their bards and rabbis, and 'tis reasonable to believe the commendable industry of translators has been such as to render several of his most accurate performances into their own language, so that their native country might receive the benefit, and themselves the reputation, of so laudable an undertaking. And how far the wings of merit have conveyed the pleasing fruits of his exuberant fancy is a difficult conjecture, considering what a continual correspondence our nation has with most parts of the universe. For it is reasonable to believe all Christian kingdoms and colonies, at least, have been as much the better for his labours as the world is the worse for the loss of him.

Those who were his enemies while he was living (for no man lives without) have now been made such friends to his memory by his death that they acknowledge they cannot but in justice give him this character, that he was one of the greatest scholars, the most correct dramatic poet, and the best writer of heroic verse, that any age has produced in England.

Yet, to verify the old proverb that 'Poets, like prophets, have little honour in their own countries', 'tis credibly reported the ingratitude of the age is such that they had like to have let him pass in private to his grave. But a true British worthy, meeting with the venerable remains of the neglected bard passing silently in a coach, unregarded to his last home, ordered the corpse (by the consent of his few friends that attended him) to be respited from so obscure an interment; and most generously undertook, at his own expense, to revive his worth in the minds of a forgetful people, by bestowing on his peaceful dust a solemn funeral answerable to his merit. The management of the funeral was left to Mr. Russell, pursuant to the directions of that honourable great man, the Lord Jeffreys, concerned chiefly in the pious undertaking.

The first honour done to his deserving relics was lodging 'em in Physicians' College, from whence they were appointed to take their last remove. The constituted day for the celebration of that office was Monday, the 13th of May, in the afternoon, at which time, according to the notice given, most of the nobility and gentry now in Town assembled themselves together at the noble edifice aforesaid, in order to honour the corpse with their personal attendance.

When the company were met, a performance of grave music, adapted to the solemn occasion, was communicated to the ears of the company by the hands of the best masters in England, whose artful touches on their soft instruments diffused such harmonious influence amongst the attentive auditory that the most heroic spirits in the whole assembly were unable to resist the passionate force of each dissolving strain, but melted into tears for the loss of so elegant and sweet a ravisher of human minds. Notwithstanding their undaunted bravery, which had oft scorned death in the field, yet now, by music's enchantment at the funeral of so great a poet, were softened beneath their own natures into a serious reflection on mortality.

When this part of the solemnity was ended, the famous Doctor Garth[1] ascended the pulpit where the physicians make their lectures, and delivered, according to the Roman custom, a funeral oration in Latin on his deceased friend; which he performed to the great approbation and applause of all such gentlemen that heard him, and were true judges of the matter. Most rhetorically he set forth those eulogies and encomiums which no poet hitherto, but the great Dryden, could ever truly deserve.

When these rites were over in the college, the corpse was

---

[1] *Author of* The Dispensary.

handed into the hearse drawn by six stately Flanders horses and adorned with plumes of black feathers, and the sides hung round with the escutcheon of his ancestors, mixed with that of his lady's; everything was set off with the most useful ornaments to move regard and affect the memories of the numberless spectators. All things being put in due order for their movement, they began their solemn procession towards Westminster. The two beadles of the college marched first with the heads of their staffs wrapped in black crepe scarfs, being followed by several other servile mourners whose business was to prepare the way that the hearse might pass less liable to interruption. Next to these moved a concert of hautboys and trumpets, playing and sounding together a melancholy funeral march, undoubtedly composed upon that particular occasion. (After these the undertaker with his hat off, dancing through the dirt, like a bear after a bagpipe. I beg the reader's pardon for foisting in a jest in so improper a place; but as he walked by himself within a parenthesis, so I have placed him, and hope none will be offended.) Then came the hearse, as before described, most honourably attended with abundance of quality in their coaches and six horses, that it may be justly reported to posterity no ambassador from the greatest emperor in all the universe, sent over with the welcome embassy to the Throne of England, ever made his public entry to the Court with half that honour as the corpse of the great Dryden did its last exit to the grave.

In this order the nobility and gentry attended the hearse to Westminster Abbey, where the choir, assisted by the best master in England, sung an Epicedium. Then the last funeral rites being performed by one of the prebends, he was honourably interred between Chaucer and Cowley. There, according to report, will be erected a very stately monument, at the expense of some of the nobility, in order to recommend his worth, and to preserve his memory, to all succeeding ages.

The cause of his death being very remarkable, it will not be improper in this place to take notice of it, as a means to put the world in mind of what slender accidents are sufficient to change the state of man, and hurry him into the darkness of Eternity. The occasion of his sickness was a lameness in one of his feet, springing from so trivial a cause as the flesh growing over one of his toe-nails which, being neglected, begot a soreness and brought an inflammation of his toe; and being a man of gross

body, a flux of humours falling into the part made it very troublesome, so that he was forced to put himself into the hands of an
able surgeon [Hobbs], who foreseeing the danger of mortification
advised him to part with the toe affected, as the best means to
prevent the ill-consequence likely to ensue. This he refused to consent to, believing a cure might be effected by less severe means
than the loss of a member, till at last his whole leg gangrened;
This was followed by a mortification, so that nothing remained
to prevent death but an amputation of the member thus putrefied.
He refused to consent to this, saying that he was an old man
and had not long to live by course of nature, and did not care
to part with one limb, at such an age, to preserve an uncomfort-
able life in the rest, and therefore chose rather to submit to death.
A little time after, according to the foresight of his surgeons and
physicians, this did unhappily happen. . . .

I shall now return to the end of Chancery Lane, where I
stood to see the funeral pass by, observing there some passages
between hackney coachmen and the mob worth delivering to the
reader. The great number of qualities' coaches that attended the
hearse so put the hackney whore-drivers out of their bias that
against the King's Head Tavern, there happened a great stop,
occasioned by a train of mourning coaches which had blocked
up the narrow end of the lane, obstructed by an entangled number of movable bawdy-houses who waited to turn up the same
narrow gulf the others wanted to go out of. Some ran their poles
into the windows of another coach, wherein fat bawd and whore,
or mother and daughter, squeaked out, for the Lord's sake, that
some merciful good man would come in to their assistance.

One impudent corrector of jade's flesh had run his pole
against the back leather of a foregoing coach, to the great damage of a beau's reins, who peeping out of the coach door, with
at least a fifty-ounce wig on, swore, Damn him! If he came out,
he would make as great a slaughter amongst hackney rogues with
his sword, as ever Samson did amongst the Philistines with the
jaw bone of an ass. Whilst he was thus cursing and swearing like
an old sinner in a fit of gout, his own coachman flinging back the
thong of his whip in striking of the horses, gave him such a cut
over the nose that he jerked in his head as if he had been shot,
not knowing from whence the blow came, and sat raving within
his leathern territories, like a madman chained down to his seat,

not daring to look out, for fear he should a second time pay for his peeping. The coachmen all the while were saluting one another with such diabolical titles, and confounding one another with bitter execrations, as if everyone were striving which should go to the devil first.

At last, by sundry stratagems, painful industry, and the great expense of whip-cord, they gave one another way, and then with their 'hey-ups', and ill-natured cuts upon their horses, they made such a rattling over the stones that had I been in St. Sepulchre's belfry upon an execution day, when the prisoner's bell rings out, I could not have had a more ungrateful noise in my head than arose from their lumbering conveyances.

In 1707 Ward was still squeezing *The London Spy* for its commercial juice by producing variations like '*The London Terraefilius, or the Satyrical Reformer*. Being Drolling Reflections on the Vices and Vanities of Both Sexes.' This was another periodical, but with a new emphasis. 'Characters' were having a brief revival at the time and Ward therefore produced 'characters', with a pretence to satire. This is his professed purpose:

... Satire, at present, is my talent; for stubborn folly and habitual vice must be corrected with severity; therefore stand off knave, have a care fool, fly hypocrite, hide harlot, run libertine, draw bully, skulk bawd, lope skellum, for I am just now going to lay about me like a country cudgel-player. ...

In case there was any doubt about his real purpose, at the end of his first issue Ward inserts a column of 'Divertisements':

Last Monday night, between the hours of eight and nine, lost out of a head-dresser's shop, in our fathers' buildings by a kind female apprentice, about fifteen years of age, a certain chimerical rarity, called a maidenhead; this is therefore to give notice to the public, that whosoever has found it, is desired not to cry it in the market-place, but to return it to the owner the next fair opportunity, after the same manner it was lost, and for his further encouragement, if another maidenhead should start up unexpectedly, madam hereby declares she has a trusy gallant, who is ready at all times to cover the shame with church-security. ...

Any young fresh country lass, who, for loss of her lover,

or perhaps her virginity, has lately popped into London, either in coach, waggon, or on pack-horse, from east, west, north, or south, if she be straight-limbed, and well-featured, shall be welcome to Mother Knab-Cony's House, at the sign of the Church-Warden and Bastard, in Shoving-Alley, near Moorfields, where she shall be furnished with gay apparel, meat, drink, washing, lodging, and physic; allowing only a moiety of her earnings in satisfaction thereof, provided she will submit her carnal endeavours to the management and discretion of the reverend old matron above-mentioned, who promises upon honour, she shall be tenderly used during the time of her servitude, and be free to remove at month's warning, from thence to the Lock-Hospital.

As for the rest, it is Ward at his coarsest walking the London streets:

... Here comes a swanking widow for you, who, I'll warrant, if she was to be weighed against a Smithfield steed, has as much flesh upon her back as a fat Lincolnshire bullock. Her face, by computation, is about the breadth of the pewter-platter in St. John's street, that the mask she wears takes up as much velvet to cover it, as a mountaineer-cap, and as much oilskin to line it as would make a butter-woman's hat-case. Her countenance is enriched with as many juicy pigments as an old drunkard's; and is here and there adorned with such ignescent carbuncles, that whoever gives her a kiss must run a great hazard of setting fire to his periwig. Her breasts are like a pair of cow's udders, when they have just calved; and her neck hangs in wallups, like an old victualler's double chin, or the hide of Langley's Rhinoceros. She is forced to wear sponges under her to catch the dripping of her serum; for though she drinks hard, yet, by the computation of her own chamber-maid, she sweats more than she pisses; though a tall woman, she's as short waisted as a sergeant's blue gown, that there is not above a moderate span between her hips and her shoulders: Her buttocks are as plump and as round as the stern of a Dutch fly-boat; but every step she takes they tremble like an Irish-bog, when trod upon, or a quaking pudding, just clapped upon the table. She is still in her widow's weeds to show her sorrow for the departure of her husband, yet suffers herself to be courted by a carrionly gallant, who is just the reverse of her own character. She has as much black cloth in a petticoat as one of Russel's skeletons has in a mourning-cloak; for her limbs are so long from her neck downwards that every step she takes is an ordinary woman's straddle: Her fiery face, set off with her charcoal coloured weeds, appears like the setting sun, surrounded with sullen clouds; and when ever she speaks, her loud masculine voice breaks through her lips like a clap of thunder. She's a notable merry matron at a gossiping, or a christening, and is never better pleased than when she is replenishing her veins with good claret; which, according to her maid's report, she often takes so immoderately, that it flows back again into the chamber pot, like pricked wine from Cheapside-conduit, upon the birthday of a Prince of Wales, into the caps of the mobile. Her mutton fists are always in such a breathing sweat, that it is two hour's hard work to draw on her gloves, and half as much to pull 'em off again: Her odoriferous petticoats, so perpetually bath themselves in their own moisture, that though she walks upon dry ground, yet she is always wet-shod, insomuch, that the dropsical juices which flow into her shoes never fail, in a week's time, to rot the stitches, and separate the soles from the upper-leathers. She is very devout of a Sunday, and a constant woman at church, where her husband, when he was living, out of a deep regard to the ease of his wife's bumfiddle, caused the seat of her pew to be amply enlarged to the breadth of her buttocks; T.H.J.B. Church-wardens; C.L.D.M. Overseers of the Poor. Her gifts and graces are principally these, viz. she has the nimbleness of a cow, and the bulk and majesty of an elephant; she is very skilful in dressing an issue; for she has had two in her own legs this ten years; she will eat like Heliogabolus, and drink like a German trooper; she is very much of a woman, and too much for any man; has abundance of love, a proportionable fortune, and no children; and having done penance in a mourning veil this six months, stands now exposed to the fairest bidder. He that carries off the prize is desired to take care of the nuptial machine, for a man's weight added to her own, will sufficiently try the strength of a sacking bedstead; nor would I advise any man to enter into an amorous engagement with her, lest he has the courage of a stone-horse; for she requires as much love as a fen-mare, that has been six months a-grazing. Now, Madam, since your magnificent Ladyship, has drawn yourself within hearing, I hope, if I tickle your ears with a gentle reproof, you

will not, out of an effeminate disgust to good advice, ridicule, or
slight what I purely intend for your own singular benefit, viz.
since you are the Leviathan of your sex, improved from a woman
by mere gluttony and ebriety into a she-monster, I would have
you lay aside the thoughts of wedlock till you can meet with your
match, or else endeavour, by a habit of temperance, to reduce
your bulkiness to a matrimonial size, lest the cart-load of blubber
that you drag about with you should not only stink your bride-
groom out of bed, but render you incapable of being a helpmate
to your husband, which is the duty of a wife to be, according to
the words of the great law-giver, Moses; for in short, as all girls
under fourteen years of age ought to think themselves too young
for a bedfellow, so all women above sixteen stone ought to think
themselves too unwieldy for nuptial enjoyment. . . .

Ward was constantly reaching out for new material and
new devices to catch the interest of his reading public. His *History
of the London Clubs* (1709), a series of portraits of both real and
imaginary clubs, was immediately popular and went through a
number of editions. Before the public appetite had jaded he had
issued a *Second Part of the History of the London Clubs*, with a
more exotic list—'The Farting Club', 'The No-Nos'd Club', 'The
Misers Club' and 'The Atheistical Club'. But whatever topical
interest there was in the 'London Clubs' is gone. It makes dull
reading now.

Ward also made his contribution to the genre of letter-
writing:

A Letter from an Enamoured Beau, to a very Beautiful Lady,
upon his seeing her make Exit from that Odoriferous Treasure of
Humane Superfluities, the House of O[ffice].
By Mr. Ward.

Madam,
When accident first dropped in my way so lovely an object as yourself, no convict, at the sight of a reprieve, or miser at
the finding a bag of old Jacobusses, could have thought his eyes
more blest than mine were with your beauty, which had so
powerful an effect upon my working imagination, that I could
not conceive you to be anything less than a piece of unknown

divinity, by chance fallen into this lower world, and by the coldness of the air you passed through frozen into a visible figure,
wherein we might clearly discern the form and deportment of those
beings about us armed with immortality.

My admiration of your perfections so deprived me of my
reason, and nourished my odd conceit to so great a height, that
I could not for my life believe a person adorned with such awful
graces, could be produced by the ordinary means of generation,
or that human acquirements could improve an object to so great
an excellence, being fully persuaded those celestial forms required
not for sustenance, such gross foods as are eat and drank to satisfy
the craving appetites incident to our feeble carcasses, which labour
under the innumerable inconveniences of a short-lived mortality,
but imagined, by your angelic looks, you were of such a chame-
leon-nature, that a bottle of *Montpelier* air would have feasted
your cherubimical prettiness, for at least the term of an apothecary's prenticeship, and that you had no more occasion for a cook
or kitchen in your family, a house or office in your garden, or a
close-stool in your bed-chamber, than a Dutch cripple has for
a pair of skates, or a dead bawd for a brandy-bottle.

I have often pursued your nimble footsteps in a dewy morning, to try if I could discover, by the print of your pettitoes,
whether so beautiful an object could be composed of such gross
matter as we common mortals; but mine eyes were still so dazzled
with the stateliness of your carriage, the proportion of your waist,
and the charming plumpness of your hindermost allurements, that
I was no more able to discern any impression of a grave substance
upon the ground you trod upon, than if I had been following
fair Rosamond's ghost upon a marble pavement, or had been
dancing after a fairy across a farmer's hall, who was running at
midnight to drop a silver penny into a bucket of water to encourage the maid's cleanliness. Having laboured for some time
under this lunatic deception, I thought myself at last in the condition of Ixion, and that I had unhappily fallen deeply in love
with a piece of divinity, that would jilt me at the long-run, and
prove but a mere shadow in my embraces, but however, after
many as serious deliberations as my frenzy would admit of, I thus
determined in myself that if you were not to be enjoyed, you were
still to be adored, so resolved if the purity of your nature was
such as could not admit of the former, I would take pleasure in

the latter; and if I found you unqualified for a bed-fellow, I questioned not but I should find you qualified for a goddess, it being my full intent to conquer you as the one, or submit to you as the other; but providence, in this ripe age of true devotion, not suffering me to straggle from the right worship, was pleased to clear my eye-sight by the following accident, and at once convinced me, I was about to turn pagan to a false divinity.

Rising early one morning to my chamber-window, about the time that Apollo's flanders had just climbed with their gilt chariots above our horizon, and having the opportunity of overlooking your ladyship's backside (that is your garden, Madam, I mean) which I always observed was so well weeded, that there was not left so much as a nettle for a scold to piss on; and as I was thus pleasing my sight with the various colours, and delighting my nostrils with the mixed effluvias of your odoriferous flowers, who should I see but your sweet ladyship pop out of a stinking conveniency, very loosely attired in your morning-dress, to my great surprise as well as disappointment; for the mist which your artful allurements had cast before my eyes, through which I had always seen you, was now dispersed by the truth of your own nature, which I found simply apparent without the least ornaments or arts to hide your imperfections; your face uncovered with pomatum, looked as freckly as the temples of a carrot-pated milk-wench, and your cheeks and lips which before seemed so rosy, by the assistance of Spanish wool, looked now as pale as if a green-sickness appetite inclined you to feed on nothing but oatmeal and tobacco-pipes; love's fleshy cushions of delight, which when trussed up with an artificial rump appeared so plump and inviting, looked as flat and as thin as the buttocks of a Barbary gelding, seemed as flabby as the udder of an old cow, and trembled as you walked, like a quaking-pudding just placed upon the table. Upon the word of an honest neighbour, Madam, I never felt a greater alteration between winter and summer, than I found in my own microcosm, for my blood, which before was so terribly inflamed with the scorching influence of your wash, paint and patches, rump-pads and buttock-bolsters, was so frozen and congealed, when I unhappily found my goddess turned into a ghost, and the wonderful blessings I expected from your beauty to be all frustrated, that I fell down at my window in a swoon under the disappointment, and instead of love, thought I should have died of an apoplexy. But recovering again, was so vexed to think that your Ladyship, whom I had chose as a deity to sacrifice my love to, should eat and drink like us common mortals, and do the more beastly offices of flesh and blood, that all my former affections were instantly changed into aversion, and I can now, with as much pleasure, look upon a Dutch mastiff, or an old cat with sore eyes, as gaze upon a piece of mortality that has so deceived me; and therefore can remain no more than your Ladyship's neighbour in charity, and that's all.

'A Letter of Advice from an old experienc'd City Lecher, to his Daughter at the Boarding-School, being Rules to raise her Fortune', is a clever parody of Halifax's 'Advice to a Daughter':

Dear Daughter,
    I hear you are a very forward baggage of fifteen, and the world thinks you handsome. Your gifts and acquirements must supply the want of money; for though your education has been large, your fortune will be but little; it being a rule with us citizens, to bestow most upon our daughter's breeding, when we have least portions to give 'em, upon this consideration, that in case we cannot make 'em fortunes to match with tradesmen, we are in hopes, if they are beautiful and well-bred, that they will have graces enough to recommend 'em to gentlemen; for if a shopkeeper takes to him a wife without a portion, he's pointed at as much for a fool, as a man is for a cuckold, whose wife is brought to bed within three months after he has married her. But gentlemen of estates may play the simpleton at any time, and its being so common a thing, makes it pass off as much unregarded as champarty in lawyers, or simony amongst clergymen; therefore, since the happiness of that part of your life to come depends upon the good management of this weighty point, matrimony, I think it necessary to arm you with these following instructions that in case Fortune flings a man of merit in your way, you may know how to counterfeit those outward signs of inward excellence, as may deceive the wisest man into a great opinion of your virtues, though your natural inclinations may be loose and vicious; or if it be your fortune to flush a well-fledged woodcock, in whom you can be happy, I shall teach you with what alluring arts and prevailing subtleties he is most likely to be taken.

If you would procure the esteem of an ingenious man, be as modest in his company as a nun at high-mass; yet let your carriage be as stately as an alderman's daughter's at a public feast; for 'tis a received opinion among the judges of your sex, that a reserved behaviour is the surest sign of virtue, and pride in a woman the best guardian to secure it. Be sure be as sparing of your words as wise men are of their promises, or courtiers of their performances; and when you do speak, let it be something that's pretty, but as concise as the prophecy of an oracle; for an ingenious man dreads the tongue of a talkative woman much more than a squirrel does the noise of a drum, or an atheist a clap of thunder. Take care to be obliging, but not free; and though reserved, yet not haughty; for scorn and fondness to a deserving man, are equally intolerable. Though you love the town as dearly as an old citizen's young wife does Tunbridge or Epsom, yet be careful how you acknowledge you are enamoured with its vanities, condemn the noisy hive, and show aversion to its vicious pastimes; speak slightingly of the play-house, though you admire it as much as a zealot does the church, or a beau a dancing-school, and show a seeming inclination to a sedate country life, though 'tis what you abominate as much as a married woman does barrenness, or a libertine the thoughts of wedlock. Be always ready to acknowledge the sovereign authority of an husband, and the duty and submission of a wife, though your headstrong temper is as great an enemy to obedience, as a fanatic is to loyalty, or a proud woman to mean apparel. Let the clergy thus be your great example, preach up passive obedience and non-resistance towards a husband, as they did towards their prince, it will please your suitor to assert it, though you never design to practice it. When he offers you a present, neither slight, nor be fond on't, but receive it with as much indifference as hypocrites say their prayers, or read a chapter in the Bible. When he offers to kiss you, neither turn your head towards him, nor from him, you may venture to let him modestly take a salute, but be sure don't you offer to give it him; be careful also that you pout not out your lip whilst he is possessing of the favour, for that's as much as to say yes, to what is often obtained without asking for. If he attempts to grip your thigh or finger, or handle the bottom of your stomacher, though you are never so well pleased with what he's going about, you must put on a counterfeit frown, and seem to be as angry as a judge, when through mistake the bribe is presented to himself, that should have been given to his lady. If he offers to touch your bubbies, you must cry, Nay, pray, Sir. If he hugs you about the middle, you must cry, O fie, Sir! And if he presumes to tickle the palms of your hands, you must then cry, Foh. Never rail against any of your own sex, for that discovers ill nature. Never commend one man in the hearing of another, for that's ungrateful to him that loves you. Though you fancy wine as much as a beau does chocolate, never be seen to drink any in the company of a prudent man that courts you, lest it washes away discretion, which is the bridle of the tongue, and causes the unruly member to betray your weakness. Never miss church, though you go to it with as ill a will as a scold does to a ducking-stool; and if you cannot answer the reader as you ought to do, dissemble with your lips and your eyes as if you did; for without a little hypocrisy you'll never be thought a devout Christian. Let your table-library in your bed-chamber be furnished with good books, and though you mind them as little as a cuckoo does her young ones, yet turn down a fresh leaf in the practice of piety every day, and lay it open in the window. Hold up your fan when anybody names smock; blush when anybody praises you; turn your head when anybody looks at you; bow when you are drank to sitting; curtsy when you are bowed to standing. And when your lover says, God Save the King, be sure you cry, Amen; and it will oblige him wonderfully; for loyalty in a woman, though it signifies nothing, will sometimes take with a man of worth as much as anything. Mind these rules with an ingenious man, and you may probably gain your ends to your life's happiness: therefore every morning, after your prayers, con this over as your next best lesson, till you have it as perfect as an actress has her part, and one time or other you may chance to find it useful.

But if it be your fortune to be liked by a fop, possessed of an estate sufficient to make your life comfortable, you must then change your behaviour as much as a chameleon does its colour, turn your reservedness into freedom, your silence into tattle, your gravity into air, your discretion into vanity, your wit into puns, and be all over action like an eel new taken, according to the following directions; for the surest way of trepanning a fool, is by humouring the cockscomb with the like folly, as the fox catches the hare by dissembling the like fear, &c.

H

In the first place you must mimic his cringes and formalities, as if you were his monkey; and show as many antic gestures in your compliments, as a kitten playing with a string. Be as singular in everything as if you would set yourself up for an original belsa, and let one word in five be French in whatsoever you talk of; stalk about the room like a peacock in the sunshine, and ape-like, never continue a minute in one posture. Laugh always when you speak, and endeavour to make everything a jest, though not a word of wit in it; talk always within his sphere; complain the weather's very hot in summer, though you find yourself in an ague, and cry it's cold in winter, though you are within two foot of a roasting fire; rail against your own sex for a parcel of tawdry minxes; but let your own apparel, in gaudy colours outshine the rainbow. Assert freedom in a woman is the only sign of virtue, and that the silent lady is the still sow that eats up all the draught. You must be sure to praise all gay fools to be pretty gentlemen; and he that flings away his money most like an ass, to be a man of wonderful generosity. You must rail against the grave wise man, and call him the world's slave, one that lives upon the earth as if he did penance for the sins of his ancestors: express a hatred to all merit; call the parson Heaven's dark-lantern, the soldier a clodskulled hero, the tradesman nasty mechanic; and seem to admire no man but the very blockhead you design to make your market on; applaud his deportment, though it is more ridiculous than a French dancing-master's; approve his wit, though it be more nauseous than a player's; and commend his dress, though it's more fantastical than Sir Fopling Flutter's;[1] rail against sermons as a useless cant in so knowing an age, and commend plays as the more edifying doctrine; call all scholars but a parcel of book-learned dunces, and justify Beau Wilson was a cunninger man than an Archbishop of Canterbury. Flatter him as if he were a prince, for the more you deceive him that way, the more he will love you. Be as expensive to him as you can, 'tis the best way to secure him, for a fool will never part with that easily he has purchased dearly, though it ben't worth keeping. Sometimes complain you have hurt your knee, sometimes that your stomacher hurts your belly, so play him round the bush where the game lies, and you'll find him the more eager for

---

[1] *The title character in George Etherege's* The Man of Mode, *or Sir Fopling Flutter, who became a by-word for the fop.*

the sport. Now and then show him the small of your leg, but seem not to know that he sees it; then clap your hand down your breasts, and complain of a flea, 'twill make him wish his fingers in the same place. Now and then spread the tossel of his neck-cloth, or stroke a straggling hair of his wig into exact order; give him a tickle of the side, or take him by the hand, play the part of a gypsy, and tell his fortune; for fools are as much to be won by love-toys, as children are with knick-knacks; therefore do but play the fool with him as much as he does with himself, and you may draw him after you as amber will a straw, and influence him far more than all the stars in the hemisphere. To show your airiness, you must flutter about the room like a bird in a cage; and when you hear him humming a minuet, you must be ready to dance to it. You'll have no occasion to alter your carriage for what company you see him in, for none will play with him but puppies of the same kind, only of another litter. The documents I have given you are sufficient for the present; and if you chance to entangle such a fool as I have hinted at, in the net of wedlock, I will then further instruct you how you shall use him. In the meantime study both your parts, that you may act either to the life, when occasion requires it; and nothing shall be wanting, but money in me, to complete your happiness, therefore take care to marry him that wants it not, and you will add great comfort to the gray hairs of your aged father.

Ward was not dedicated to his Grub Street condition. At the height of his success, in 1712, at the age of forty-five, he bought an ale-house and turned to trade. With all his popularity he had not prospered. He was growing older, and it was evidently becoming more and more difficult to reach for new tricks to sell his wares. He knew that the route from Grub Street to debtor's prison was short. He must have seen how wretchedly many of his associates ended their lives. Roger L'Estrange, for all his former eminence, died a broken old man. John Dunton, for all his successes and prodigious activity, was hopelessly in debt. Tom Brown lived his last years in poverty and ill health and died relatively young. John Tutchin, editor of the *Observator*, was beaten up for a supposed libel and died soon after. William King was diseased and in debt and was to die shortly. George Ridpath, of the *Flying-Post*, had to leave the country. For a pamphleteer, life's heights and depths depended on whether your party was in power, and during our period neither Whigs nor Tories were in power long enough to ensure a prosperous life for the hack. The life of the Grub Street hack was neither safe nor secure. It had no dignity, it was not respectable. Part of the hardship the hack endured was the direct result of a gay and dissolute life. But that merely hastened the end; it was not the cause. The time was still not ripe, not quite, for one to live simply by the pen. Life was easier in trade, especially if one was growing older. So Ward retired to his ale-house.

The Political Pamphleteers

After all the pandering to public taste, the libels, obscenities and seemingly pointless trivia of Grub Street, the freedom of
the press may not seem an important issue. But the Grub Street
struggle against government interference was an important part of
the struggle for civil rights. Regulation of the press was almost
entirely political at the turn of the 18th century. It was used as an
instrument of government to subdue the opposition, and it was used
inconsistently. Apart from its arbitrary nature, generally speaking, if a man wrote in favour of the government, he was smiled
upon. If he wrote against the government, he wrote at his peril.
This was the situation until well on in the 10th century. When the
Licensing Act lapsed in 1695, the courts merely used the Common
Law for their indictments. Yet life was easier for the pamphleteer
after 1695, because he could print without permission, and the
penalties for breaking the vaguely-defined libel laws were not
severe. Instead of hanging and mutilation there were imprisonment and the pillory. But these were distressing enough.

To understand the situation which the political pamphleteers of our period inherited we must go back to 1660 and sketch
in the momentous struggle between the writers and the government which, as party government developed, became a battle between the Whig writers and the Tory. In 1660 Charles II returned to the throne with the noisy approval of the majority of

his subjects. But the Civil War did not end; it merely shifted ground. It became a war of pamphlets. To meet the pamphlet menace, the government imposed the Licensing Act of 1662, which limited the number of printers, appointed licensers to assess the political loyalty of printed material, and appointed a king's messenger with powers to enter and search for unlicensed presses and printing. The power behind the Licensing Act was Roger L'Estrange,[1] who was made chief licenser: Surveyor of the Imprimery.

L'Estrange's first notable success was in the case of John Twyn, a printer. The title of the book Twyn printed suggests the crime: '*A Treatise of the Execution of Justice:* wherein is clearly proved that the Execution of Judgment and Justice, is as well the Peoples as the Magistrates duty, and if the Magistrates pervert Judgment, the people are bound by the Law of God to execute judgment without them and upon them.' In effect, it justified the execution of Charles I. Twyn was indicted for high treason, found guilty and sentenced to be drawn upon a hurdle to the place of execution, there to be hanged, cut down while alive, his privy parts and entrails to be taken out and burnt before his eyes, his head to be cut off, his body divided into four quarters 'to be disposed of at the pleasure of the King's Majesty.' And the Lord was formally requested to have mercy upon his soul. The sentence was carried out almost to the last grisly detail. It was the usual sentence for high treason. But for printing a book, such a sentence was severe even in the Restoration period, when the slightest opposition was felt to be treasonable. Twyn, unfortunately, had enraged the judge by refusing to tell the name of the author.

The prevailing attitude to censorship was reflected not in the judgement on Twyn, but in L'Estrange's *Considerations and Proposals in order to the Regulation of the Press* (1663). His proposals show the essentially political nature of the censorship and, since L'Estrange was chief censor, indicate the principles which governed him:

What books, libels, and positions are to be suppressed, and

---

[1] *L'Estrange (1616-1704) was a strong royalist. He helped form the* London Gazette *and later became editor of the Tory newspaper,* The Observator. *He was also a translator of some note.*

First, all printed papers pressing the murder of the late King.

Secondly, all printed justifications of that execrable Act.

Thirdly, all treatises denying His Majesty's title to the Crown of England.

Fourthly, all libels against the person of His Sacred Majesty, his blessed Father, or the Royal Family.

Fifthly, all discourses manifestly tending to stir up the people against the established Government.

Sixthly, all positions terminating in this treasonous conclusion, that, His Majesty may be arraigned, judged, and executed, by his people. . . .

Now to the several sorts of penalties, and to the application of them.

The ordinary penalties I find to be these; death, mutilation, imprisonment, banishment, corporal pains, disgrace, pecuniary mulcts: which penalties are to be applied with regard to the quality of the offence, and to the condition of the delinquent.

The offence is either blasphemy, heresy, schism, treason, sedition, scandal, or contempt of authority.

The delinquents are the advisers, authors, compilers, writers, printers, correcters, stitchers, and binders of unlawful books and pamphlets: together with all publishers, dispersers and concealers of them in general: and all stationers, posts, hackney-coachmen, carriers, boat-men, mariners. Hawkers, mercury-women, peddlars, and ballad-singers so offending, in particular.

Penalties of disgrace ordinarily in practice are many, and more may be added.

Pillory, stocks, whipping, carting, stigmatizing, disablement to bear office, or testimony. Public recantation, standing under the gallows with a rope about the neck, at a public execution. Disfranchisement (if free men), cashiering (if soldiers), degrading (if persons of condition), wearing some badge of infamy. Condemnation to work either in mines, plantations, or houses of correction.

Under the head of pecuniary mulcts, are comprehended, forfeitures, confiscations, loss of any beneficial office, or employment, incapacity to hold or enjoy any: and finally, all damages accruing, and imposed, as a punishment for some offence.

Touching the other penalties before-mentioned, it suffices only to have named them, and so to proceed to the application of them, with respect to the crime, and to the offender.

The penalty ought to bear proportion to the malice, and influence of the offence, but with respect to the offender too: for the same punishment (unless it be death itself) is not the same thing to several persons; and it may be proper enough to punish one man in his purse, another in his credit; a third in his body, and all for the same offence.

The grand delinquents are, the authors or compilers, (which I reckon as all one), the printers and stationers.

For the authors, nothing can be too severe, that stands with humanity, and conscience. First, it is the way to cut off the fountain of our troubles. Secondly, there are not many of them in an age, and so the less work to do.

The printer, and stationer, come next, who besides the common penalties of money, loss of copies, or printing materials, may be subjected to these further punishments:

Let them forfeit the best copy they have, at the choice of that surveyor of the press, under whose cognisance the offence lies; the profit whereof the said officer shall see thus distributed: one-third to the King, a second to the informer, reserving the remainder to himself.

In some cases, they may be condemned to wear some visible badge, or mark of ignominy, as a halter instead of a hatband, one stocking blue, and another red; a blue bonnet with a red T or S upon it, to denote the crime to be either treason, or sedition; and if at any time, the person so condemned shall be found without the said badge, or mark, during the time of his obligation to wear it, let him incur some further penalty, provided only, that if within the said time, he shall discover and seize, or cause to be seized, any author, printer, or stationer, liable at the time of that discovery and seizure to be proceeded against, for the matter of treasonous, or seditious pamphlets, the offender aforesaid shall from the time of that discovery be discharged from wearing it any longer.

This proposal may seem fantastic at first sight; but certainly there are many men who had rather suffer any other punishment than be made publicly ridiculous.

Twyn was executed in 1664. For a number of years after, Roger L'Estrange's zeal for inspection kept the press relatively quiet. (Even so, from 1660 to 1680, sixty-five short-lived news sheets were published, many of them unlicensed.) Then came the Popish Plot and the murder of Sir Edmund Berry Godfrey in October, 1678. England was stirred into a frenzy of fear and the Whigs played on the menace of Popery for their political ends. It took Charles II four years to bring the opposition Whig pamphleteers under control.

On February 5, 1680, the Whig publisher, Benjamin Harris, and editor of the anti-government newspaper, *Protestant Domestick Intelligence*, was tried for publishing *An Appeal from the Country to the City* ... which supported the claims of the Duke of Monmouth (the illegitimate son of Charles II) to the throne. This trial, which was published as a broadsheet, shows very clearly the political bias of the courts and the difficulties of opposition pamphleteering and publishing. The assumption from the beginning of the trial seems to have been that the book was seditious. Before any witnesses were called the Lord Chief Justice made his judgement on the book: 'There was hardly ever any book more pernicious to set us together by the ears than this, nor anything a greater incendiary; one can hardly write a worse. . . .'

Witnesses were called to prove that Harris sold the book in his shop; other witnesses testified that the publisher was a quiet and peaceable man. To this the Lord Chief Justice replied: 'There is scarcely any but Smith,[1] that is so factious a seller of books, as Harris: All your *Domestick Intelligences* are so; for which, you know, you have forfeited your recognizance almost in every book.

Robert Stephens (Robin Hog, the Messenger of the Press) was called as a witness:

Stephens: My Lord, I have seen this book several times in his shop, and others too: and I have asked him why he would so publicly vend them? (I did not indeed buy one of them myself, but I caused a man to buy one for me) and he said he had several

---

[1] *Francis Smith, another opposition publisher of the time who got into considerable difficulties with the government. He edited* Smith's Protestant Intelligence. *The reference to Smith and Harris's* Domestick Intelligence *shows that Harris was being tried not merely for publishing the* Appeal, *but for all his publishing transgressions against the government.*

H*

thousands to stand by him: and he is accounted an Anabaptist.
He said so before the masters and wardens of the Company [the
Stationers Company]; who questioned him why he sold such scandalous things. And he said he had several thousands to stand by
him.

Then spoke the Lord Chief Justice to this purpose.

Because my Brother shall be satisfied with the opinion of
all the judges of England what this offence is, which they would
insinuate, as if the mere selling of such a book was no offence.
It is not long since, that all the judges met, by the King's Command; as they did sometime before too: and they both times
declared unanimously, that all persons, that do write, or print, or
sell any pamphlet, that is either scandalous to public or private
persons; such books may be seized, and the person punished by
Law: that all books, which are scandalous to the Government,
may be seized; and all persons so exposing them, may be punished.
And further, that all writers of news, though not scandalous, seditious, nor reflective upon the Government, or the State; yet if they
are writers (as there are few others) of false news, they are indict-
able, and punishable upon that account.

So that, your hopes of anything of that kind, will be vain;
for all the judges have declared this offence, at the Common-
Law, to be punishable in the seller, though in the way of his
trade: the books may be seized, and the person punished. . . .

You have nothing more to do, ⎱ Speaking to the Jury,
but to give your Verdict: ⎰ who presently withdrew.

If there be anything in Law, let me know it; because you
go out.

Then one of the Jury asked my Lord, if they might not
have the book with them, which was there in the Court, and it
was answered in the negative.

Before the Jury went out, Mr. Harris would fain have
spoken to them for himself, but it was not permitted him.

Then, after a little while tarrying, they returned to the
Bar.

And being, as is usual, asked if they were agreed on their
Verdict, and who should speak for them; they answered yes, and
appointed their foreman, who said he was guilty of selling the
book.

At which there was a very great and clamorous shout.

Lord Chief Justice said, that was not their business, they were only to determine whether barely guilty, or not guilty.

The Recorder would have had them give their Verdict by the poll, but they all unanimously cried out, they were all agreed, and then the foreman gave the Verdict again, Guilty.

Mr. Recorder then prayed, that he being for the King, Mr. Harris might stand committed; who was thereupon presently delivered to a tipstaff to be carried to the King's Bench.

Mr. Harris earnestly beseeched his Lordship, that he might be sent to any other prison, and named Newgate three or four times, but it was not granted him. Thereupon he said, I hope God will give me patience to go through it.

Then my Lord Chief Justice spoke to the jury to this effect.

I am sorry you gave countenance to this cause so much, as to stir from the Bar, when the evidence was so full, and when I told you plainly, not only my opinion, but likewise that of all the judges of England, that selling this book was an offence at the Common Law, for which they ought to be punished: and yet with your scruples, you give the party (with their hollows, and shoutings) to take advantage; though you did mean upon the matter the same thing then, you do now. Yet you see, upon every little occasion, when a thing shall seem to thwart the Government, how ready they are to send up their loud hollowings. It was not so prudently done as might have been done.

We had need look about us, for if at such a time, and for such a base book, such clamorous noises shall be made, what shall become of us? Our lives and fortunes are at stake. Would I knew some of those shouters, I would make them know, I would punish them. I am incensed in the behalf of the Government, and of all our lives and fortunes, that such shall go unpunished.

Harris was fined £500 and sentenced to the pillory. This was not as trivial as it may seem. The fine was enormous for the time—£500 has the equivalent value of about £3500 today. Victims in the pillory were usually surrounded by a mob and pelted not only with cabbages and rotten eggs and other refuse, but sometimes with more dangerous missiles. The experience could be fatal. But the Whigs set up a protective cordon around Harris and he was returned to prison pending payment of the fine. Twice the Whig Parliament petitioned the King for Harris's release and were refused. Finally it managed to inveigle his release without the King's knowledge. Harris promptly celebrated his deliverance with a pamphlet, *Triumph of Justice over Unjust Judges.*

May, 1680: The King issued a proclamation restricting all newspapers:

Whereas it is of great importance to the state, that all news printed and published to the people, as well concerning foreign as domestic affairs, should be agreeable to truth, or at least warranted by good intelligence, that the minds of his Majesty's subjects may not be disturbed, or amused by lies or vain reports, which are many times raised on purpose to scandalize the government, or for other indirect ends: and whereas of late many evildisposed persons have made it a common practice to print and publish pamphlets of news without licence or authority, and therein have vended to his Majesty's people all the idle and malicious reports that they could collect or invent, contrary to law; the continuance whereof would in a short time endanger the peace of the Kingdom, the same manifestly tending thereto, as has been declared by all his Majesty's judges unanimously. His Majesty, therefore, considering the great mischief that may ensue upon such licentious and illegal practices, if not timely prevented, has thought fit by this his Royal Proclamation (with the advice of his Privy Council) strictly to prohibit and forbid all persons whatsoever to print or publish any news-books or pamphets of news not licensed by his Majesty's authority.

The King's proclamation checked the newspapers for several months. Then the Whig pamphleteers began again, particularly against L'Estrange, who was accused of being a Papist. L'Estrange replied with the pamphlet, *L'Estrange no Papist,* which in turn brought replies with ingenious titles like, *Dialogue upon Dialogue: or, L'Estrange no Papist nor Jesuite, but the Dog Towzer.* Towzer became one of the pet names that the Whigs gave L'Estrange.

The attack on L'Estrange was one of the minor skirmishes. The main battle was over the succession to the throne: James, the Roman Catholic brother of the King, or a Protestant candidate—the Tories against the Whigs.

Throughout this period the pamphleteers complicated each other's lives by writing obviously seditious pamphlets and signing them with the names of their opponents.

In December, 1680, the popular Whig pamphleteer, Henry Care, was arrested for libel.

April, 1682: 'Popish' Nat Thompson was arrested for libel, released on bail and arrested for debt the same day. Even the Tory pamphleteers were having their difficulties.

There were other arrests, and editors fled the country, usually to Holland. By the end of Charles II's reign, the press was 'in order' again. The Whig papers were all but stamped out and the King ruled supreme. The Popish Plot and the Whig effort to exclude the Roman Catholic Duke of York from the throne, was one of the last great pamphleteering flurries before the lapse of the Licensing Act in 1695.

In 1688, James II was deposed and William III came to the throne. Roger L'Estrange's position as former bloodhound for the Stuarts was delicate in the extreme. For twenty-five years he had tried to stifle the press, in the name of order and political unity. He did not quite succeed, but his term of office was one long harassment. Then in 1688 the Whigs came to power, L'Estrange was dismissed and became a favourite target of abuse. It was not until 1695, however, with the lapsing of the Licensing Act, that the press became significantly more free.

With William III came new provocations and new pamphlet wars. Some Whigs felt that the interests of William's Dutch friends at Court were not England's interests, a point which John Tutchin[1] made in his satire, *The Foreigners*, August 1, 1700. The response to Tutchin's satire was immediate. Within a month appeared *The Reverse: or the Tables Turn'd. A Poem. An Answer to a late Scurrilous and Malicious Medley of Rhimes called 'The Foreigners'*. Shortly after that came *The Natives. An Answer to 'The Foreigners'*. But the main reply was Defoe's[2] *The True Born Englishman*, which demonstrated the crystal purity of the English breed:

---

[1] *Editor of the Whig* Observator.

[2] *Defoe does not quite qualify as a Grub Street writer. In fact, he is one of the great writers of the language. Yet some of his tactics have all the flair of Grub Street and some of them, indeed, are so brilliant that as a Grub Street tactician he is second to none. We shall concern ourselves only with those aspects of Defoe's career that touch on Grub Street.*

Thus from a mixture of all kinds began,
That heterogeneous thing, an Englishman:
In eager rapes, and furious lust begot,
Betwixt a painted Briton and a Scot.
Whose gendering offspring quickly learned to bow,
And yoke their heifers to the Roman Plough:
From whence a mongrel half-bred race there came
With neither name, nor nation, speech or fame.
In whose hot veins new mixtures quickly ran,
Infused betwixt a Saxon and a Dane.
While their rank daughters, to their parents just,
Received all nations with promiscuous lust.
This nauseous brood directly did contain
The well-extracted blood of Englishmen.

This was powerful satire. It attacked aristocratic pretensions and so wittily made the political point that William's interests were England's that it had an immediate success. In fact, it was one of the most popular pamphlets that Defoe wrote, and quickly went through several editions. But it also aroused as much opposition as Tutchin's work and there was another round of replies, for example: *An Answer to a late Pamphlet Entitled 'The True Born Englishman'; 'The English Gentleman Justified*: A poem on the occasion of a late Scurrilous Satyr entitled *The True Born Englishman'*; and a delightful diatribe entitled, *The Fable of the Cuckoo: or, The Sentence on the Ill Bird that defiled his own Nest. Shewing, in a Dissenter's Dream, some Satyrical Reflections, on a late Infamous Libel, call'd, 'The True-Born Englishman'.* Here is a sample of it:

Bane of my life, thou wretch so very vile,
That but to name thee does the tongue defile,
Unnatural cannibal, so barbrous grown,
Instead of other's flesh to gorge thy own. . . .
    You monster! Is this fit for you to tell?
Must my dishonour be your subject matter,
Who share a portion of my human nature?

Curs'd forge of scandal, could you find no other
To bring to show her postures, but your mother?
Are you to turn me up, ye Hell-born imp:
Suppose I am a whore, must you be pimp?
Must the dark closet, where so close you lay
Nine months, ye wretch, be opened by your key?
Or, grant that you my nakedness had seen,
By chance surprised your parent, and your Queen,
You should have gone, you brute, with backward feet,
To cover, and not call folks in to see't.
      The Roman tyrant that his mother wrong'd[1]
Though once to see his place of birth he long'd,
Had yet so great a sense of filial duty,
Not to expose the Venus of her beauty
To the lewd crowd; but chose a silent few
For his mad frolic in that interview.
But thou, to be a witness of my shame,
Call'st all the world, and fill'st the mouth of Fame,
French chattering jays, Scotch daws, and Irish rooks,
Fat German geese, Low-Country Belgic ducks,
Grave Spanish crows, Italian sparrows, pies
Of Poland, almost every bird that flies,
Whether home-bred, or foreign tramontano,
Must pore into my *fistula in ano.*
. . . .

      Near a famed Tower, of old built to oppose
Rude insurrections of Augusta's[2] foes,
Where ancient Thames, with crooked winding glides,
Repletes and ebbs, with her alternate tides,
A forlorn spot, called Execution Dock
Appears to view; on it, of timber-stock
A gibbet stands, a dire memento made,
To frighten those that use the thieving trade,
Poor common slaves, unskill'd in great affairs,
That purloin sheep, and sometimes cows and mares,
And now and then some pirates that have shares
In robberies at sea; and such like deeds,
. . . .

[1] *Nero.*   [2] *London.*

Oft dangle there; the scum of all the nation,
That can't arrive to Tyburn-exaltation;
'Tis neither England, Scotland, Ireland, Wales;
Nor any other land we know of else;
But on bleak sands, its bending forehead shows,
Just where the humorous water ebbs and flows;
There, as fit place, I charge thee in few words,
To scape due vengeance from the injur'd birds.
Advance, and boldly daring wind and weather,
Hang up thy self and Satyr both together;

This controversy was sweetness itself compared to the storm stirred up by Defoe's next pamphlet, *The Shortest Way with the Dissenters* (1702), in which he suggested as a *reductio ad absurdum* that the best way to solve the problem of the Dissenters in England was to kill them off or transport them to the colonies. The occasion of Defoe's satire was the fierce controversy over Occasional Conformity, the device that enabled Dissenters to qualify for public office by taking the Anglican communion, thereby making a show of conformity and avoiding the restrictions of the Test Act. This turn of events came about with the death of William III in March, 1702. His successor, Queen Anne, was intensely High Church and consequently Tory, and for the first years of her reign the Tory pamphleteers flourished. In the House of Commons the Tories gained power and immediately tried to pass a Bill against Occasional Conformity. The bill successfully passed the lower house and was defeated by the Low Church bishops of the House of Lords. This happened several times, and each time public opinion on both sides was aroused until a full-scale pamphlet war developed between the Whigs and the Tories.

Defoe himself considered Occasional Conformity hypocritical. But he was even more opposed to the Tory plan to outlaw Occasional Conformity, which he saw as one more blow against the civil liberties of the non-conformists. *The Shortest Way* is a brilliant example of satiric irony. Defoe assumed the role of a rabid High Church Tory advocating a kind of 'final solution' for the troublesome Dissenters. But irony is a treacherous, double-edged weapon and Defoe's argument was so compelling that at first both Whigs and Tories were taken in. Some High Church

Tories seriously thought it an excellent idea, and the Dissenting Whigs, of course, were appalled. When Defoe, somewhat alarmed, tried to clarify the situation in his *Brief Explanation* by showing his satire to be an attack on the High Church party, it infuriated both sides still more. He was charged with libel and a warrant went out for his arrest. The Government at last had an excuse for punishing a dangerous opposition writer.

On January 11, 1703, the following announcement appeared in the *London Gazette*: 'Whereas Daniel de Fooe is charged with writing a scandalous and seditious pamphlet entitled *The Shortest Way with the Dissenters,* whoever shall discover the said Daniel de Fooe to one of Her Majesty's principal secretaries of state so as he may be apprehended, shall have a reward of 50 pounds which Her Majesty has ordered immediately to be paid upon such discovery.' In the *London Gazette* of January 14, his description was given: 'He is a middle-sized man about 40 years old, of a brown complexion, but wears a wig, a hooked nose, a sharp chin, gray eyes, and a large mole near his mouth; he was born in London, and for many years was a hose factor in Freeman's Yard in Cornhill, and now is owner of the brick and pantile works near Tilbury Port in Essex.'

On May 20, Defoe was betrayed by an informer, 'was taken on Thursday in a private house in Spittle Fields' (*Daily Courant,* May 24), and, according to the *Post Man* of May 25, 'after having been examined, he was committed ... to Newgate.' On July 7 he was tried at the Old Bailey, found guilty and sentenced. The following announcement appeared in the *London Gazette* of August 2: 'On the 29th instant, Daniel Foe, alias de Foe, stood in the pillory before the Royal Exchange on Cornhill as he did yesterday near the Conduit in Cheapside, and this day at Temple Bar, in pursuance of the sentence given against him at the last session at the Old Bailey for writing and publishing a seditious libel entitled *The Shortest Way with the Dissenters.* By which sentence he was also fined 200 marks, to find sureties for his good behaviour for 7 years and to remain in prison till all be performed.'

Defoe himself, with a splendid defiance, wrote his *Hymn to the Pillory,* continuing his attack, and at the pillory itself the Dissenters of London swarmed around Defoe, hailed him as their champion and pelted him with flowers. It was a brief moment of popularity for Defoe. He was returned to Newgate and kept there for five months until Robert Harley, the new Tory leader, decided that he could be useful and had him released. This was interesting, since Defoe was not a Tory, but a Whig. For many years after his release from prison Defoe was to remain outwardly a Whig and work undercover for Harley. It was only in 1714 after Harley was disgraced that Defoe was able to become outwardly a Tory and work undercover for the Whigs. He had lost his tile works as a result of his imprisonment and he now had to support himself and his large family by his political activities and the skill of his pen.

As for Defoe's *The Shortest Way,* there was a flood of replies, ranging from the restrained to the scurrilous, from simple titles like *Remarks on De Foe's Explanation of his Short Way,* to John Dunton's *The Shortest Way with Whores and Rogues ... the whole dedicated to Mr. Daniel de Foe.* The most impressive title was announced in the July 14th issue of the *Daily Courant*:[1] '*The Shortest Way with the Dissenters, or Proposals for the Establishment of the Church,* with the Author's brief Explication considered, his Name exposed, his Practices detected; and his hellish Designs set in a true Light, that the Party which stickles for him may rightly know him; and that which is against him may continue to triumph over him ... To which is added a Postscript by way of Answer to some malicious Aspersions. ...'

Even Ned Ward got into the battle over Occasional Conformity: '*Helter Skelter: or, the Devil upon two Sticks*: In a Comical Dialogue between High Church and Low Church, relating to the Times'; *All Men Mad: Or, England A Great Bedlam; The Dissenting Hypocrite, or the Occasional Conformist,* which was directed particularly against Defoe and Tutchin. But his main contribution was *The Secret History of the Calves-Head Club,* of which he was at least part-author. The Calves-Head Club was purported to be a blasphemous society of Dissenters who, on January 30th of each year, got together to drink to the memory of Oliver Cromwell and his fellow regicides. *The Secret History* was to expose the foul practice by publishing a report of their meeting and the seditious songs they sang to the destruction of the government. The songs published were feeble. But the mere

---

[1] *The first daily newspaper, which came out in 1702. Until the* Daily Courant, *most of the newspapers were published three times a week.*

device of publishing a *Secret History* on January 30th of each year from 1703 to 1713—one edition appeared even in 1721—had most people convinced that there was such a thing as a Calves-Head Club. The 1704 edition was dedicated ironically to the Whig John Tutchin as the Club's chief inspiration and 'Secretary to the abominable Society of King-Killers', and the dedication continued to appear for several years after Tutchin died in 1707.

It should be pointed out that Ned Ward was not a party hack in the pay of the Tories. Possibly he wrote because the subject was ripe and he smelt a quick sale. But in their politics the Grub Street hacks were usually sincere. Ward was in fact, militantly High Church and Tory and he wrote what he believed.

The battle over Occasional Conformity resolved itself into a battle of champions: For the Whigs, Defoe and Tutchin, for the Tories, Charles Lesley, editor of *The Rehearsal* and James Drake, editor of the *Mercurius Politicus*. This, of course, is over-simple for Grub Street. Defoe and Tutchin had not yet forgotten their own battle over *The True Born Englishman*. Outwardly they were still enemies, though how much so is not clear, as we see from the following title, *The Republican Bullies: Or, a Sham Battel between two of a side, in a Dialogue between Mr. Review* [Defoe] *and the Observator* [Tutchin], *lately fall'n out about keeping the Queen's Peace . . .*, dated 1705. The fight between the Whigs and the Tories was not a fair one. The Whig pamphleteers were at a continual disadvantage until the Tories were defeated in 1705. They were in constant danger of arrest and both Defoe and Tutchin had been taken into custody. The difficulties of opposition pamphleteers are clearly illustrated in the pages of Tutchin's *Observator* of the period. The following excerpt, the Preface to the first volume of his *Observators,* shows embattled Tutchin in the role of St. George:

The
PREFACE
To The
READER.

I have now finished one volume of *Observators*, notwith-standing the inveterate malice, and envy of the enemies of our country, against the design of this paper, which was only to set things in a true light, and to show who have been the betrayers of our country and who have impoverished the kingdom by their piracies on the public; as also to defend my Queen's title to the Crown, which was opposed by the Jacobites and High-Flyers, High Church Tories, before it was placed on her head; as also of her successors, the Princess of the House of Hanover.

I must confess many pens there are in England more cap-able of such a performance than mine: but very few there are will make themselves public in the service of their country; be-cause thereby they make themselves a mark for the enemies of our country to shoot at. If I have done what no man else dare do, I think I have deserved the applause, and not the censure of my Countrymen.

The *Observators* were written in the form of a dialogue between Country-Man and Mr. Observator. Here in the July 1st to 4th issue of 1702 is the first of a series of vindications of the *Observator's* policies:

Country-Man. When I was last at London in a bookseller's shop, I heard one that looked like a gentleman, say, that in a short time they would exalt your Worship to the pillory for writ-ing this *Observator*. You see, how you must expect to be treated; for he that justifies Queen Anne's title, is as odious in the eyes of the Jacobites and Tories, as is anyone that has saved the life of King William.

Observator. All their threats I don't value. I know they threaten me with the Privy-Council, with messengers and Secre-tary of State's warrants, and abundance of frightful stories; against all which, I hold up my target of English Law, and if that don't secure me, I must fall a sacrifice to Arbitrary Power. I am yet within the protection of the Law; for in this nor any other paper have I written one word against our Constitution. I have scandalized nobody by falsehoods and malicious calumnies: but, if speaking the truth, if vindicating my Queen's title, (which none except myself has done) if asserting the Constitution of my dear country, its ancient laws and liberties, be a crime, then I acknowledge myself a criminal; but such times I hope will never happen in England.

Country-Man. But, Sir, if the great men in power will crush you, you are undone, they'll tell you, it is not for men of your quality to meddle with state affairs, and that you are busy and troublesome, and ought to be suppressed.

Observator. I don't meddle with state affairs, I take not the business of the Ministers out of their hands; I only reflect on things that have happened, and give my judgement on them as they are a benefit or detriment to the public, and this is lawful for any man of the meanest quality in England to do.

Country-Man. But they say you are no capable judge of what is or is not for the interest of your country.

Observator. Why not I, as well as another?

The cry against John Tutchin seemed to increase with every issue. In 1703 a mock trial was published, foreshadowing Tutchin's real trial a year later:

THE

EXAMINATION, TRYAL,

AND

CONDEMNATION

of

Rebellion Ob——r, &c.

We the Grand Inquest for the body of this City, upon our oaths, do say, that Rebellion Ob——r, not having the fear of treason or scandal before his eyes, but moved by the instigation of the Devil's children the Republicans, did villainously, traitorously, maliciously, feloniously, rascally, and injudiciously, without appearance of reason on his part, make his endeavour by the assistance of pen, ink, and paper, three poisonous weapons to stab the Church established and the present constitution, to the heart, in order to bring in anarchy and confusion; and them to murder, and utterly extirpate, did publish weekly on Wednesdays and Saturdays, for this year and half past, a libel in breadth six inches, and ten in length, and yet continues publishing and setting it forth, to the great grief of Her Majesty's true friends and subjects, and the unspeakable dishonour of a government who gives him its protection. In regard therefore to our duties to the Queen, aforesaid, we the Jurors aforesaid, pursuant to the depositions made upon oath before us, do return him the said Rebellion Ob——r, to fall under the cognizance of this Honourable Court, as a false traitor and incendiary, an enemy to Her Majesty and the present ministry; and do think in our consciences, notwithstanding he has been teaching us our duty in his late papers, and he had those who brought in their verdict *Ignoramus* the last session, that he is guilty of the crimes aforesaid, and has attempted the murder, aforesaid, and ought to suffer as in cases of treason and sedition, aforesaid, &c.

On February 25, 1704, the government finally made its move against Tutchin and issued a proclamation for his arrest. The ostensible reason was a particular passage in the February 9-12 issue of *The Observator* which was called libellous, but it is clear that this was the excuse the government was waiting for. The proclamation was issued on a complaint made to the House of Commons. A reward of £100 was offered for Tutchin's discovery and apprehension and £50 each for the apprehension of John How, the printer, and Benjamin Bragg, who sold the *Observators*.

For several months before he was brought to trial Tutchin fought his case through the pages of his *Observator*, an expedient which today's laws would not have permitted him. Even on the morning of his trial he continued his defence against the charge. The following description of Tutchin's trial was issued as a broadsheet:

THE
TRYAL AND EXAMINATION,
of
MR. JOHN TUTCHIN,
For Writing a certain Libel, call'd the
OBSERVATOR;

Before the Right Honourable the Lord Chief Justice HOLT, &c.

at Guild-Hall in the City of London, on Saturday the 4th of November 1704.

On Saturday the 4th of November 1704 Mr. John Tutchin was brought to his trial at Guildhall upon an information, for writing a scandalous, and seditious paper, called the *Observator*; at which time the Court being sat, and the jury sworn, his indictment was read to this effect, viz. that John Tutchin, Gentleman, did falsely, maliciously and seditiously write a libel, called the *Observator* to the disturbance of the peace, and tranquillity of this Kingdom of England, and to the great scandal and reproach, of our Sovereign Lady the Queen, and her Government, against the peace of our Lady now Queen, her crown and dignity, &c.; he the said John Tutchin, being a seditious person, and a daily inventor and publisher of false novelties, and of horrible and false lies, and a perpetual disturber of the peace; to which the defendant by his council pleaded Not Guilty: whereupon the Queen's council opened the cause, and ordered to be read several of the defendant's papers, called the *Observators*, that reflected upon the government, and Ministry of State in general; and accordingly several paragraphs of the said papers and libels were audibly read in court; after which Her Majesty's Attorney General spoke very learnedly to each particular circumstance of the indictment, which concerned both Prince and people, and that it tended to the disturbance of the peace, as well as to the creating a misunderstanding between Her Majesty's subjects; the said libel was scandalous, seditious and malicious, reflecting upon the Ministry in general, and on Her Majesty's Government in particular.

Then one of the Queen's evidence were called, who declared in court that the defendant John Tutchin, brought a certain paper called the *Observator* to him in writing some years ago, and made an agreement with him, to have it printed and published twice a week, viz. Wednesdays and Saturdays, which he said was done accordingly. But being asked if he printed it word for word as it was brought him in writing, he answered, that he oftentimes took out words that he did not like, and put in others that he thought more proper: and being further asked whether Mr. Tutchin himself inserted to his said paper the title of *Observator*, or whether he advised him to it, to which he answered in the affirmative.

From which the defendant's council took occasion to insinuate, that Mr. John Tutchin could not, in a positive sense, be the author of the libel mentioned in the indictment, in regard those words that were taken out, and others that were put in their steads, might so far alter the intent and design of the first author, that consequently it could not properly be called his. In answer to which the Queen's council made it plainly appear, that the defendant had actually owned the said paper to be his, by causing the said printer to publish a set of the said libels in a volume together, to which said volume, the said Mr. Tutchin had not only prefixed a preface, but subscribed his name at large.

Another evidence for the Queen declared in court, that the said defendant John Tutchin, did acknowledge and own before Her Majesty's principal Secretary of State, that he was the author of the said libel called the *Observator*, and consequently there was no room to doubt the contrary.

Then the defendant's council entered into a debate, whether the said paper entitled the *Observator* amounted to the charge laid in the indictment against the defendant; viz. scandalous, seditious, malicious &c. in regard no part whereof mentioned any particular person by name, only in general terms, that there were mis-managements in the Ministry in several offices &c. from whence they argued that no person whatsoever in any station had thereby received any scandal or damage. nor the government any prejudice upon that account.

But the Queen's council very learnedly argued, that since the defendant had in some of his papers in a manner positively asserted that the Ministry was corrupted with French gold, and that great men in offices took bribes (as it were) to betray the nation, and several other scandalous expressions that he often used in his said papers, it sufficiently amounted to reflections on the government in general, and on Her Majesty in particular in employing men in the Ministry as would betray the nation, &c. and therefore consequently made good the charge contained in the indictment viz. scandalous, malicious and seditious &c.

Then the defendant's council raised some scruples relating to the indictment, which charged the defendant with writing, printing and publishing the said libel in the City of London, when it was written in Surrey, and afterwards sent to the printers in Gracechurch Street: to which Her Majesty's council replied that

since it was printed and published in London, and the agreement
was made in that City, where first written, it was no error in
the indictment, because it was proved, and more than that, he
acknowledged himself the author of it, therefore it was not material
nor indeed possible to know in what place he composed it always;
and thereupon very largely insisted upon several branches of the
indictment, setting forth the ill effects such scandalous papers
might by degrees have upon the public, by instilling wicked principles into the minds of men, sheltering themselves under the
plausible pretences of defending the rights and liberties of the
people. And that if mercenary scribblers were allowed such an
uncontrolled freedom, no government could be safe, or enjoy any
peace and tranquillity under such an unbounded liberty.

And further added that the government having from time
to time in an indulgent manner, gently admonished him to forbear writing such a scandalous paper; but instead of taking their
good advice, he rather increased his reflective expressions, and
as it were, seemed to defy both law, justice, and authority.

After which the council on both sides engaged in several
learned debates, as to the nature and consequences of libels in
general, and this of the defendant's in particular, the Queen's
council insisting that it was a scandalous and pernicious libel, and
the defendant's endeavouring to prove the contrary; so that having maintained near four hours dispute pro and con, relating to
the matter in question, the Lord Chief Justice Holt gave his
charge to the jury, and in a very large and excellent discourse,
opened and explained the particular circumstances contained in
the trial, both for the Queen and the defendant, as also the nature
and consequences of such libellous and scandalous papers, and
what evil effects such libels might produce if not in time prevented; with other notable arguments too tedious to repeat; so
that leaving the decision thereof to the jury, they thereupon withdrew for about a quarter of an hour, and then returned and
brought Mr. Tutchin in Guilty, of the said indictment.

His sentence, and punishment, is to be ordered as Her
Majesty's judges of the Queen's-Bench-Bar at Westminster shall
think fit to appoint.

The Court was crowded on this occasion in an extraordinary manner, so that the whole hall was not sufficient to contain them, nay, even King's Street, especially that end next Guild

Hall was so thronged and crowded with people as scarcely ever was known upon such an occasion, in the memory of man.

Tutchin escaped sentencing on a technical flaw. The prosecution was unable to establish his responsibility for the publication. For one month no *Observators* were published. Then on December 6, 1704, publication was resumed with a hearty, 'Here's our old friend Master *Observator* come again.'

Tutchin continued his *Observator* until three years later, in 1707, when he was beaten by persons unknown and died of his injuries. In the October 1, 1707, issue of his own *Observator* it is recorded that 'upon opening him, the surgeons found his lungs sound, but his kidneys and his head damaged by their blows. . . .'

Defoe might have come to a similar end but for his political connections. On February 19, 1704, he founded his famous *Review*. Three months later Harley supplanted the Earl of Nottingham as Secretary of State and Defoe got himself a second job. He was to make enquiries about men hostile to the Tory administration, to establish relationships with the Whig editors and to act as an *agent provocateur* by writing articles in his *Review* attacking Harley. In this way he could not only act the part of a healthy Whig, but bring Harley's Whig enemies out in the open, which would be satisfying to both sides. Defoe had one more duty, to get lists of those financing the opposition papers. By joining both the Whigs and the Tories at the same time Defoe had hit on how to be a successful pamphleteer and keep alive. Defoe's dishonesty cannot be defended, but his party principles have a certain consistency if we are to accept at face value his pamphlet, *Rogues on Both Sides*, written in 1711:

> . . . The violencies of parties are now come to that extravagant bigotry to men, and not principle; that if any demagogue cries out in a shower of rain, that it rains buttered turnips, the whole party will face one down, that it is so, nay, believe it so far themselves, that they'll bring out their pewter platters and earthen dishes, and copper and brass vessels, to catch them; and eat whatever these receive with a perfect Israelitish faith, since it seems to them to be no other, than their leaders tell them it is.

> Nannius, a zealous Whig, was consulting with three or four companions, what tavern to spend the evening in; and the Vine

in Long-Acre being proposed, Nannius cries out, Dammee, 'tis a Tory Tavern, and the Dog cannot have good wine; never considering, that it was no damage to the Whig cause, that the Tories know, and love good wine, and they have ever since their birth, to the day of the date hereof.

Tabitha, a good pious painstaking sister, lives within the precincts of Lambeth Marsh; she washes linen with that address, that every customer recommends her to his acquaintance; but it happens, that she frequents the morning lectures of the Saints, and remembers not only the text, but the whole sermons of the gifted. She was recommended to Furius, a Tory, and a beau, whose faith was much in clean linen, who understanding she was a Whig, cried, Stap my vitals, the bitch can never wash well, for she is a Whig; not considering, that a Whig may love clean linen, as well as a Tory.

I confess, for my own part, I was always so unfortunate, as not to be able to continue long of any party, that was uppermost; because both Whig and Tory have still been guilty of things complained of in each other. Both sides have shown dexterity enough to gain their point, but neither has yet discovered ability, moderation, or justice enough to maintain themselves in their posts, but have hitherto lost them as weakly and shamefully as they got them, with address and judgement; like generals, who are very successful in battles, but never know how, or do not care to pursue the victory. . . .

By the summer of 1705 the Tory cry that the Church was in danger was too extreme even for Queen Anne. She withdrew her support from the Tories, a new election was held and the Whigs were returned with a majority. The Tory pamphleteers very soon were in the same dangerous position that their brother Whigs had occupied. The Queen's attitude to the Dissenters became more moderate, and Ned Ward, disgusted with the turn of events, wrote his most powerful attack on the Dissenters, *Hudibras Redivivus*. But Ward miscalculated the new temper of the times, and when one issue attacked the Queen the Whigs had him arrested on June 13, 1706. These were the offending lines:

But that which makes the Church-men wonder,
And strikes them worse than bolt of thunder,

Is that an English heart of oak,
Who, like a friend, so kindly spoke,
Should put upon them such a joke,
And make 'em by experience find,
That Woman's words are only wind
. . . .

Good deeds become an English heart,
Fine words don't contervail a fart.
Heroic actions are alone
The glories of a camp and throne.

On November 14 the *London Gazette* announced: 'Edward Ward, being convicted of writing, printing, and publishing, several scandalous and seditious libels entitled *Hudibras Redivivus, or a Burlesque Poem on the Times,* highly reflecting upon Her Majesty and the government; was likewise on Thursday last fined for the same by the court of Queen's-Bench 40 marks, and ordered to stand in the pillory on Wednesday next at Charing Cross for the space of one hour, between twelve and two in the afternoon, with a paper on his head denoting his offence; and also to stand in the pillory on Thursday next near the Royal Exchange in Cornhill in like manner; and, before he be discharged out of prison, he is to give security for his good behaviour for one year.'

William Pittis, another Tory pamphleteer, got into one scrape after another, for the same reason—defending the Church. Most of his difficulties arose from one book, James Drake's *Memorial of the Church of England,* an extreme High Church attack on the new policy of moderation. Pittis persisted in vindicating Drake's position with a single-tracked perversity that one must admire. *The Memorial* was published early in 1705, and when the Whigs came into power they issued a proclamation offering a reward for the capture of the author. Although they arrested the printer, David Edwards, and promised him a pardon if he revealed the author's name, he refused and the Whigs never discovered who the author was. *The Memorial* itself was burned by the Grand Jury of London in August, 1705.[1]

---

[1] *J. Drake's career as a Tory pamphleteer was almost as colourful as Pittis's. He attacked the Whig government in his* History of the Last Parliament *(1702), was brought before the House of Lords and acquitted. His* Historia Anglo-Scotica *offended the Presbyterians and it was burnt at Mercat Cross, Edinburgh, June 30, 1703. In 1706 he was convicted of a libel in his journal* Mercurius Politicus *and acquitted on a technicality. The government was in the process of re-phrasing the charge when he died in 1707.*

On October 11, 1705, William Pittis was committed for writing *The Bonfire*, a derisive comment on the burning of *The Memorial*. This was his third entanglement with the courts. Earlier, in March, 1704, even the Tories had found him offensive and took him up for libel for his periodical *Heraclitus Ridens*, which suddenly ceased publication. But *Heraclitus Ridens* was merely transformed into the *Interloping Whipster*, Pittis was taken up again, and this time made his first acquaintance with the pillory. In 1706 he wrote a lengthy defence of *The Memorial* entitled, *The Case of the Church of England's Memorial Fairly Stated*. On April 27 Pittis 'was ordered in the Court of Queens-Bench to stand in the pillory three times, and to pay 100 marks for writing the *Vindication of the Memorial of the Church of England*. At the same time Mr. Sawbridge[1] the bookseller was fined 200 marks for printing the same, and ordered exposed in Westminster Hall with a paper affixed to his hat signifying his crime.'

But this was not the end of Pittis's career in the courts. In 1707 he made another defence of *The Memorial* in a half-sheet entitled, *Fire and Faggot*, for which he was again committed, but managed to escape sentencing. As for Pittis's booksellers, frequently they were arrested with him. But at least Pittis's escapades provided them with excellent advertising copy:

ADVERTISEMENT.

Just published, *Fire and Faggot*, or the City Bonfire, for which the printer and publisher are bound over by order from above.[2]

Although the Tories were solidly in power in 1710, Pittis still found a way to get into trouble. In December, 1712, the government was looking, unsuccessfully, for the author of a Jacobite pamphlet entitled *Jus Sacrum*, this time not about the Church, but about the right of kings, particularly of the Stuart pretender to the throne. It was the work of Pittis. Finally, in December, 1714, with the Whigs back in power, Pittis was jailed for his *Reasons Against a War with France*. This last experience must have been discouraging, because we hear little about him after 1714. Between his politics and his debts, drunken Pittis had spent a good part of his Grub Street life communing with the courts.

---

[1] *George Sawbridge the younger. See above, p. 113.*
[2] *From Pittis's own journal,* The Whipping-Post, *Oct. 2 1705.*

With the Tories back in power in 1710, the Tory pamphleteers were again triumphant and the Whigs on the run. The political writer by this time had become an important element of party government. He had acquired status. The best writers in the country had ranged themselves on either side of the party struggle. But even the best had their difficulties. Richard Steele was expelled from the House of Commons for *The Crisis*, which accused the government of plotting against the Protestant succession. He got off lightly. Swift himself was pursued by the House of Lords in March, 1714, for his pamphlet, *The Public Spirit of the Whigs*—mainly an attack on Steele, with some slighting references to the Scottish nobility—and a reward of £300 was offered 'for discovering the author of [that] false, malicious, and factious libel.' His publisher and printer were taken into custody, while Swift, by virtue of his position and the protection of Robert Harley, was untouched. Defoe, after his experience at the pillory and Newgate Prison, wrote for both sides at the same time which gave him a special status in Grub Street. Yet even he got into difficulties again, as John Oldmixon describes in his *History of England during the Reign of Queen Anne:*

About this time [1713] too appeared three pamphlets with the following titles:

> *Reasons against the Hanover Succession, &c.*
> *What if the Queen should die?*
> *What if the Pretender should come?*

In each of these pamphlets there were several passages highly treasonable; and it was easily perceived they were writ by Daniel Foe. Mr. Benson, who, as I said before, was under a sham prosecution, was resolved to carry on a real one against this tool of the ministers. He spared neither pains nor expense on this occasion, and in a few days he got into his own possession the original manuscripts of all those three pamphlets, written in D. Foe's own hand, or rather hands, for they were every one of them different; but all the three being proved by one of the printer's servants, before the Lord Chief Justice Parker, to be the handwriting of D. Foe, his Lordship granted a warrant to take him up; which being done, tho' not without much trouble and charge, his Lordship committed him to Newgate. But what was matter of great surprise was, that the very person whose proper business it was to appear against him, appeared for him, and approved of his bail, namely, Mr. Borret, Solicitor to the Treasury, which he durst not have done without order from his masters. Mr. Benson immediately applied to Sir Edward Northey (then Attorney-General) and offered him no less than ten guineas to retain him against D. Foe; but he declined it, and told Mr. Benson, he could not be concerned in the prosecution without an order from a Secretary of State. Mr. Benson then went to another eminent Council (now one of the greatest ornaments of Westminster Hall) who made no difficulty, but entered very heartily into the prosecution, and it was brought near to a day of trial; at which time the same person who had procured D. Foe to be bailed, procured his pardon, which Foe produced in the Queen's-Bench.

Here the reader may observe the unparalleled impudence of the then Ministers,[1] who had made the Queen so often declare to her parliament, how much she had the House of Hanover at heart, and who had themselves so often solemnly sworn to it, yet here, in defiance to all sense and conscience, they appeared as openly for the Pretender, especially the then Lord Bolingbroke (who countersigned the warrant for D. Foe's pardon) as if they had been at that very instant, what Bolingbroke has been since, the Pretender's own Ministry.

This prosecution, however, which was begun and followed by a private gentleman, and entirely at his own expense, and was carried so far that the Royal Pardon only could protect the criminal, had the good effect, that the tools of the Ministers were afterwards obliged to be more cautious.

It was on the first day of Easter term, that Daniel Foe, for whose appearance J. Grantham, Printer, and T. Warner, Publisher, had been bound in £400 a piece, did appear, among others, at the Court of Queen's-Bench; and her Majesty's Attorney-General acquainting the Court that he was ordered to prosecute him for the above-mentioned libels, he was continued upon his recognizance; but before he went out of Court the Lord Chief

---

[1] *As a Whig historian, Oldmixon had a built-in bias against the Tory ministry.*

Justice Parker caused the two *Reviews*[1] of the 16th and 18th of April to be shown to him, and asked him whether he was the author of them, which, after some hesitation, he confessed; whereupon his Lordship declared, that those two papers were very insolent libels against him in particular, and also against the laws of England; but that his Lordship being personally concerned, he would leave it to the other judges to do what they thought fitting in that matter; and the two *Reviews* being then distinctly read their Lordships concurred in opinion, that they were highly insolent to the Lord Chief Justice, and a notorious contempt to that Court, and the laws of the nation, and that the said Daniel Foe should be committed prisoner to the Queen's-Bench for his said offence.

The Court was unanimous, that the books for which he was bound over were scandalous, wicked and treasonable libels; but D. Foe endeavouring to excuse himself, by saying the books were writ ironically, he was told by Judge Powis, after several learned arguments to prove the absurdity of that pretence, that he might be hanged, drawn and quartered for those books. But Daniel Foe had the good luck to escape the gallows, in the manner as has been mentioned. There was a search at this time for Pittis, the author of *Jus Sacrum*, but he could not be found. This wretch had been at Oxon, sold his fellowship of New-College, went to London, turned quack, Jacobite and libeller, and was soon reduced to beggary and infamy, which well qualified him for the service of the cause he now espoused.

Thanks to Harley's intervention, Defoe was released from prison. The maximum penalty of hanging, drawing and quartering could still have been imposed for Defoe's offence, though it was unlikely. Yet it was an unnerving experience, which put him even further in Harley's power. Now everyone knew that he had been a two-layered pamphleteer, Whig on the outside and Tory on the inside. The Whig crowds who once pelted him with flowers at the pillory did not appreciate his virtuosity. The Whig hacks were merciless: 'Judas discovered and caught at last ... a thorough-paced, true-bred hypocrite, a High Churchman one day, and a

---

[1] *Defoe's famous* Review *(1704-1713) was one of the great achievements of early 18th-century journalism. He wrote it single-handed while engaging at the same time in a multitude of other literary activities.*

rank Whig the next.' This did not do justice to Defoe's agility, since he was both Whig and Tory at the same time. Defoe's later journalistic career was no less agile. He was involved in two more libel suits and each time was saved by Harley. And when Harley was removed from office and the Whigs returned to power, Defoe merely reversed himself. He became outwardly a Tory convert and secretly controlled the Tory press for the Whigs. Finally, in 1719, at the age of sixty-one, he wrote *Robinson Crusoe* and embarked on a new career which was to make him one of the great novelists of English literature. It was certainly a less dangerous career.

Modern scholars have been inclined to be lenient with Defoe's political gymnastics. Like most men of letters of the time, they argue, Defoe repudiated the label of party man, whether it was Whig or Tory. And it is true, as we have seen in *Rogues on Both Sides,* that Defoe claimed to prefer truth to faction, and truth was not always confined to one party. The inference is that he worked for what he believed to be the best interests of his country, regardless of party labels. But there is still a great deal of duplicity that cannot be explained away. And it is not surprising that many of Defoe's contemporaries, not blessed with a 20th-century perspective, were not so charitable.

The times in which Defoe wrote were difficult for political pamphleteers, despite the abolition of the Licensing Act. A certain amount of subterfuge was undoubtedly necessary in order to survive. Even for the major writer with good connections, political pamphleteering was dangerous. But for the common run of pamphleteers, the result was likely to be Newgate Prison and financial ruin. As for the government, it viewed the situation of an unbridled press as calamitous and did everything it could to curtail its activities. In 1711 Bolingbroke, the Secretary of State of the Tory government, apprehended fourteen booksellers, printers and publishers for "printing and publishing Libels and Ballads, some of which write really scandalous invectives against the Ministry and Government."[1] Although the Tory government was unable to limit the press by direct legislation, they were responsible for the Stamp Tax of 1712, by which they intended to destroy the Whig

[1] *Abel Boyer,* The Political State of Great Britain *(London, 1934), Vol II, p. 645, from Ronbesterg, Publishing . . . in England, II, pp. 401-402.*

opposition. It is interesting that Jonathan Swift opposed the Stamp Tax, even though he was a friend of Harley and Boling-broke, the Tory leaders, and was the author of one of the most formidable satires on Grub Street ever written, *A Tale of a Tub* (1704). 'They are here intending to tax all little printed penny papers a halfpenny every half-sheet, which will utterly ruin Grub Street, and I am endeavouring to prevent it,' he said in his *Journal to Stella*. Even for Swift, despite his satire, Grub Street was an institution to be preserved. Swift did not prevent the tax, and it did cripple Grub Street. Many newspapers ceased publication, the number of pamphlets was reduced. But Grub Street survived, and it is still with us. It is not so raucous, perhaps, it has become rather respectable and very much duller, but life would be duller still without it.

Payment and Dedications

Despite the vinous example of writers like Pittis and Tom Brown, many of the hack authors did not lead particularly gay lives. The Grub Street myth of the carefree, irresponsible hack dancing through life one step ahead of the bum-bailiff did not remotely fit the facts, for instance, of John Oldmixon's life. 'It is said of this man [Oldmixon],' Isaac Disraeli remarked, 'that "he had submitted to labour at the press, like a horse in a mill, till he became as blind and as wretched." '[1] This is not to suggest that the Oldmixons were martyrs of unrewarded virtue, but simply that they worked hard at their Grub Street trade and for all their prodigious efforts lived in misery and squalor.

Some figures are available which roughly indicate the pay the hack writers of the period received for their literary labours. To be meaningful, these figures, of course, must be translated into modern values. According to the Bank of England, £1 in 1700 would have the purchasing power of about £7 today. And there is Dr. Johnson's remark in Boswell's *Life*[2] about the Irish painter who managed to live in London on £30 a year in about 1730. However, this was looked on as a phenomenon of frugality and even Oldmixon might not have managed it. The most helpful way of interpreting the value of money at the time is to know what it could buy. By studying the account-books of the period,

[1] Calamities and Quarrels of Authors *(1859), p. 10.*
[2] The Life of Samuel Johnson, *ed. G. Birkbeck Hill and Rev. L. F. Powell (Oxford, 1934), Vol. I, pp. 104-5.*

economists[1] have been able to collect a very comprehensive list of the prices of commodities. Bread was a penny for a 16-oz. loaf; butter from 6d. to 9d. a pound; beef 4d. a pound; bacon about 6d. a pound. Coffee was expensive and the price seemed to fluctuate from 9s. to 15s. a pound. As for clothing, an ordinary hat would have cost about 2s. 6d.; a pair of stockings, 1s. 10d.; a pair of common shoes, 4s.; a plain suit, about £2 14s. The apparel of the Grub Street hacks, however, who usually made some pretence to style, would not have been so cheap. Drink, the Grub Street staple, was inexpensive. Ordinary claret was 4s. to 5s. a gallon; port, 5s. a gallon; red and white ordinary wine, 6s. a gallon; Madeira, 7s. a gallon, the best Bordeaux and Canary, 9s. a gallon. Information on wages is relatively meagre. An ordinary labourer was paid from 9d. a day in the country to as high as 1s. 8d. a day in London. Carpenters and masons in London were paid 2s. 6d. a day. These facts should give us some idea of how to interpret the figures below.

Until the Copyright Act of 1709 the author had to sell his copy outright. After the Act he was required to sell only one edition or only for a period of fourteen years—that is, if he was prepared to brave the wrath of the publisher upon whom he depended for his livelihood.[2] How much did the publisher pay for his copy? Isaac Disraeli came upon an interesting document, the account-book of Bernard Lintot, who published some of the major writers of the period, including Pope. Precise figures are given.[3] Pope himself did very well. From 1712 to 1716 he received over £4000, which included £7 for his *Rape of the Lock* and £32 5s. for *Windsor Forest*. The bulk of the money came from Pope's *Homer*, which was published by subscription, with all the subscription money going to the author. But there was only one Pope. For roughly the same period, from May 12, 1713, to January 8, 1717, John Gay received £234 10s. for his writing, including the *Trivia*. He got only £2 10s. for *The Mohocks, A Farce*. Dr. William King, a minor satirist who was very popular at the time, received

---

[1] *The above information was gathered from Sir William Beveridge,* Prices and Wages in England from the Twelfth to the Nineteenth Century, *Vol. I, London, 1939, and from James E. Thorold Rogers,* A History of Agriculture and Prices in England, *Vols. VI and VII, Oxford, 1887.*

[2] The English Book Trade, *p. 118.*

[3] Calamities, *pp. 328ff. John Nichols,* Literary Anecdotes of the Eighteenth Century *(1812), has a fuller note on Lintot's account-book.*

£10 for both parts of his *Useful Transactions in Philosophy,* a satire on the Royal Society, but £32 5s. for his *Art of Cookery. In Imitation of Horace's Art of Poetry.* These prices are for the more fortunate writers with a wide following.

But for writers like John Toland, whose book on Deism, *Christianity not Mysterious* (1696), caused considerable controversy, who devoted a lifetime to writing works of criticism, history and theology, the financial return was meagre. 'All this author [Toland] seems to have reaped from a life devoted to literary enterprise, and philosophy, and patriotism, appears not to have exceeded £200,' said Disraeli.[1] According to Richard Kingston,[2] Tom Brown received £4 for his pamphlet, *The Welsh Levite.* Brown also 'writ a lampoon of half a sheet upon the late Dr. H——k, for a dozen of beer, and some bread and cheese.' And he received at least £3 for his 'banter upon ... the Philadelphians,' which he neglected to write. John Dennis, the critic, received £2 12s. 6d. each for his *Essay upon Publick Spirit* (1711) and for his *Reflections ... upon ...* [Pope's] *Essay upon Criticism* (1711).

It is interesting to note that Edmund Curll's scale of payment, despite his reputation for squeezing authors, was not much below Lintot's. He paid Susannah Centlivre twenty guineas each for her three plays, *The Wonder, The Cruel Gift* and *The Artifice* (May 18, 1715); John Durant Breval was paid four guineas for his poem, 'The Art of Dress' (February 13, 1716); Robert Samber got four guineas for his pamphlet, *The Praise of Drunkenness,* and twelve copies (February 20, 1723); Thomas Stackhouse got ten guineas for *The Life of Bishop Atterbury* (September 16, 1723); and Thomas Cooke £5 for Andrew Marvell's *Life* (April, 1726).[3] The last two items may seem low for an entire book, but Lintot only paid £4 for Elsum's *Book of Painting* and £5 7s. 6d. for David Edward's *Journals of Parliament.* It would seem that the going rate for a substantial pamphlet by a popular writer was from £2 to £4—though Toland received £10 15s. from Lintot for his pamphlet *Naturalizing the Jews* (1714). And £4 to £5 would often buy outright the entire book of a minor author.

[1] Ibid., *p. 332.*
[2] *See above, pp. 23ff.*
[3] *These details of Curll's payments were taken from William Roberts,* The Earlier History of English Bookselling *(1892), pp. 239-240.*

I*

As for playwrights, they received money from at least two sources, the sale of their work to the publisher and the profits from the theatre. As Beljame points out,[1] the only return for the playwright when his play was performed was the profit of the third performance. But plays had very short runs then and they did not always last that long. If a playwright received £70 for the third performance, according to Beljame, he considered himself incredibly lucky. In fact, he was lucky if he made £50, and Tom Durfey speaks of making only £20. A prologue or epilogue for a play brought at the most, even for Dryden, according to Beljame,[2] five guineas. Dryden never made more than £100, says Beljame,[3] for even his most successful plays, which included profits from the third performance, the sale of the manuscript to the publisher and the dedication. Beljame calculates this as follows:[4] about £70 for the third-night performance, £20 to £25 for the sale of the manuscript and £5 to £10 for the dedication. And this was for the great Dryden.

The dedication was another source of income for the more reputable writer. Disraeli[5] points out that there was even a fixed fee for the dedication, from five to ten guineas, 'from the Revolution to the time of George I, when it rose to twenty.' But this source of income was not frequently open to the hack writer, who, willy-nilly, had an independence denied people like Dryden.

From the above figures one can still only guess how much writers like Ward, Pittis and Brown actually made from their writing. We can only be sure that they had a wretched time of it trying to keep alive, though their taste for claret and for punks, the vitality of much of their writing, suggest a gaiety not easily suppressed.

By the end of the 17th century, with the increase of political patronage, the hack writers found another source of income, provided that they wrote for the right side. There was a corresponding decline of court patronage: the time for fulsome dedications was almost over. Dryden was not the last respectable author to write dedications with a straight face. But after Dryden,

[1] *Alexandre Beljame,* Men of Letters and the English Public in the Eighteenth Century, 1660-1744 *(English Edition, 1948), pp. 108ff.*
[2] Ibid., *p. 113.*
[3] Ibid., *p. 112.*
[4] Ibid., *p. 121.*
[5] Calamities, *p. 30.*

dedications, for the most part, were self-conscious and double-edged, and frequently satiric.

One of the most brilliant satires on dedications is Thomas Gordon's *A Dedication to a Great Man, Concerning Dedications,* written in 1718. Gordon was a Whig pamphleteer and one of the editors of the *London Journal* (1721) and the *Independent Whig* (1728). He is rather late for the period we are considering and it is, perhaps, questionable to consider him a Grub Street hack. But this satire is a superb piece, virtually unknown to the modern reader, and shows an aspect of the Grub Street world we have not yet seen:

A

DEDICATION

TO A

GREAT MAN

Concerning

Dedications, etc.

My Lord,

Your Lordship and I are not at all acquainted; I therefore take leave to be very familiar with you, and to desire you to be my patron, because you do not know me nor I you: Nor can this manner of address seem strange to your Lordship, whilst it is warranted by such numerous precedents. I have known an author praise an Earl for twenty pages together, though he knew nothing of him, but that he had money to spare. He made him wise, just, and religious for no reason in the world, but in hopes to find him charitable, and gave him a most bountiful heart, because he himself had a most empty stomach. This practice being general, it is a very easy matter to guess, by the size of the panegyric, how wealthy the patron may be, or how hungry the author; if it exceeds three pages, you may pawn all the blood in your body upon it, the writer has fasted three days; and that his Lordship, among all his other good parts, has at least ten thousand pounds a year.

From all this we may learn that a great man's fortune is as easily known from a dedication to him, as from the rent-roll of his estate, and that his bounty to the author is only wages for publishing his wealth to the world.

It is likewise evident, that no Lord of a low fortune must expect an humble admirer amongst us wits and writers, unless he bargain with us at a set price, and give us so much a piece for every good quality he has occasion for.

We must not therefore judge of the high and mighty as they are described in the frontispiece of books and poems. Your dedicators are a sort of intellectual tailors, that cut out cloths for a great man's mind without ever taking measure of it. They have indeed two rules from which they never depart: first, the dress must be gaudy; and secondly, it must never fit. Their business is to make it of a vast dimension, and to cover it all over with tinsel. If the suit be bulky and shining, the poet has the reputation of a skilful tradesman, for the stuff and the exactness are never consulted.

I would upon this occasion congratulate the quality upon the advantage which it is to them, to have their characters drawn by such as either do not, or dare not, know them, and consequently will be sure not to put their graces, and Lordships, and Ladyships, out of countenance—A convenient piece of good breeding! for which, I hope, they are thankful.

For myself, when I see a long drift of excellencies and talents crammed down a Nobleman's throat, who has no relish of them, or right to them, I am not at all surprised, because I am sure it is not meant as an encomium upon his honour, but merely as a declaration of the author's wants, and a heavy complaint of nakedness and hunger.

Some may reckon a dependance on a great man the best reason and foundation for dedicating to him; but I am not of their opinion. For my part, I have no manner of dependance on any Star and Garter in Great Britain, as any one may observe from the cheerfulness of my looks, and the integrity of my life. I own, that setting up for a writer, I judged it convenient to me and my book, to call in your Lordship for an assistant, but no farther than just to set off and honour my title page. I at first indeed intended to let the whole credit of the thing remain with you, by entitling my pamphlet, *An Essay of a Man of Quality*; but my book-seller, who is a smokey fellow, and understands the pulse of the people perfectly well, fell into a great rage, and asked me for the five shillings again, which he had advanced to me by way of encouragement, a week before. He told me he had neither plea-

sure nor profit in selling waste paper to the grocers at two pence
a pound. Why, says he, the famous Daffy might as rationally have
written *aqua fortis* upon his elixir: *The Essay of a Man of Quality!*
If I were to chain the book to my counter, it would not make it
a more everlasting shop-keeper than this very title. It is as bad
as a spell; and the most adventurous reader will not presume
to open the book that is fortified with it.—I have followed his
advice, and am the other five shillings the richer for it.

But, as I was telling your Lordship, reliance on a great
man is not a good reason for dedicating to him; for either he will
receive the present of your praise as a just tribute for such your
dependance, (and then where is your pay, and the due hire of your
sweat and invention?) or else he will reward you with a sort of
coin, called promises, stamped with his honour, but never current
amongst shopkeepers and victuallers. Alas! Who will give you an
ell of cloth, or a cut of beef upon it? It is a lamentable thing the
world should be arrived to such a pitch of ill breeding, that now-
a-days a great man's word and honour are as little minded by
the rest of the world, as by himself.

And so I will proceed to assert that the only proper patron
for an author to inscribe his works to is one to whom he is an
utter stranger, who, having had no manner of commerce with the
aforesaid author, can understand his dedication to be nothing
else but an elegant demand for such a sum of ready money. Dedications are therefore bills of exchange, drawn by the witty upon
the great, and payable at sight. But, lest the worthy offering
should not be understood, or recompensed as it ought to be,
through the deplorable ignorance of the quality, whose high characters place them far above the reach of knowledge and the im-
pulses of humanity, I have, for the benefit of my worthy companions in the labours of the Standish, drawn up the following
form, with which I would have all dedications to conclude.

The Right Honourable Dives Earl of Widefield,

Debtor to Paul Poorwit, for the following Goods
sold and delivered.   l.   s.   d.

Impris, for a large stock of learning,
very much wanted, ———————————— 02 10 00

Item, for a barrel of rare eloquence,
   admired by all the world, but never
   yet used, ───────────────────── 05 00 00

Item, for as much justice and honour as a
   great man has occasion for, ──────── 00 01 1½

Item, for a hogshead of courage that never
   saw the sun, ───────────────── 10 00 00

Item, for half a pound of wit and humour, being
   all I had to spare, but very good in their
   kind, and dog-cheap, ──────────── 01 00 00

Item, for a long line of lineage, and great
   quantities of ancient blood, neither of
   them measured, but only guessed at, ── 05 00 00

Item, for praising your ancestors,
   unknown, ──────────────────── 01 10 00

Item, for admiring your Lady's beauty,
   unsight, unseen, ───────────── 00 10 00

Item, for a graceful person, all of my own
   making, ─────────────────── 02 10 00

Item, for several thimble-fulls of generosity,
   a scarce commodity! ─────────── 00 02 05

                                    ──────────
                          Sum Total   28 03 6½

My Lord,
      I have sent you the above mentioned goods, being the best
my garret affords, and at the lowest price. I hope they will please
you. You will find in the cargo several things which I have not
itemized, viz. A large parcel of virtue, and another of good nature,
because I knew you wanted them as much as any of the rest.—
These two articles will raise the whole to, at least, even thirty
pounds; and I have drawn a bill upon your Lordship accordingly,
which I beg your Lordship to pay at sight; for, I assure you, I
have had pressing occasion for the money long before it was due.
I might have found chap-men for these goods among very many
of the nobility and gentry, as unprovided with them as yourself;
but out of pure respect to your Lordship, I resolved you should

have the refusal.—In firm expectation of your approaching
bounty,

> I am,
>> My Lord,
>>> Your Lordship's most obliged,
>>> Most devoted,
>>> Most obedient,
>>> Most, &c.

In this plain manner would I have authors treat their patrons. The said thirty pounds may probably be all the poet's stock,
and wits, dealing the least upon credit, either in selling or buying,
of any trading people in the world, have the more occasion for
ready money.

Your Lordship may by this perceive, how I expect to be
treated and rewarded for the following panegyric on yourself.

In attempting your character (to use the fashionable phrase),
I shall begin with the antiquity of your house, equally old and
illustrious. Your ancestors won honours, and you, my Lord, wear
them; how well they become you, I need not say, the same being
as evident to the whole world as to me. You would no doubt
acquire new ones, were there any room left for them; but what
occasion have you to toil and struggle for that which is already
provided for you by others? And it is a plain instance of your
consummate prudence, that your ease is by no means interrupted
by any the least pursuit of this kind. If any dare insolently call
in question your glory, show them your coat of arms, and the
number of your manors; strike them dumb by telling them of
the nobility of your blood, and blind, by showing them the splendour of your race.

Nobility is held by patent, and where is the necessity of
another tenor by virtue? A piece of parchment is a much more
portable instrument. Your Lordship seems apprised of the difficulty
of excelling in anything, and therefore wisely forbears drudging
for fame. Your ancestors excelled for you. They, by having many
accomplishments, have saved you the trouble of having any. The
lustre of their names shines still upon you, though exceedingly
weakened by the length of the journey, having spent many of its
rays in its passage through three or four generations, who wanted
its influence as much as yourself. Thus, if we trace the merit of

a great family, it is like the course of a river inverted, largest towards the fountain.

Should anyone make an ill bred comparison, (which God forbid) between your Lordship and the founders of your house, you could show him, or I for you, that you possess several arts and acquirements, which the old-fashioned fellows, with all their abilities and long beards, were utter strangers to. If one of your forefathers was a great orator, and could do wonders with his mouth, your Lordship is as dexterous in the exercise of the organ next to it, and can take snuff with great volubility of nostril. What though another of your grandsires was an able politician, a person of great cunning and brains? The outside of his head was not half so well instructed as your own: you have more curls in the covering of yours, than he had wiles in the lining of his: his was equipped by painful study, yours is edified by your painful barber. A third was a brave soldier, but were he put to handle your cane or your snuff-box, he would be at as great a loss, as you, my Lord, would be to handle his truncheon. A fourth sat up at nights, and lived by his clients; but your Lordship, more happy and less learned, lies abed all day, and lives by your tenants. All these laboured for your grandeur and support, foreseeing, as one would imagine, that you would have need of their aid. And it cannot be denied, that it is possible one may be so great a man as to be good for little. Wisdom and worth, we see, cannot be entailed like titles and acres. It were, indeed, to be wished, that a wise head and an honest heart could beget their likeness, and that famous men could transmit their parts with their titles to their posterity; but since that cannot be, their descendants must comfort themselves with being akin to merit, though ever so remotely.

Nothing is more frequent and natural than to value ourselves upon that which is none of ours. Of this I have, in my time, seen several merry instances. I knew a thrasher in Wiltshire, who was so elevated upon his brother's being made a parson, and promoted to a curacy of twenty pounds a year, that he threw away his flail, as a discredit to one who was nearly related to so great a man, and betook himself to poaching in the river, as a more gentleman-like way of life. It was observed of him, that ever afterwards he rolled his stockings, whereas he had before always humbly buttoned his breeches over them. It is said he threatens to leave the village where he was born, because the ill-bred inhabitants still continue to style him no higher than bare Gaffer Thump, as they used to do, notwithstanding that his brother is a curate. But it is thought this high-spirited person will be disappointed, for that no parish will receive him without a certificate. I would, out of the benignity of my nature, comfort all great men who have noble blood, but vulgar understandings, with the repartee of a West Country blacksmith, who, in a dispute with a barber that called him ignorant fellow, answered, with equal scorn, that though he could neither read nor write, his Father had been game-keeper to the Lord of a manor. The barber, who was but the son of a barber, finding himself out-matched in family, very re-spectfully gave up the dispute to his betters.

It is scarcely to be conceived how diffusive and multiply-ing a little good blood is. The increase of the blessed Virgin's milk, by the magic and management of popish monks, is not more mira-culous. How many thousands find themselves enriched by it, or rather impoverished! for nothing is more apt to turn the brain; and it is often got into the head, when there is not half a drop of it in the arteries.

We may observe, by the way, that we are ever nearest re-lated to the greatest man of our blood, though removed seven generations from him. If our great-grandfather, for instance, was a wise man, and our grandfather and father a brace of fools, we skip the two last, and become, after a wonderful manner, the im-mediate descendants of the first. Thus a man becomes the very next in blood to, perhaps, the first of his name, who lived 300 years ago, and scorns to be in the least akin to the person that begot him. You shall not meet with a Jew who is the son of his father—No, he's the son of Abraham, who has been dead so many thousand years, and yet is still forced to father a swarthy race of brokers and b—g—ers, In the same manner has King Cadwallader begot every mother's son that has been born in Wales for five hundred generations. I know a lady, who is far gone in genealogy and pride, whose father had, with a great title and estate, a great faculty, likewise, of drivelling. Him she never men-tions as being, I suppose, no ways related to him; but a great man of her name, who lived in the reign of William Rufus, is her good and right well-beloved kinsman—He was, I take it, either her Uncle, or at farthest, her cousin-german.

This picking and culling of our ancestors, as if it lay at

our mercy, after we are brought into the world, who should bring us thither, shows great ambition, but small policy. For, certainly, we should be exceeding careful not to mention ourselves with such of our ancestors with whom we cannot stand a comparison. A dwarf may strut upon the shoulders of a giant, but still his dwarfship is the more conspicuous from the company he keeps; and many a man climbs only to show his elevated littleness. This is all wrong—They that would appear tall, ought to converse only with the short, if they would take a natural method of coming at the scope of their ambition. I therefore approve the prudence and policy of our worshipful country squires and fox-hunters, who, for the sake of having daily companions, at least something below themselves in speech and understanding, spend all their time with dumb creatures, and live and die among horses and dogs. An honest gentleman, whose speaking organs would be of no use to him in the Senate or in conversation, shall be very eloquent in an assembly of hounds, and, with great force and fluency of throat, outdo his brother-orators in their own way. The wisdom of these worthies, who are educated in the kennel, goes farther yet; for every man chooses for his tutor that beagle whose voice he is most capable of imitating: insomuch, that as soon as I hear one of those academics begin his exercise, that is, to open, I can presently pronounce whose pupil he has been, whether bred under Doctor Fowler, or Doctor Sweetlips. At present, Doctor Ringwood is more famous than all the rest for the number of scholars he has trained up; I know several of them myself, and particularly a hopeful young gentleman, the eldest son of a Baronet, who is a great proficient in this kind of throat-learning.—It is believed he is now fit to head the pack himself in the absence of his said master, the polite Dr. Ringwood. When this ingenious young heir displays his wind-pipe, his mother's heart beats for joy, and the old knight tells the company, with a wink and a nod, Harry is father's own son.—Now thus far all is well, when ambition goes hand in hand with capacity. But, Sir John, not content with these excellencies in himself and his son, will be ever and anon mentioning the virtues and talents of his ancestors, who were indeed great men. However, the knight never concludes without insinuating his own praise, and that of his heir, by asserting, that not one of his forefathers could compass a bumper, or fill a hunting-horn.

Having thus, my Lord, done justice to your pedigree, I shall proceed next to the consideration of your fortune.

The founders of families are generally provident enough to support the titles they leave behind them with suitable estates; which is a most commendable care, for, alas! as the world runs, what is blood without riches? Money and land are the very touchstones of quality. Antiquity may be overlooked, but acres are visible honours. Nothing is more illustrious than a long rent-roll; without it, the most sounding and splendid patent has no power over the hearts or hats of an assembly. It is confessed, neither family nor riches make the least alteration in the human frame. An earldom cannot cure a stinking breath, nor make the skull half an inch thinner; and a great man may be a dwarf or a scoundrel, with half a million of money, or half a country in his possession. Alexander the Great had a wry neck, (perhaps with carrying the globe upon his back) of which the propriety of the world could not cure him. But I am only talking of reputed, and not real, greatness, and cannot but congratulate your Lordship upon the real kindness which is done you, in particular, by this distinction.

You, my Lord, have a double right to respect, from your title, and from your affluence. The latter is indeed the less worthy; and yet, such is the bigotry of the world to wealth, that were it not for that, the former would hardly be regarded. Nay, to deal ingenuously with your Lordship, had I not known you to be rich, I should, perhaps, never have known you to be noble; and then your Lordship and I should never have been patron and client, nor mankind been instructed in your character. I would not therefore, for less than thirty pounds, that your Lordship should have wanted this opportunity of obliging posterity and myself. Go on, my Lord, in the paths of honour, that is, in the art of getting; and continue to be deserving, that is, to be rich.

From your Lordship's wealth it is natural enough to make a transition to your Lordship's wit; since, according to the laudable civility of the world, the man who has sufficiency of bags is sure to be endowed with sufficiency of brain. It is very observable, that though wit has seldom or never the sense to fall into the road of gain, and therefore your witty men are the foolishest fellows in the world, that is to say, the poorest, yet riches, on the contrary, never fail to dub a fool a wise man; and a dunce no sooner ceases to be poor, but he is transmuted into a shrewd cunning fellow. The reason of this must be, that the wit of a poor man, lying only in the inside of his head, is altogether invisible and unregarded; whereas the wit and parts of the wealthy being entirely without the skull, and consisting of assets and effects, are honoured, because they are obvious. A man who has wit in chestfuls, and a genius that consists of several manors, will never want the praises which are due to such uncommon talents. I could mention many worthy citizens who have vast capacities at sea, and are wonderfully witty in ware-houses, and most ingenious in bankstock, besides others, whose abilities are as conspicuous in the Exchequer.

I cannot but lament, on this occasion, with a feeling concern, the invincible obstacles which hinder that unhappy wit, which is merely internal, from rising into notice and reputation. Alas! (*absit invidia verbo*) there is no wit at all in being hungry, and where is the jest of having but one shirt? A wig without buckle is but dull entertainment, and a threadbare coat has no manner of force upon the muscles. I can speak it from experience, there is no joke in an empty purse. I had therefore no expedient left to procure me a little wit, but the letting out my parts to hire, as I now do to your Lordship. Thirty pounds, my Lord, frugally managed, will make me a wise man for three months together. Your Lordship, who hath talents of a vast extent for several miles round you, and vast parts in cash and bank bills, has not only a sufficient bulk of penetration and wisdom to serve you for life, but will doubtless transmit the same substantial accomplishments undiminished to your posterity. My Lord Clarendon tells us, that Oliver Cromwell's abilities seemed to rise in proportion to his advancement in power: And your Lordship's wit and sense, that are now so bulky, and of such mighty circumference, would certainly have been invisible to the buzzard world to this hour, had not your fortune lifted them and you into observation.

I do not say all this to prove to your Lordship that your Lordship has a great deal of wit; it is the last thing you want to be convinced of—But it is my ambition to get myself a little wit and wisdom with your money; and it is but reasonable I should do something for it. I owe my landlady for a quarter's lodging, and my laundress for a month's washing; they are the two first whom I intend to satisfy that I am a sensible man: for I already find, by their sour looks, they begin to question my parts. My shoe-

maker too, and several other tradesmen, want sadly to handle
some proofs and instances of my wit and genius. It would be barbarous in your Lordship to let me pass any longer for a fool
amongst these fellows whom one cannot live without. For a small
matter of that sort of good sense, which is called money, I shall
find admiration among them, and, which is better, credit, and
new shoes. I have often been witty, to the best of my skill, at the
tavern over a bottle of wine; but the blockhead, the vintner, is so
dull and covetous, that he can see no wit about me, but what
I tell out between my finger and my thumb, a piece of ingenuity
which I am not always master of. O, the degeneracy of the Age!
Ben Johnson has frequently paid his reckoning in a couplet,
and lived comfortably and merrily a whole winter's night upon
a pun. Alas! I do not believe, in this Iron Age, a canto of a hundred staves would bring a quart of sherry, or a pound of salmon.
Many a wit would be forced to pawn his coat (if any person
would take it) for a dinner, did not the charitable bookseller advance him half a crown on his new poem, and by that means pay
him half in hand.

If a certain eminent merchant had not manifested his uncommon understanding in the uncommon number of his ships,
and his harmonious disposition (tuneful would have done better)
in the chiming of his bags, the bluntness of the incomparable
Mr. Durfey's nature would never have raised so many plauditory
plants in the large field of the said merchant's commendations:
but that venerable lyric knew too well the easiness of his patron's
humour, not to expect from it an order upon his goldsmith, where
the harmonious knight keeps the opulent marks of his uncommon
understanding. How large taste he afforded Mr. Durfey of his
parts, I know not; what I am to expect from yours, my Lord, I
know, and so will your Lordship too, when you have perused this
uncommon dedication.

I have, by this time, I hope, with sufficient clearness, displayed to my readers, that is, to the whole world, the quality and
extent of your Lordship's wit. If I have but little to say of your
eloquence, it is because you have hitherto shown but little. But
this is owing to nothing but choice and reservedness, on your
part: your modesty, my Lord, like a pot-lid, smothers the overflowings of your spirit, and suppresses the ebullition of your rhetoric. It becomes me to believe you could do wonders this way, if

you would. Why will you thus neglect and conceal your abilities, and obstinately persist to be only a hearer in the Senate? I do not question, but even this omission and seeming indolence is praiseworthy and public-spirited. Your Lordship, no doubt, considers that the very listeners, in public assemblies, are promoting the trade of their country, while they consume snuff, and wear out handkerchiefs. Thus is the interest of mankind advanced by idleness and incapacity itself.

Besides, when I reflect how much tongue artillery is daily wasted without doing the least execution, I must applaud it as a piece of prudence and humanity in your Lordship, to avoid the shedding of innocent words. How many excellent orators have we, who are instructive without being understood, severe without being felt, and loud without being heard. What pity is this! Commend me to those that sit still and take snuff, because they have nothing else to say. I have often lamented and sighed in my closet, that men's tongues should have more speed than their understandings. When our spirits are heavy and grave, it is but reasonable the tongue should be shod with lead. But, alas! our chops, when once they are set a-going, generally show our intellects a pair of heels, and gallop away with such fleetness, that even the memory itself is distanced, as swift as it is.

Were the tongue only to move by the direction of good sense, how many worthy English gentlemen and fine ladies would live and die discreetly dumb? This putting of the jaws upon hard labour without profit, and committing a rape upon people's ears without the consent of their hearts, is a notorious nuisance and breach of the peace. It is an offence to others, and a distemper in ourselves. This disease I call the Upward Looseness; and it is in several respects as nauseous as that below; nay, it sometimes equally affronts the sense of smelling, as when the speaker's lungs are not over orthodox, or so.

It is really a miserable case, that, when a chattering booby finds himself loaded with a turbulent quantity of words and wind, which he has a mind to discharge, I must be obliged to stand the shot of his noise and nastiness for perhaps an hour or two together. This, I am sure, is contrary to the rules of equity and cleanliness; but it seems I am bound to it by the laws of courtesy and good breeding.

What I have here said of loquacity concerns only private

conversation: but when this insult upon our senses appears in public assemblies, it is yet more intolerable. Why must prating oafs (empty of everything but froth and clamour) be forever suffered, without rebuke, to be spewing up their ill-scented crudities in the faces of men that are either wise or brave? I would humbly propose, for the ease of this Christian country, that whenever an orator of this sort begins to gape and strain, one of the company shall go up to him, and, taking hold of his button, tell him, Sir, I am sorry to see you troubled with so violent a vomiting: or, perhaps, it may be more proper, without saying a word, to run with a chamber-pot, and hold it up to his chin. For this purpose, I would decree that every place of public meeting in this island be provided with one or more of these necessary vessels, either to receive or restrain the overflowings of indigested oratory. If one of these emetic speakers cannot conveniently be come at, it is only crying, To the chamber-pot; and, if he has shame in him, he will grow well, and sit down.

There is something exceeding insolent in these long-winded talkers. What right has any man living to lay an embargo upon my throat, when at the same time he keeps his own open? He that usurps the whole discourse lays this modest injunction upon the whole company; namely, to be silent, and hear him.

The ladies, indeed, who understand their privileges much better than we do ours, are not enslaved by our rules; but, though there be a score of them together, exert the faculty of speech all at once: and really, if we do but remember that it is their whole business and ambition to be only voluble, without troubling themselves with being intelligible, we cannot blame them for exercising their tongues, as they do their fans, in all weathers, merely for a little parade, or because they are used to it. Ladies, therefore, when they are fluttering either of these inoffensive instruments, ought not to be interrupted with an offer of the chamber-pot; for if it be only the depravity of the intention that makes actions criminal, it is evident they can be no offenders, who speak without any intention at all. I know the fair prattlers are so overstocked with self-denial, that they will humbly disown this my justification of them, as what they do not deserve; but I am resolved to persist, and make them innocent in spite of themselves. But as for those of my own sex, who are addicted to purge at the mouth, I shall never revoke my decree against them, or any of them, except such as honour the truth, and freely confess that, though they talk much, they mean nothing. And indeed it cannot be denied that very many well-meaning persons are rhetorical for no reason in the earth, but because they are not retentive; and so are forced to break words purely for their ease. When a man's tongue is always ready bridled and saddled, he cannot help it if it will run away with him.

This kind of eloquence, like an ill breath, is curable but one way, and that is, by tying a certain ligature, called a halter, round the patient's neck, and girding it, until you have quite stopped up the gutter through which the aforesaid excrements do issue.

But as this remedy might prove somewhat dangerous to many thousands of his Majesty's good subjects, I shall be cautious in recommending this public-spirited project, though I am fully convinced it would effectually destroy all his enemies within these his Dominions. But as I am a friend to the tranquillity and noses of mankind, I will make bold to prescribe a *succedaneum*; that is to say, an equivalent for hanging.

As a specific, therefore, against the dreadful effects of this fetid and epidemical distemper, I would advise the sick body, when the fit is coming upon him, which he will perceive by an ungovernable agitation in his jaws, and an incessant rattling in his throat, to withdraw himself immediately from company, and employ these indefatigable organs in running over a chapter or two in the Bible. People, I know, particularly my patients, will make a horrid outcry against the distastefulness of this remedy, but that can be no objection against the use of it, since the bitterest drugs are often the most successful. Besides, it is well known, that all medicines that dispose to sleep, are harsh and unpalatable. Of this nature are the numerous and powerful opiates, which come daily from the press and the pulpit. A dose or two of Scripture, if people would but be persuaded to take it (*sed hic labor, hoc opus est!*) would compose those convulsions of the chops, and that flux of speech, which hitherto have been thought incurable. But let none despair; for though their mouths be dry, and their lips chapped with the perpetual evacuation of eloquence and spittle; though their heads ache with nodding, and their eyes with winking; nay, though their throats should be riven with hemming, and their wind-pipes with straining; nay, even though their very arms should be jaded with explaining their stories, and their canes worn out with enforcing their orations, yet I, the doctor, will, by the blessing of the Bible on my endeavours, work a perfect cure.

This secret, which I found out by great industry and long study, I might, like other great physicians, have kept to myself; but I prefer knowledge and the good of mankind to living in ignorance, and keeping a coach.

For your many excellent speakers that cannot read, I must find out some other cure. Perhaps it may be no ineffectual method to ask them, whether they will give what they say under their hands, and to present them at the same time with pen, ink, and paper. You shall find they will immediately grow shy of attesting it in so solemn a manner, and so recover to avoid disgrace. N.B. This remedy effectually cures talkative beaux.

As to the ladies, who hate everything that is unpleasant or unfashionable, I know my Scripture-specific will never go down with them without a great deal of art. These genteel well-bred patients would think me a strange, rude fellow, should I advise them to so vulgar a thing as the reading of an old book; and so I find I must grow cunning, that I may not be thought clownish. Being well acquainted with the inquisitive spirit which is in them, I intend to recommend the Bible to them as a book that contains many strange adventures, and many secrets which they never heard of before: there they will find gallantry and intrigues, songs, dances, and pretty fellows; mobbings, rebellions, and the Church; hereditary right, and a Jewish pretender, who was a very handsome man, but had his title and complexion both ruined by the gallows; and there they will find courts, ravishings, and adultery, and everything that can please and entertain them. Besides, the book is finely bound and gilt. I mention the strongest motive last, because they may remember it most.

I am sensible few of our fine ladies are furnished with this useful book, the same being got entirely into the hands of their servants, and other mean people, who are poor enough to be good Christians, I must therefore acquaint the quality, that the said book, called a Bible, may be met with at the booksellers'; Mr. Baskett, encouraged, I suppose, by this project of mine having not long since ventured upon a new impression; otherwise, it is thought, Bibles might, in a small time, have been out of print.

To convince the whole world that I am altogether disinterested in this useful discovery, I must, in justice to myself, declare that I have never seen the colour of Mr. Baskett's money; for, though I belong to the Society for the Reformation of Manners, I do utterly decline the usual perquisites arising from the execution of that office. If Mr. Baskett indeed should force a bribe upon me, I know the courtesy of my nature will by no means suffer me to affront so worthy a person, by a rigid refusal, it being my steadfast principle to suffer rather than resist, upon such powerful trials, as many of our good and modest doctors are forced into greatness and bishoprics, in spite of their obstinate and repeated *nolo*. But, though I shall not fall out with Mr. Baskett for a small matter, I protest beforehand, that if he offers me above a hundred guineas, I shall be strangely surprised. . . .

I should now proceed to display and extol, as becomes me, your Lordship's great piety and gallantry, the gravity of your carriage and the liveliness of your behaviour, the grandeur of your deportment and the humility of your conversation; and, most particularly, I should celebrate your great generosity to myself, and your great frugality to all the world: and your Lordship may depend upon it, I will very soon gratify my own ambition, by equipping you with all these great gifts, and many more.

At present a thing has happened, which interrupts me in the discharge of this my necessary duty. A thing, which the shyness of my nature will have me to conceal from all the world but so good and loving a friend as your Lordship. My Lord, it is now twelve o'clock, and I want a dinner; and, alas! I doubt my bookseller will not trust me with a shilling, without mortgaging these my papers into his hands for the sum aforesaid. Thus must half your Lordship, that is, half your character, be pawned that I may dine. Be assured of hearing from me soon, for I have your measure, and, as becomes your faithful tailor, will finish your suit with all speed. I am, with wonderful devotion, and great haste (it is now a quarter after twelve)

My very good Lord,

Your Lordship's most dutiful,

and most obedient humble servant.

P.S. To avoid the envy that eminent writers must ever expect, I have determined not to put my name to my work, until the thirtieth edition of this treatise, which perhaps may not be this month yet; by which time it is presumed, that all those who detract from its excellencies, will be hissed into silence and shame by the whole world.

I designed to have subjoined at the end a table of the principal matters, as other great authors have done, but, going about it, I quickly found I must transcribe the whole book into an index, and so gave it over.

Penny Broadsheets and other Trivia

Grub Street was continually flooded by an almost infinite variety of penny broadsheets: large single sheets of paper about 9 inches by 12 inches to 14 inches, printed on one side only, whose authors were usually anonymous. They provided the kind of general entertainment found in our popular magazines today. There were lampoons, serious verse, bantering treatments of various subjects, 'characters', and sub-literary miscellanea like 'An Account of a Great and Famous Scolding Match' (1699), an opportunity for displaying the linguistic wonders of Billingsgate—a multitude of subjects and forms that defy classification. The 'character' was a set description of a composite individual, a social type—such as the pedant, the non-conformist, the virtuoso, the astrologer—which, in the last part of the 17th century, was usually satiric. It was very much in vogue in our period and varied in form from the brilliant, particularized sketches in the satires of Dryden and Pope to the stock pieces of the penny broadsheets like the 'Character of a Town-gallant' (*c.* 1680) and its companion-piece included here:

The

CHARACTER

Of

A Town-Miss.

A miss is a new name, which the civility of this age bestows on one that our unmannerly ancestors called whore and strumpet.

A certain help mate for a gentleman, instead of a wife; serving either for prevention of the sin of marrying, or else as a little side pillow, to render the yoke of matrimony more easy. She is an excellent convenience for those that have more money than wit, to spend their estates upon; and the most that can be said in her commendation, is that she will infallibly bring a man to repentance. Yet you may call her an honest courtesan, or at least a common inclosed; for though she is an out-lier, yet she seems to be confined within the pale, and differs from your ordinary prostitute, as wholesale men from retailers; one perhaps has an hundred customers, and the other but two or three, and yet this gets most by her trade. Indeed, she may well thrive, seeing she always carries her stock above her, and every man is desirous to deal in her commodity: for she is a gallant's business, a citizen's recreation, a lawyer's estate in fee-tail; a young doctor's necessary experiment, and a parson's comfortable importance.

The royal preacher calls her a strange woman, but we usually term her a common woman, and have reason so to do; for sins that were strange in Solomon's days, are common in ours. She is a caterpillar that destroys many a hopeful young gentleman in the blossom, a land-siren far more dangerous than they in the sea: for he that falls into her hands, runs a three-fold hazard of shipwrecking soul, body and estate.

She talks high of her family, and tells a large story how they were ruined by the late wars. But the true history of her life, is generally to this effect: she is only the cub of a bumkin, licked into a genteel form by town conversation. Nature gave her a good face, and an indifferent stock of confidence, which she by prudent management has improved into impudence; like a forward rose bud she opened betimes, and lost that trifle they call a maidenhead, so early, that she cannot remember she ever had any such thing. She was scarcely thirteen when her father's ploughman and the squire, their landlord, (the verier clown of the two) went joint tenants to her copy-holds, but proving with child, she had the wit to lay it to the last, who for his credit, dispatched her incognito, with a sum of money on a carrier's pack, to be disburthened at London, the goodliest forest in England, to shelter a great belly. There the bantling was exposed to the tuition of the parish in a handbasket, and the charitable midwife (who counts

K

procuring in a civil way a necessary part of her office) soon brought
her acquainted with a third-rate gentleman, who took her a lodging in a garret, and allowed her six shillings a week. But making
a sally abroad one night, picked up a drunken cully, and at a
tavern (whilst he was no less pleasantly employed) picked his
pocket of a gold watch, and some straggling guineas, and left him
to pawn his sword and periwig for the reckoning. After this lucky
adventure, she discards Monsieur Shabby (her former customer)
and her lofty lodging; puts herself in a good garb, gets a maid
(forgive me, for I lie, I mean a she-servant) whom she coaches
to call her Madam, and Your Honour, and hires noble rooms,
richly furnished, about Covent Garden; there she takes state upon
her, and practices every day four hours in the glass, how greatness will become her. Her first business is to make herself to be
taken notice of, to which purpose, like Dinah, she walks the streets;
sometimes she, like Jael, stands at the door; and sometimes, like
Jezebel, she looks out at the window: But her main market-place
is the balcony, which she frequents as constantly as any lady in
a romance; and the language of her eyes is, What do you lack,
sir? By which she at last attracts a wealthy gallant, who, with a
little address, obtains the mighty honour of her acquaintance;
but she seems extremely nice, reserved and modest, protests she
would not go to a tavern for a world, when the whole business
is, she is only afraid of being pawned there. In brief, she manages
him so discreetly, that she cheats him into love insensibly, like a
tailor's bill, wherein a man sees himself rooked abominably, yet
knows not where to find fault. Having thus got the woodcock
into the pitfall, she resolves to pluck him. When he importunes
her for the great kindness, she talks of honour and conscience,
and vows she will never stain her reputation but for valuable
considerations: this brings them to articles; he promises to allow
her a hundred and fifty pounds a year, and she swears a thousand dissembling oaths, how infinitely she loves him, and that she
will prove constant, and true to him alone, and never be concerned with any other man in the world; and the silly fop is so
fatally bewitched as to believe her; and continues a long time in
that fool's paradise of dotage, whilst in the meantime, she drives
a trade privately, with two or three more. For the concealing of
which, from the first, it is the whole employ of the little harlotry,

her chambermaid, to study lies, pretences and excuses, and she makes them pay her even to extortion; to quicken her invention; sometimes she is gone abroad in her aunt's coach; sometimes one of her cousins; a woollen draper's wife in the city is sick, and she must visit her. Nor is Madam herself less full of plot and intrigue to bubble her gallant: sometimes, having pleased him well, she begs the best ring he has on his finger, or pretends herself to be in debt; and that, unless he will suffer her to be scandalized with an arrest, bound he must be for her (to one of her confederates, you may be sure) for fifty pounds, and the everlasting changeling cannot find in his heart to deny her. At other times she shall purposely give him occasion to be jealous, and when he has raved and sworn, and cursed and ranted for two hours, as if he had been possessed with a hundred and fifty devils, she shall cleverly wipe off the suspicion, upbraid his jealous coxcombship; fall a-snivelling and call herself the most unfortunate of women, to love a man with so much passion, that thus abuses her. Then he submits, begs her pardon on his knees, and coaxes her with all imaginable kindness; but still she pouts, looks sullen, and will not let him have a bit of that same, until he has given her a new gown, or a necklace of pearl, for atonement, and reconciliation.

But in time, his appetite being cloyed, his purse exhausted, or his eyes enlightened, he begins to withdraw, and she soon finds out another, a verier fool than he; but for security, will not trade, unless he settle an annuity of £300 a year on her for life; which being firmly done by an able conveyancer in sheep-skins, half as large as the premises. Within one month she abandons him for a more noble and strenuous gallant. And now being arrived at the zenith of her glory, she has her boys in livery, her house, splendidly furnished, and scorns to stir abroad without a coach and six horses. She glitters in the boxes at the play house, and draws all eyes after her in the street, to the shame and confusion of all honest women, and encouragement of each pretty girl that loves fine clothes, good cheer, and idleness, to turn harlot, in imitation of such a thriving example.

She takes upon her, more pride, than would have served six of Queen Elizabeth's countesses; uses Sirrah at every word, and to a lady of the best quality, and old enough to be her Mother: nothing but—I tell thee sweetheart! She despises her sister, for losing her reputation, by being kept by a meaner gal-

lant than her own; and gets one to attempt to steal her, that she
may be thought an extraordinary fortune.

She has always two necessary implements about her, a
blackamoor and a little dog; for without these, she would be
neither fair nor sweet. The rest of her retinue consists of her she-
secretary, that keeps the box of her teeth, her hair and her painting, an old trot, that understands the town, and goes between
party and party, and a French merchant to supply her with dil-
does; or in default of those, she makes her gallant's purse maintain two able stallions (that she loves better than him) for performance of points wherein he is defective. Her skin is much
clearer than her conscience, which makes her go with her neck
and shoulders bare; and she has reason, for her upper parts are
the shop of Cupid, and those below, his warehouse: but all that
you are like to buy there, is damnation and diseases. She is a very
butcher, that exposes her own flesh to sale by the stone; or, if you
please, a cook that is dressing herself all day with poignant sauces,
to be tasted with the better appetite at night. Like a disabled
frigate, that has received many shots between wind and water, she
is forced once a year to put in at Tunbridge, or Epsom, to wash
and tallow, and refit her leaky bottom: after which, she cruises
up and down the town as briskly as ever; until age spoils her
sailing, and engraves wrinkles, where she once painted roses. Then
her former adorers despise her, the world hates her, and she becomes a loathsome thing, too unclean to enter into Heaven; too
diseased to continue long upon earth; and too foul to be touched
with anything but a pen, or a pair of tongs: and therefore it is
time to leave her;—For, foh, how she stinks.

Single broadsheets frequently served to cover the topical
news:

THE TOWN RAKES:

or

The Frolics of the *Mohocks* or *Hawkubites*.

With an account of their frolics last night and at several
other times; showing how they slit the noses of several men and
women, and wounded others, several of which were taken up last

night by the guards, and committed to several prisons, the guards being drawn out to disperse them.

There are a certain set of persons, amongst whom there are some of too great a character to be named in these barbarous and ridiculous encounters, did not they expose themselves by such mean and vulgar exploits.

These barbarities have been carried on by a gang of them for a considerable time, and many innocent persons have received great injury from them, who call themselves Hawkubites; and their mischievous invention of the word is, that they take people between hawk and buzzard, that is, between two of them, and making them turn from one to the other, abuse them with blows and other scoffings; and if they pretend to speak for themselves, they then slit their noses, or cut them down the back.

The watch in most of the out-parts of the town stand in awe of them, because they always come in a body, and are too strong for them, and when any watchman presumes to demand where they are going, they generally misuse them.

Last night they had a general rendezvous, and were bent upon mischief; their way is to meet people in the streets and stop them, and begin to banter them, and if they make any answer, they lay them on with sticks, and toss them from one to another in a very rude manner.

They attacked the watch in Devereux Court and Essex Street, made them scour; they also slit two persons' noses, and cut a woman on the arm with a penknife that she is lamed. They likewise rolled a woman in a tub down Snow Hill, that was going to market, set other women on their heads, misusing them in a barbarous manner.

They have short clubs or bats that have lead at the end, which will overset a coach, or turn over a chair, and tucks in their canes ready for mischief.

One of these persons supposed to be of the gang, did formerly slit a drawer's nose at Greenwich, and has committed many such frolics since. They were so outrageous last night, that the guards at Whitehall were alarmed, and a detachment ordered to patrol; and it is said, the train-bands will be ordered to do duty for the future, to prevent these disorders; several of them were taken up last night, and put into the round houses until order is given what to do with them.

Then, as now, some of the most popular reading were descriptions of the lives of criminals. But at the turn of the 18th century, the publishing circumstances were more dramatic, since they were ghost-written in the first person and hawked on execution day at the foot of the gallows.

Memoirs of the Right Villainous John Hall was an elaborate variation of this form which went through at least three editions, with extensive pieces added each time. John Hall's particular claim on posterity is described in this excerpt by the Newgate Chaplain published in broadsheet form:

> II.   What sort of judgement that shall be, which Christ behaviour, Confessions and Last Speeches of the Malefactors that were Executed at Tyburn, on Wednesday, December 17, 1707.

At the sessions held at Justice Hall in the Old-Bailey, on Wednesday, Thursday, Friday and Saturday, being the 10th, 11th, 12th and 13th instant, there were nine persons convicted of capital crimes, and received sentence of death accordingly. Of these nine, two obtained a gracious reprieve, (which, I hope, they will take care to improve to God's glory), the other seven were ordered for execution. But the last of these seven was reprieved at the gallows.

On the last Lord's Day, the 14th instant, I preached to them, both in the morning and afternoon, upon this text, 2 Cor. 5, 10, 11: for we must all appear before the Judgment Seat of Christ, that everyone may receive the things done in his body, according to that he has done, whether it be good or bad. Knowing, therefore, the terror of the Lord, we persuade men. From which words, first paraphrastically explained in general, I considered and discoursed upon these following particulars, viz.

> I.   That all men shall be called to judgment, and must certainly appear before Christ.
>
> II.   What sort of judgment that shall be, which Christ will then pass upon them. It will be a judgment either of eternal condemnation or absolution. Here I endeavoured to represent to them the horrible torments of Hell, and the surpassing joys of Heaven.

III. By what means condemnation might be avoided, and absolution obtained, namely, by faith and repentance.

IV. And lastly, how these graces, faith and repentance, might be wrought in us, viz. by the spirit of God, which we ought earnestly to pray for.

Having enlarged upon these particulars, I exhorted my auditory, chiefly the condemned, that they would seriously consider and examine themselves, and earnestly pray to God for His divine assistance, that they might steadfastly believe in Christ, and truly repent of all their sins, both known and unknown, and through the merits of our Blessed Redeemer, who has shed His most precious blood for all repenting sinners, obtain mercy and pardon at God's hands, and the eternal salvation of their immortal souls.

To all this they seemed to give great attention; and I observed them all along to behave themselves with decency and devotion; indeed, much better (in my judgment) than any one else in the congregation, though very numerous. They continued in a very tractable temper, and desired to receive Christian instruction, which they all very much wanted, as having lived the most part, if not the whole, of their time in sin and ignorance, which they now acknowledged with trouble and grief of heart.

I: John Hall, condemned for felony and burglary, viz. for breaking the house of Captain John Guyon, of the Parish of Stepney, and taking thence a blue cloth wastecoat, and other things of a considerable value, &c. He said he was about 32 years of age, born in Bishops-Head Court near Grays-Inn Lane, in the Parish of St. Andrews-Holbourn; that he was in the sea service about 15 years off and on; and had followed also the business of chimney-sweeping, when at land. He owned, in general, that within these 3 years last past he had committed a great many robberies, some of them very considerable, in and about London; but he would not come to particulars, saying he had forgotten them in a great measure, and it would signify nothing to any person to know every ill thing he had done; for he could make no other amends to the persons he had wronged, than to ask their pardon. Upon my asking him, whether any servants or neighbours of the persons he had robbed at any time, were ever concerned with him, he answered, No, so far as he could remember. He readily acknowledged he had been a very ill liver; that he had committed all manner of sin but murder. I found him very ignorant in matters of religion, though he said he formerly went to church. He could neither read nor write, which, he told me, was a great misfortune to him; for had he known those things, he might have spent his time better. He further said, that he was much addicted to idleness and gaming, which two vices brought him to the commission of others, particularly that of robbing at such a rate as he did; and, that when of late he had some thoughts of leaving off thieving, he found his inclinations were still that way. He expressed himself as if he was now willing to die, desiring nothing in this world but that God, of His infinite mercy, would forgive whatever he had done amiss, and dispose him to die well, so as he might avoid the eternal condemnation he had deserved. I pressed him to confess the fact for which he was condemned; but he denied it, though at the same time he acknowledged God's justice in bringing him to this untimely end. At the request of a certain person, I asked him whether (as it was reported by some) he had made a contract with the Prince of Darkness, for a set time to act his villainies in; he answered, he never did, nor said any such thing. He and all the rest being asked, whether they knew anything of Mr. Hampson's murder, they all declared and protested, that they knew nothing of it. . . .

Here are John Hall's professional observations on thievery and on Newgate Prison, a kind of third-person commentary on his own experience taken from the beginning of his *Memoirs*:

. . . Every man in this community [of thieves] is esteemed according to his particular quality, of which there are several degrees; though it is contrary often to public government, for here a man shall be valued purely for his merit, and rise by it, too, though it be but to a halter, in which there is a great deal of glory in dying like a hero, and making a decent figure in the cart to the tune of the two last staves of the 51st Psalm. They have there several classes, too, and a pickpocket is no more a companion for a reputable house-breaker, than an informer is for a Justice of Peace, or a player for a man of the first quality. And since I have now begun with their several qualities, I shall show them by their distinct titles.

An Interpretation of the Several
Qualities of Rogues.

Hoisters, such as help one another upon their backs in the night-time to get into windows.

Sneakers, such as sneak into a house by night or day to steal.

Sneaking Budgers, such as pilfer things off of a stall.

Tail-drawers, such as take gentlemen's swords from their sides, at the turning of a corner, or in a crowd.

Clouters, such as take handkerchiefs out of folk's pockets.

Files, such as dive into folk's pockets for money or watches.

Dubbers, such as rob dwelling-houses, warehouses, coach-houses, or stables, by picking the locks thereof.

Cheiving-layers, such as cut the leathers which bears up coaches behind, and whilst the coachmen come off their boxes to see what's the matter, they take a box or trunk from under his seat.

Wagon-layers, such as wait just out of town for wagons coming in or going out of town in a dark morning, to take boxes, or any portable bundles out of them.

Prad-layers, such as cut bags from behind horses as people ride along in the dark.

Horse-pads, such as rob in the highway on horseback.

Foot-pads, such as rob passengers.

Mill-layers, such as break into houses, by forcing doors or shutters open with betties or chisels.

Till-divers, such as go into shops with pretence to buy something, and with several excuses of seeing this thing, and that thing, to make the shopkeeper turn his back often, they put a small whalebone, daubed at the end with bird-lime, into the till of the counter, and draw up the money; but this employment is now grown something out of date.

Running-smoblers, such as go into a shop in the night, where people are busy in the back-room, or elsewhere, and, snatching something that's nearest them, they run away with it.

Fam-layers, such as go into goldsmith's shops, with pretence to buy a ring, and several being laid upon the counter, they palm one or two by means of a little ale held in a spoon over the fire, with which the palm, being daubed, any light thing sticks to it.

Faggot and Stall, such as break into people's houses, and, taking away what they please, gag all therein.

Impudent Stealers, such as cut out the backs of coaches, and take things out of them.

Sweetners, such as drop money before people, and, taking out of sight, inveigle a man (after a hot dispute with some of their accomplices, who earnestly claim halves of what they find) into a tavern they use, where they draw him into cards, dice, or buckle and thong, which they planted in some visible place, and win all his money: these sort of vermin likewise go about the country to cheat people of their money, by the legerdemain slight of cups and ball, and luck in a bag; this is a function too that has not flourished since the late Act for Vagabonds.

Night-gamester, such as rob parks at nights for venison, which proves to be dear if they are taken.

But of all these, house-breaker, under three denominations, viz. hoister, dubber and mill-layer, is the most famous and heroic employment of them all, and in one time exceeds that of the highway.

Some are ingenious at the lob, which is going into a shop to have a guinea or a pistole changed, and the change being given the bringer palms two or three shillings, and then says there wants so much, which the shop-keeper, telling over again, says it is true, and very innocently makes up the sum.

As for the female proficients, they consist chiefly in these:

Shop-lifting, which almost everybody understands.

Buttock and Twang, which is walking to be picked up, and, frightening him that does it with her pretended husband, after she has picked his pocket, so that the fool runs gladly away without his watch or money.

Buttock and File, which is the same with the other; only this is the better-natured beast of the two, and performs her stage before she takes her wages, which may be some satisfaction to the ass she carries.

There are also setters of both sexes, that make it their business to go about upon information, to pry into the disposition and avenues of houses, and bring notice of the booty, of which

they have a share when the robbery is performed, and are generally used as scouts in the time of action.

Having thus briefly run through their several functions, I
come now to give a description of that famous college they usually
take their degrees in, to wit, Newgate. This ancient structure was
founded and endowed by the famous Whittington; and as the
design was good, it cannot be said that it has not brought up many
to preferment, in which there are as many orders to pass through
as at any other of our learned universities. He that has been once
at the Bar may be said to commence Bachelor; twice at the cart's
arse makes him a Master of Arts; three times in the juggler's box
makes him at least a Fellow of a College; but to have been once
under the Ordinary's tuition, the very merit of a condemned sermon institutes him Head of his Order, be it in what respective
function it will. But to return.

Newgate, so called, is divided into three parts, (viz.) the
Press Yard, Master-side, and Common-side, of which the first
has the pre-eminence. They who have the honour to be sent hither,
may in some measure fancy themselves going into Paradise, for
narrow is the way that leads to it. The rooms, according to modern
calculation, are very commodiously furnished. Those who have
experienced it are the best judges, and yet those who have not
may give a near guess by the price; a man may have a palace,
and all its appurtenances, elsewhere, at an easier rent than one
individual mansion here, to swing a cat in; but this is peculiar
to places of great concourse and trade. The windows to these
apartments for decency and human distinction are generally
glazed, yet are inwardly so well fortified by Vulcan's craft, that
there is hardly any danger of tumbling out at the casements, when
the students are either too deeply elevated by domestic Nantz, or
liable to melancholy suggestions in their retirement. The air they
enjoy here is in a yard that scarcely outmeasures a tailor's ell,
and reasonably not above the breadth of a concise bill in Chancery; yet here they find room to measure out the day, which they
may do by tale, so many steps to an hour. The sun appears to
them in perspective, and is visible in this world no time but just
in its meridian, which transitory hour they set apart to worship
it, and then take their sorrowful leave of until the next day; for
as to the rising and setting of it they are utter strangers. . . .

Here are to be seen the miserable wrecks of several un-

fortunate gentlemen, the rocks they split on being generally treason, murder, rape, scandal, debt, and some voluntary decayed
bankrupts, that mistook the late Act, promiscuously jumbled together.

Now, as concerning the humours of the Master-side, when
a scholar in iniquity comes there by virtue of a *mittimus*, he is
delivered up to the paws of the wolves, lurking continually in
the lodge for a prey; where as soon as he's adorned with a pair
of iron boots, and from thence conducted (provided he has gilt)
over the way to hell, for really no place has a nearer resemblance
of that eternal receptacle of punishment than the Master-side;
for the cellar (where poor relentless sinners are guzzling in the
midst of debauchery, and new-invented oaths, which rumble like
thunder through their filthy throats) is a lamentable den of horror
and darkness, there being no light but what they procure from the
help of one of that greasy company, whose mystery is, by a subtle
metamorphosis, to turn night into day with what they get from
butchers and kitchen-wenches' industrious savings. In this boozing-
ken, (where more than Cimmerian darkness dissipates its horrible
gloom) the students, instead of holding disputes in philosophy and
mathematics, run altogether upon law; for such as are committed
for house-breaking swear stoutly they cannot be cast for burglary,
because the fact was done in the day-time; such as are committed
for stealing a horse-cloth, or coachman's cloak swear they cannot
be cast for felony and robbery, because the coach was standing
still, not stopped; and such as steal before a man's face swear they
value not their adversary, because they are out of the reach of
the new Act against private stealing. Thus, with an unparalleled
impudence, every brazen-faced malefactor is hardened in his sin,
because the Law can't touch his life. But when night has spun her
darkness to the length of nine o'clock, then are they hurried up
before their drivers (like so many Turkish slaves) to their kennels,
which are joined like so many huts, as though they took their
order from martial discipline: and as in all places of disorder and
confusion all things go by contraries, so here, instead of the men
lying over the women, the women lie over the men, in whose
several apartments both male and female are confined until they
distil a little oil of argentum for the favour of going into the cellar,
to spend their ill-gotten coin with speed, to make the old proverb

good, Lightly come, lightly go, or rather, What's got over the
devil's back is spent under his belly. . . .

But now passing by that part of the Master-side, into which
prisoners are brought upon real suspicion of debt, their talk being
altogether upon an Act of Grace, I shall proceed to the humours
of the Common-side. Those scholars that come here have nothing
to depend on but the charity of the Foundation, in which side
very exact rules are observed; for as soon as a prisoner comes
into the turnkey's hands three knocks are given at the stair-foot,
as a signal a collegian is coming up . . . and no sooner are the
three strokes given, but out jump four truncheon officers (who only
hate religion because it condemns their vices) from their hovel,
and with a sort of ill-mannered reverence receive him at the grate;
then, taking him into their apartment, a couple of the good-
natured sparks hold him whilst the other two pick his pockets,
claiming sixpence as a privilege belonging to their office; then
they turn him out to the convicts who hover about him (like so
many crows about a piece of carrion) for garnish, which is six
shillings and eight pence, which they, from an old custom, claim
by prescription time out of mind for entering in the Society, otherwise they strip the poor wretch if he has not wherewithal to pay
it. Then cook ruffian (that scalded the Devil in his feathers) comes
to him for three pence for dressing the charity-meat, which charit-
able-disposed persons send in every Thursday . . . but yet the
caged person is not clear of his dues, for next, two other officers,
who have a patent for being swabbers, demand three halfpennies
apiece more for cleaning the gaol of its filth, which requires the
labour of Sisyphus, and is never to be ended. Then at the signal
of the gray-pease woman, which is between seven and eight, he
is conducted downstairs, with an illumination of links, to his lodging, and provided he has a shilling for civility-money, may lie
in the Middle-Ward, which (to give the devils their due) is kept
very neat and clean, where he pays one shilling and four-pence
more to his comrades, and then he is free of the College, and
matriculated.

But the Lower-Ward, where the tight, slovenly dogs lie
upon ragged blankets, spread near Sir Reverence[1] one would take
to be Old Nick's back-side, where all the damned go to ease their

---

[1] *Dung.*

roasted arses; and trampling on the floor, the lice crackling under their feet, make such a noise as walking on shells which are strewn over garden-walks. To this nasty place is adjoined the Stone Hold, where convicts lie until a free pardon grants them liberty from tribulation; but not making good use of mercy, come tumbling headlong in again. This low dungeon is a real house of meagre looks, and ill smells; for lice, drink and tobacco is all the compound.

When the prisoners are disposed to recreate themselves with walking, they go up into a spacious room called the High-Hall, where, when you see them taking a turn together, it would puzzle one to know which is the gentleman, which the mechanic, and which the beggar, for they are all suited in the same form or kind of nasty poverty, which is a spectacle of more pity than executions; only to be out at the elbows is in fashion here, and a great indecorum not to be threadbare. On the north side is a small room called the Buggering Hold; but from whence it takes its name, I cannot tell, unless it is a fate attending this place, that some confined there may or have been addicted to sodomy. Here the fines lie, and perhaps, as he behaves himself, an out-lawed person may creep in among them. But what degree of lati-tude this chamber is situated in, I cannot positively demonstrate, unless it lies 90 degrees beyond the Arctic Pole; for instead of being dark here but half the year, it is dark all the year round. The company one with another there is but a vying of complaints, and the causes they have to rail on the ill success of petitions, and in this they reckon there is a great deal of good fellowship. There they huddle up their life as a thing of no use, and wear it out like an old suit, the faster the better; and he that deceives the time at cards or dice thinks he deceives it best, and best spends it. Just by them lie the tangerines, in a large room, called Tangier, which next to the Lower Ward is the nastiest place in the goal. The miserable inhabitants hereof are debtors.... These poor wretches are commonly, next their creditors, most bitter against the lawyers, as men that have had a stroke in assisting them there; a bailiff, likewise, they mortally hate, because he makes them fear the Queen's name worse than the Devil's. But in this apartment lie, besides, real debtors, such as are called your thieving debtors; who, having for theft, satisfied the Queen, by being burnt in the face, or whipped, which is no satisfaction to the wronged subject, their adversaries bring an action of trover against them, and keep them there until they make restitution for things stolen.

Up one pair of stairs over them is Jack Ketch's kitchen, where, in pitch, tar and oil, he boils the quarters of those traitors who deservedly suffer for the several sorts of high treason. Near this place are adjoining several rooms, which prisoners hire that have a mind to live retired; and opposite to the kitchen, where man's flesh is dressed, is a lightsome room, called Debtor's Hall, so named from such unfortunate men lying there, where every man shows like so many wrecks upon the sea, here the ribs of £20, here the ruins of a good estate, doublets without buttons, and a gown without sleeves. And a pair of stairs higher lie women that are fines and debtors, thinking, like their suffering companions below them, every year seven until they get abroad....

Now if there should be any great tumult or uproar among the prisoners, whose deepest endearment is a communication of mischief, then a bell, which hangs over the High Hall stairs, (to call the turnkey, when out of the way, by single ringing, to let people in and out), is rung double, and at the alarm several officers belonging to the gaol come running up to quell the mutiny; which being appeased, the ringleaders thereof (who are such high-spirited fellows that would sooner accept the gallows than a mean trade) are conducted to a low dungeon, as dark as the inside of the Devil's arse in the peak, and hung all over with spider texture, and are there sheared, or put into bilboes, and handcuffed; but in case the place of punishment should be first taken up by any factious woman, that's given to pattin and pen-knife, then they are punished in the press-room, where men that stand mute at their trial are pressed to death, by having their hands and feet extended out to four iron rings fixed to the ground, and a great heavy press of wood, made like a hog-trough, having a square post at each end, reaching up to the ceiling, let up and down full of weights by ropes upon them, in which torment he lies three or four days, or less time, according as he is favoured, having no food or drink, but black bread, or the channel water which runs under the goal, if his fainting pains should make him crave to eat or drink.

But now I am arrived to the women felons' apartment, in the Common-side, where there are a troop of hell-cats lying head and tail together in a dismal, nasty, dark room, having no place to divert themselves but at the grate, adjoining to the foot passage under Newgate, where passengers may, with admiration and pity, hear them swear *extempore*, being so shamefully versed in that most odious profanation of heaven, that volleys of oaths are discharged through their detestable throats whilst asleep. And if any of their acquaintance gives them *l'argent*, then they jump into their cellar to melt it, which is scarcely so large as Covent-Garden cage, and the stock therein not much exceeding those peddling victuallers, who fetch their drink in tubs every brewing day. As for the suttler there I have no more to say of her, than that her purity consists in the whiteness of her linen; and that the licentiousness of the women on this side is so detestable, that it is an unpardonable crime to describe their lewdness. . . .

But now, having shown in what manner they enter students, and conform themselves in their college, let us see how they take their degrees for farther preferment, and make their progression out again; in which it is observed that few are ever expelled for any irregular demeanour. But when the days of Oyer and Terminer approach, and the gates of Janus in the Old-Bailey are thrown open, the whole College betimes in the morning are conducted down, making as they go along a jingling with their fetters like so many Morris dancers in the Christmas holidays; and such malefactors as will not give half-a-crown to be in the bail-dock, where criminals, both male and female, are secured, go in a hold, where they resemble so many sheep penned up in Smithfield on a market-day: There the prisoners claim twelve-pence apiece of the youngest for hold-money, with which collection they make shift to get drunk before they go up to the Bar to be arraigned or tried; the same odious custom is likewise observed by the women in their hold. And if it should be a prisoner's good luck to be acquitted, he kneels, and cries, God bless the Queen, and all the honourable Court; then joyfully returning to his comrades, they make him spend his quit-shilling for his happy deliverance. But when they are all tried, the Judge (after the fire is made, and the burning engine put up) proceeds to pass sentence on the several offenders, then those cast for single felony are brought up; but such as never broke their friends for learning, not venturing a *non legit*, throw themselves on the mercy of the Court, and escape marking with an ignominious T, by entering themselves in Her Majesty's service; and such as can read claim the benefit of the clergy; a favour only designed at first for scholars, but now through long custom claimed by the illiterate, are forced (upon the account of clearing the land of villains) to save their bacon by listing, too. But profligate women (having not this advantage) are glimmed for that villainy, for which rather than leave it, they could freely die martyrs. Next sentence of death is passed on malefactors; but upon this point, the women have a great advantage over the men, by pleading their bellies, who are then searched by a jury of matrons, impanelled for that purpose; but either for favour or profit some are brought in quick with child, when it is of a church, to the great abuse of the Honourable Court; not but that they deserved for it; but as the saying is, no grass grows on the highway. Those cast for petit-larceny shove the tumbler, i.e., whipped at the cart's tail; and others are made city surveyors, being appointed to overlook Penance Board at Temple Bar, Cheapside Conduit, and the Royal Exchange; but I cannot properly call one so exalted a captain over tens, hundreds, or thousands, because the number of the spectators is uncertain.

The Court being broken up, and by an Oyez appointed to begin again at another certain time, the prisoners not cast for their lives return from whence they came, the thief-takers ogling them as they trudge along (to know their shameless faces another time) as wishfully as a gypsy does ignorant country wenches hands to tell their fortune. But those sentenced to go to the Condemned Hold, there being two, one for males, another for females; who being relentless wretches, unmindful of a future state, make their dark, dismal den the rendezvous of spittle, where they dialogue (as in tobacco shops) with their noses, and their communication is smoke; where being in hopes of the Queen's mercy, their words are still so many vomits cast up to the loathsomeness of their hearers. In sum, the whole life of these distressed wretches is a question, and their salvation a greater, which death only concludes, and then they are resolved.

To fit them for another world, they are immediately after condemnation carried out of this into a place, that whoever were to be conveyed thither in his sleep, when he awakened and looked about him, (that is, I mean, would look if he could see anything), would absolutely, without much hesitation, conclude he had departed this life in some melancholy slumber, and was arrived in the gloomy mansions of Eternity, without knowing anything of it. For food here you'll conclude they have no extraordinary appetites; nor are they fed with anything but the spoon-meat of the Gospel; and not every one of them has any stomach to that neither. The Ordinary is their dry-nurse, and gives them constant attendance in this their visitation, who, poor souls, may very properly be said to lie upon their deathbeds, for, generally speaking, all his patients die upon his hands.

Next Sunday, following their fatal doom, they go to the chapel to hear the condemned sermon, which is so near Heaven, as to be situated on the very top of all Newgate, and possibly sometimes is their *ne plus ultra*, the farthest stage they make that way. Here Mr. Ordinary expounds some useful text of Scripture, which he applies to the purpose in hand, viz. holy dying; for to preach up amendment of life, as I have hinted before, would here be eloquence thrown away.... And now, after two hours' discipline under the Ordinary's hands, one would think their persecution should end; but the bell-man, who is the prelude to the hangman, like a flourish before a damned melancholy tune, comes next to torture them with his inhuman stanzas, as if men in their condition could have any stomach to unseasonable poetry; for the night before execution, placing himself under their window, he harangues them with the following serenade, set to the tune of the Bar-bell at the Black Dog.

> All you that in the Condemned Hold do lie,
> Prepare you, for tomorrow you must die:
> Think well upon your sins, in time repent,
> Lest you are headlong unto Satan sent.
> Watch then, and pray, that so you may be fit
> T'appear so soon before the Judgment Seat;
> And when St. Pulcher's bell tomorrow tolls,
> The Lord above have mercy on your souls.

The next morning they are conveyed up to the chapel again, where they receive the last portion of Grace from the Ordinary, who takes them to auricular confession, and is as diligent in inquiring out the particulars of their lives, as though he were to send a catalogue of their sins along with them for a passport. Having thus done, and compounded the necessary ingredients for their dying speeches, he gives them the finishing stroke, and delivers them over to the secular arm. Then they are conveyed to a place called the Stone Hall, where, having those great obstacles of their liberty knocked off, they are installed by the Yeoman of the Halter with the ensigns armorial of his office, and by some of his attendants conducted down to the cart, having, perhaps, made it the greatest of their care to make a decent appearance to the spectators, for pride is the last sin that leaves them in this world, and that bears them company to the gallows; so that one would take them for bridegrooms going to espouse their old Mrs. Tyburn, being as spruce as a powdered wig, a Holland shirt, clean gloves, and a nosegay, can make them. The great comfort of having it said, There goes a proper, handsome man, something meliorates the terrible thoughts of the meagre tyrant's death; and to go in a dirty shirt were enough to save the hangman a labour, and make a man die with grief and shame of being in that deplorable condition. It is but saying they are dead by the law, and the cavalcade to Tyburn may serve for a funeral procession; there is something of magnificence in it; the lamentable ditty from St. Sepulchre's wall is the sum of their great achievements, and the doleful knells at St. Andrew's and St. Giles's is the spiritual music that ushers on the pomp. Being come to Tyburn, the Ordinary renews his acquaintance with them, where they never part without one lamentable merry hymn together, and indeed, to speak truth, they are very loathe to spoil company; but the dearest friends in the world must part. The hangman, having tied them up for his greater security, gives the Ordinary the pre-eminence of finishing his office first, and is in the meantime surveying their ornaments, and putting them into lots for the easier accommodation of the sale. Being admonished to say something to the spectators, it is natural enough to hear a poor, shivering malefactor come out with his last dying speech, as follows (turning to the spectators), I desire you all, good people, to pray for me; I confess I have been a very wicked offender, and have been guilty of many heinous sins, especially whoring, drunkenness, Sabbath-breaking, and all the rest, which has brought me to this shameful end; therefore pray take example by me, that you may mend your lives.

This is in substance literally followed by a great many that hear it; and now their time being expired, their caps are pulled over their eyes, and they are turned off with a sentence they hardly ever made use of in their life-times before, Lord, have mercy on us. After a few jerks and unmerciful thumps to dispatch them, they expire with the contempt, and hardly the pity, of any that behold them. Having hung there the space of half an hour, come some of their relations with a deal coffin cross the doors of a coach to take them away; but there is first a bargain to be made with the hangman for their clothes, which they purchase at a market price; for, having intimated to him to which person they have the honour to be related, he takes a careful survey of every individual button-hole, and being a man of few words, conscientiously tells them so much is the price if they have him clothes and all; which, if they disagree to, he is stripped, and the miscellany of rags are all crowded into a sack, which his *valet de chambre* carries on purpose, and, being digested into Monmouth Street, Chick Lane, &c. are comfortably worn by many an industrious fellow. Others that have no friends, or at least none that want the grace to disown them, have their length and breadth in unconsecrated clay, under or near the dark dimensions of the gallows.

Thus, I have given you the character, life and tragic end of a thief; that is, one that is so much master of his trade as to venture his neck for it; there being some so very diligent, that their constant practice is to live within the purlieus of the Law, and not to venture above a whipping, or a burning at most. If what I have inserted here (as I was in hopes it would) does but become serviceable to the public after my death, it will answer the design of those who advised me to the publication thereof, to which I consented to give what necessary hints I could for that end.

Your Departed Friend,
John Hall.

EPITAPH

Here lies Hall's Clay,
Thus swept away;
If bolt or key
Obliged his stay,
At Judgment Day
He'd make essay
To get away;
Be't as it may,
I'd better say,
Here lies Jack Hall,
And that is all.

[AMORY, THOMAS]. *Life of John Buncle, Esq.* . . . 2 vols. London: J. Noon, 1756.

[BLACKMORE, RICHARD]. *A Satyr against Wit.* London: Samuel Crouch, 1700.

BOSWELL, JAMES. *Life of Samuel Johnson,* 6 vols. Ed. G. B. Hill, Rev. L. F. Powell, Oxford, 1934.

BOYER, ABEL. *The Political State of Great Britain.* . . . London: J. Baker et al., 1711-1740. (Boyer was editor until 1729).

BROWN, TOM. *The Works of Mr Thomas Brown, in Prose and Verse.* . . . 3 vols. London: Sam Briscoe, 1707–08.

———— *Works* . . . The Fifth Edition, corrected, etc. . . . 5 vols. London: Sam Briscoe, 1720–21.

———— *A Collection of Miscellany Poems, &c.* 2nd ed. London: J. Nutt, 1700.

———— *Letters from the Dead to the Living.* Vol. 2 of *Works,* London, 1707.

———— *Amusements, Serious and Comical.* London: John Nutt, 1700.

———— [*The Auction of Ladies*] *Characters of Several Ingenious Designing Gentlewomen.* . . . [London: Abel Roper], 1699.

————*A Description of Mr D[ryde]n's Funeral.* London. 1700. Broadsheet.

———— [?] *An Elegy on the Death of the Author of the 'Characters, &c. of the Ladies Invention',* who dyed on the 13th of this instant May at the Rose Spunging-House in Woodstreet under an Arrest. . . . London, 1700 [?].

———— *The Late Converts Exposed*: or the Reasons of Mr Bays's Changing his Religion Considered in a Dialogue. Part the Second, London, 1960.

———— *Physick Lies a Bleeding, or the Apothecary Turned Doctor.* . . . London: C. Whitlock, 1697.

BROWN, TOM. *The Reasons of Mr Bays Changing his Religion*. Considered in a Dialogue between Crites, Eugenius and Mr Bays. London, 1691.

—— *The Salamanca Wedding*: or, A True Account of a Swearing Doctor's Marriage with a Muggletonian Widow. . . . London, 1693.

—— *A Satyr upon the French King*. Written by a non-swearing Parson. . . . London, 1697.

COLLIER, JEREMY. *A Short View of the Immorality and Profaneness of the English Stage*. London: S. Keble, 1698.

T.C., SURGEON [EDMUND CURLL?]. *The Charitable Surgeon*: or, The Best Remedies for the worst Maladies, Reveal'd. London: Edmund Curll, 1708.

CURLL, EDMUND. *Curlicism Display'd*. London: Printed for the Author, 1718 [?].

DEFOE, DANIEL. *The True-Born Englishman*. A Satyr. 1701.

—— *R[ogue]'s on both Sides*. . . . London: John Baker, 1711.

DENNIS, JOHN. *A True Character of Mr Pope and his Writings*. London, 1716.

DE LA CROSE, JEAN. *The Works of the Learned*, An Historical Account and Impartial Judgement of Books newly printed, both Foreign and Domestick, to be published monthly. London: Tho. Bennet, 1691.

DRAKE, JAMES. *The Memorial of the Church of England*. London, 1705.

DUNTON, JOHN. *Dunton's Whipping Post or, A Satire upon Every Body*. To which is added . . . the Whoring-Paquet: or News of the St[allio]ns and Kept M[istres]s's. London: B. Bragg, 1706.

—— *Dying Groans from the Fleet Prison*: or the National Complaint. London: Printed for the Author, 1723 [?].

—— *The Life and Errors of John Dunton*, Late Citizen of London; Written by Himself in Solitude . . . Together with the Lives and Characters of a Thousand Persons now Living in London &c. . . . London: S. Malthus, 1705.

—— *The Living Elegy*: or Dunton's Letter (being a Word of Comfort) to his Few Creditors: With the Character of a Summer-Friend. . . . London, 1706.

DURFEY, THOMAS. *New Poems*. London, 1690.

SCRIBLERUS SECUNDUS [HENRY FIELDING]. *The Author's Farce*. . . . London: J. Roberts, 1730.

[GORDON, THOMAS]. *A Dedication to a Great Man, concerning Dedications*. . . . London, 1718.

ISCARIOT HACKNEY [RICHARD SAVAGE]. *An Author to be Lett*. Being a Proposal . . . to the Solid and Ancient Society of the Bathos. London: Alexander Vint, 1729.

[KING, WILLIAM]. *Dialogues of the Dead* relating to the present controversy concerning the Epistles of Phalaris. London, 1699.

[KINGSTON, RICHARD]. *Impudence, Lying and Forgery Detected and Chastiz'd, Etc.* London, 1700.

—— *A Modest Answer to Captain Smythe's Immodest Memoirs*. London, 1700.

L'ESTRANGE, ROGER. *Consideration and proposals in order to the regulation of the Press.* . . . London, 1663.

―――― *L'Estrange no Papist* : In Answer to a Libel Entituled L'Estrange a Papist. . . . London, 1681.

[OLDMIXON, JOHN]. *The History of Addresses.* London, 1709.

[OLDMIXON, JOHN]. *The History of England during the Reigns of King William and Queen Mary, Queen Anne, King George I.* . . . London, 1735.

―――― *Memoirs of the Press, Historical and Political, for Thirty Years Past, from 1710 to 1740.* London: T. Cox, 1742.

PARKER, GEORGE. *Ephemeris for the Year of our Lord, 1708.*

―――― *J. Partridge's Scurrilous Reflections in his Almanack for the Year 1699, Answered.* 1700 [?].

―――― *Merlinus Hewson, or Johannodion's Ignorance in Trigonometry Exposed.* 1707 [?].

[PARTRIDGE, JOHN]. *Flagitiosus Mercurius Flagellatus: or the Whipper Whipp'd* : Being an Answer to a Scurrilous Invective Written by George Parker. . . . 1697 [?].

PITTIS, WILLIAM. *The Case of the Church of England's Memorial Fairly Stated.* London, 1706.

―――― ed. *Miscellanies over Claret.* London, 1697.

[POPE, ALEXANDER]. *A Full and True Account of a Horrid and Barbarous Revenge by Poison, on the Body of Mr Edmund Curll, Bookseller.* . . . London: Roberts, Morphew, Baker, Popping, 1716 [?].

ROPER, ABEL [?]. *A Full and True Account of A Terrible & Bloody Fight between Tom Brown, the Poet, and a Bookseller.* [London, 1700] Broadsheet.

SHEPHEARD, FLEETWOOD [?]. *A Petition of Tom Brown, Who was Taken up on Account of the 'Satyr upon the French King'.* From *The Flying-Post* for November 23–25, 1698.

SMITH, MATTHEW. *Memoirs of the Secret Service.* . . . London, 1699.

―――― *Remarks upon the D[uke] of S[hrewsbury]'s Letter to the House of Lords, concerning Capt. Smyth.* . . . London, 1700.

―――― *A Reply to an Unjust, and Scandalous Libel, intituled A Modest Answer to Captain Smith's Immodest Memoirs.* London, 1700.

SPINKS, J. *Quackery Unmasked or, Reflections on the Sixth Edition of Mr Martin's Treatise of the Venereal Disease.* . . . London: D. Brown, 1709.

TRIPE, DR ANDREW [WILLIAM WAGSTAFFE]. *Some Memoirs of the Life of Abel, Toby's Uncle.* . . . London: T. Warner, 1726.

TUTCHIN, JOHN. *The Examination, Tryal, and Condemnation of Rebellious Ob[servato]r, &c.* 1703.

―――― *The Foreigners.* London, 1700.

WARD, EDWARD. *The Second Volume of the Writings of the Author of 'The London Spy'.* London, 1703.

―――― *The Third Volume Consisting of Poems on Divers Subjects.* By the Author of *The London Spy.* London, 1706.

WARD, EDWARD. *The Batchelor's Estimate of the Expences of a Married Life.* . . . London, 1725.

―――― *The Delights of the Bottle*: or, The Complete Vintner. . . . London, 1720.

―――― *Female Policy detected*: or, the Arts of a designing Woman laid open, etc. London, 1695.

―――― *A Frolick to Horn-Fair.* With a walk from Cuckold's-Point thro' Deptford and Greenwich. 1699.

―――― *The History of the London Clubs.* London, 1709.

―――― *Hudibras Redivivus*: Or, A Burlesque Poem on the Times. London, 1705.

―――― *The London Spy.* 1698–1700.

―――― *The London Terraefilius*: or, the Satyrical Reformer. 1707.

―――― *The Poet's Ramble after Riches . . . with the Author's Lamentation.* London, 1691.

―――― *A Step to the Bath*: with a Character of the Place. London, 1700.

―――― *A Step to Stir-Bitch-Fair*: with Remarks upon the University of Cambridge. London, 1700.

―――― *A Trip to Jamaica.* London, 1698.

―――― *A Trip to New-England.* London, 1699.

―――― *The Woman's Advocate,* or the Baudy Batchelor out in his Calculation: being the genuine Answer . . . to 'the Batchelor's Estimate'. . . . London: A. Moore, 1729.

Anonymous and Miscellaneous

The Character of a Town-Miss. London: Rowland Reynolds, 1680. Broadsheet.

Commendatory Verses on the Author of the Two Arthurs, and the Satyr against Wit; by some of his particular Friends. [A miscellany by various authors.] London, 1700.

The Fable of the Cuckoo; or, The Sentence on the Ill Bird that defiled his own Nest. Shewing, in a Dissenter's Dream, some Satyrical Reflections, on a late Infamous Libel, call'd The True-Born Englishman. London, 1701.

Memoirs of the Right Villainous John Hall, The Late Famous and Notorious Robber, Penn'd from his Mouth some time before his Death. . . . London: Ben Bragg, 1708.

Neck or Nothing: A Consolatory Letter from Mr D[u]nt[o]n to Mr C[u]rll Upon his being Tost in a Blanket &c. London: Charles King [?], 1716.

The Ordinary of Newgate, his Account of the Behaviour, Confessions, and last Speeches of the Malefactors that were executed at Tyburn, on Wednesday, Decemb. 17, 1707. London: Ben J. Bragg, 1707.

A Short, but Just Account of the Tryal of Benjamin Harris, upon an Information brought against him for printing and Vending a late Seditious Book called *An Appeal from the County to the City, For* the Preservation of His Majesties Person, Liberty, Property, and the Protestant Religion. London, 1679.

The Town-Rakes: or, The Frolicks of the Mohocks or Hawkubites. London: J. Wright, 1712. Broadsheet.

The Tryal and Examination Mr John Tutchin, For Writing a certain Libel, call'd the Observator ... on Saturday the 4th of November 1704. Broadsheet.

Journals

The Athenian Gazette (Mercury). Ed. John Dunton, London, from 1691.

The Daily Courant. London, from 1702.

Flying-Post. Ed. George Ridpath. London, from 1695.

Heraclitus Ridens. Ed. William Pittis. London, from 1703.

The Infallible Astrologer. Ed. Tom Brown. London, from 1700.

The Interloping Whipster. Ed. William Pittis, from 1704.

The London Gazette. From 1666.

The London Mercury. Ed. Tom Brown. London, 1691. Later entitled *The Lacedemonian Mercury*.

Merlinus Liberatus. Ed. J. Partridge [Benjamin Harris]. London, from 1706.

Merlinus Liberatus; being an almanack for 1690, etc. Ed. John Partridge. London.

Mist's Weekly Journal. London, from 1725.

The Observator. Ed. Roger L'Estrange. London, from 1681.

The Observator. Ed. John Tutchin. London, from 1702.

Post-Boy. Ed. Abel Roper. London, from 1695.

Post-Man. Ed. Jean de Fonvive. London, from 1694.

Protestant Domestick Intelligence. Ed. Benjamin Harris. London, from 1679.

The Rehearsal. Ed. Charles Leslie. London, from 1707.

The Whipping-Post. Ed. William Pittis. London, from 1705.

Secondary Material

BELJAME, ALEXANDRE. *Men of Letters and the English Public in the Eighteenth Century, 1660–1744*. (English Edition.) London: Kegan Paul, 1948.

BEVERIDGE, SIR WILLIAM. *Prices and Wages in England from the Twelfth to the Nineteenth Century*. Vol. I. London: Longmans & Co., 1939.

BOYCE, BENJAMIN. *Tom Brown of Facetious Memory*. Cambridge, Mass.: [Harvard Studies in English, Vol. 21], 1939.

CRANE, R. S., and KAYE, F. B. *A Census of British Newspapers, 1620–1800*. Chapel Hill: University of North Carolina Press, 1927.

D'ISRAELI, ISAAC. *Calamities and Quarrels of Authors*. London, 1859.

—— *Curiosities of Literature*. London: Edward Moxon, 1838.

HOWELL, T. B. *A Complete Collection of State Trials....From the Earliest Period to the Year 1783* Vol. XVII. London: Longman's et al, 1816.

MUDDIMAN, J. G. *The King's Journalist, 1659–1689*. Studies in the reign of Charles II. London: John Lane, 1923.

NICHOLS, JOHN. *Literary Anecdotes of the Eighteenth Century*. . . . 9 Vols. London: Nichols, Son, and Bentley, 1812–15.

PLANT, MARJORIE. *The English Book Trade*. London: Allen & Unwin, 1965.

PLOMER, HENRY ROBERT. *A Dictionary of the Booksellers and Printers who were at work in England, Scotland, and Ireland from 1668 to 1725*. London: Bibliographical Society, 1922.

ROBERTS, WILLIAM. *The Early History of English Bookselling*. London: Sampson Low, 1892.

ROGERS, JAMES E. THOROLD. *A History of Agriculture and Prices in England*. . . . 7 Vols. Oxford: Clarendon Press, 1887.

ROSTENBERG, LEONA. *Literary, Political, Scientific, Religious and Legal Publishing, Printing and Bookselling in England*. 2 Vols. New York: B. Franklin, 1965.

STRAUS, RALPH. *The Unspeakable Curll*. London: Chapman & Hall, 1927.

TROYER, HOWARD. W. *Ned Ward of Grub Street*. Cambridge: Harvard University Press, 1946.